THE RUSSIAN REVOLUTION IN SWITZERLAND

THE RUSSIAN REVOLUTION IN SWITZERLAND 1914–1917

Alfred Erich Senn

THE UNIVERSITY OF WISCONSIN PRESS

Madison, Milwaukee, and London

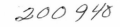

Published 1971
The University of Wisconsin Press
Box 1379, Madison, Wisconsin 53701

The University of Wisconsin Press, Ltd.
27-29 Whitfield Street, London, W.1

First printing

Printed in the United States of America
Heffernan Press, Inc.
Worcester, Massachusetts

ISBN 299-05941-3; LC 76-143766

To Philip E. Mosely

Contents

Acknowledgments

In preparing this study I have enjoyed the aid and encouragement of many people. In particular I would like to thank Professor Georges Haupt, Dr. M. Tucek, Professor Witold Sworakowski, Mr. Alexander Rolich, and Dr. Ferdinand Böhny. I am deeply indebted to the staffs of the Schweizerisches Sozialarchiv, the Staatsarchiv in Zurich, the archive of the *Neue Zürcher Zeitung,* the Bundesarchiv in Bern, the Bibliothèque Publique et Universitaire in Geneva, the Bibliothèque Cantonale et Universitaire in Lausanne, the Bibliothèque de la Ville in La Chaux-de-Fonds, the archive of the Auswärtiges Amt in Bonn, the Haus-, Hof-, und Staatsarchiv in Vienna, the Columbia University Russian Archive, the Hoover Institution in Stanford, California, the Yale University Library, and the University of Wisconsin Library.

In addition I want to acknowledge the assistance which I have received from the Research Committee of the University of Wisconsin Graduate School and from the University's Russian Area Studies Program. I completed the study under a fellowship from the John Simon Guggenheim Foundation.

None of the persons or institutions mentioned above, of course, can be held responsible for any of the opinions or statements in the work. Its shortcomings are all mine.

A. E. S.

Zurich
June 1970

List of Abbreviations

AAB	Auswärtiges Amt, Bonn, Politisches Archiv
AAM	Auswärtiges Amt, Bonn, Politisches Archiv, Microfilm. Series/Roll/Frame
Aleks. Ar.	Archive of G. A. Aleksinskii, Columbia University Russian Archive
All. et la paix	André Scherer and Jacques Grunewald, eds., *L'Allemagne et les problèmes de la paix*. Paris, 1962
Ar. Monatte	Jean Maitron and Colette Chambelland, eds., *Syndicalisme révolutionnaire et communisme. Les archives de Pierre Monatte*. Paris, 1968
BBAr	Bern, Bundesarchiv
BStAr	Bern, Staatsarchiv
Ber. Brunner	*Bericht des Ersten Staatsanwaltes A. Brunner an den Regierungsrat des Kantons Zürich über die Strafuntersuchung wegen des Aufruhrs in Zürich im November 1917 (vom 9. November 1918)*. Zurich, 1919
Ereig. Ukr.	Theophil Hornykiewicz, ed., *Ereignisse in Ukraine 1914–1922*. 3 vols. Graz-Philadelphia, 1966–68
Forel Ar.	Fonds de Auguste Forel, Bibliothèque cantonale et universitaire, Lausanne
HHSAr	Haus-, Hof-, und Staatsarchiv, Vienna
IISH	International Institute for Social History, Amsterdam
OAr	Okhrana Archive, Hoover Institution, Stanford, California
Obzor	*Obzor deiatel'nosti rossiiskoi sotsial-demokraticheskoi rabochei partii za vremia s nachala voiny Rossii s Avstro-Vengriei i Germaniei po iul' 1916 goda*. N.p., n.d.
PRO	Public Records Office, London
PSS	V. I. Lenin, *Polnoe sobranie sochinenii*. 5th ed. Moscow, 1960–64
Vperiod Ar.	Cercle d'idées Vperiod, 1909–17, Archive, Bibliothèque publique et universitaire, Geneva

ZSSAr	Zurich, Schweizerisches Sozialarchiv
ZStAr	Zurich, Staatsarchiv
Zimm. Bew.	Horst Lademacher, ed., *Die Zimmerwalder Bewegung*. 2 vols. The Hague, 1967

Introduction

The prehistory of the Russian revolutions of 1917 involves an enormous number of virtually independent stories, ranging from the vicissitudes of the Romanov dynasty to the conspiratorial meetings of fugitive revolutionaries. Among these stories, the activity of Russian political emigrés in Switzerland during the First World War demands special attention because of the presence there of so many well-known revolutionary leaders. Although these emigrés played almost no role in the events leading to the downfall of the Tsarist regime in March 1917, their activities embodied the issues which culminated in the Bolshevik seizure of power in Russia in November 1917, and they themselves contributed heavily to the international significance of that second revolution.

The emigrés represented almost all the major nationalities of Russia —Russians, Ukrainians, Jews, Poles, Georgians, Armenians, Latvians, Lithuanians, and Estonians. They found their common ground in their opposition to the Tsarist government. Beyond this, however, they differed sharply in their political programs, in which they mixed together political and social convictions, national prejudices, and even personal antagonisms. Some favored the disintegration of the Russian state into its national components, others, the democratization of Russia and the maintenance of its existing territorial unity.

Historians have already probed many aspects of emigré activity. In the last few years the Zimmerwald movement, which drew together socialists opposed to the First World War, has in particular received a great deal of attention, and the publication in 1967 of the archives of the

Swiss Socialist Robert Grimm can only intensify this development.[1] The long-standard works of Angelica Balabanova, Merle Fainsod, Alfred Rosmer, and Branko Lazitch maintain their significance, but the newer works by Julius Braunthal and Jules Humbert-Droz reflect the greater breadth of documentation which has become possible in the last ten years.[2] Recent Soviet works, such as those by N. E. Korolev and Ia. G. Temkin, have offered an introduction to the archival holdings of the Soviet Union,[3] and the biographies of Martov, Radek, Plekhanov, and Trotsky have helped to add a personal dimension to the historiography.[4]

A number of Western authors have taken up the problem of German intrigue among the emigrés, and they have particularly attempted to show collusion between the Germans and Lenin, a line of thought that can be traced to the wartime writings of G. A. Alexinsky. Recent authors subscribing to this view have singled out several men as possible channels of communication between the emigrés and the German government: Alexander Kesküla, Alexander Siefeld, Alexander Parvus-Helphand, Alexander Tsivin, and Karl Moor.[5]

Swiss writers have produced an impressive literature of their own in discussing the impact which the emigrés had on their hosts. In particular, the question of Lenin's role in the formation of the Swiss Communist Party and the emotional consequences of the Swiss general strike

1. Horst Lademacher, ed., *Die Zimmerwalder Bewegung,* 2 vols. (The Hague, 1967).

2. Angelica Balabanova, *Die Zimmerwalder Bewegung, 1914–1919* (Leipzig, 1928); Merle Fainsod, *International Socialism and the War* (Cambridge, 1935); Alfred Rosmer, *Le Mouvement ouvrier pendant la première guerre mondiale,* 2 vols. (Paris, 1936–53); Branko Lazitch, *Lénine et la IIIe Internationale* (Paris, 1951); Julius Braunthal, *History of the International,* 2 vols. (London, 1967); Jules Humbert-Droz, *Der Krieg und die Internationale* (Vienna, 1964).

3. N. E. Korolev, *Lenin i mezhdunarodnoe rabochee dvizhenie* (Moscow, 1968); Ia. G. Temkin, *Tsimmerval'd—Kintal'* (Moscow, 1967) and *Lenin i mezhdunarodnaia sotsial-demokratiia 1914–1917* (Moscow, 1968).

4. Israel Getzler, *Martov: A Political Biography of a Russian Social Democrat* (Cambridge, 1967); Samuel H. Baron, *Plekhanov: The Father of Russian Marxism* (Stanford, 1963); Warren Lerner, *Karl Radek: The Last Internationalist* (Stanford, 1970); and Isaac Deutscher, *The Prophet Armed: Trotsky, 1879–1921* (New York, 1965).

5. See George Katkov, *Russia 1917: The February Revolution* (London, 1967); Stefan Possony, *Lenin: The Compulsive Revolutionary* (Chicago, 1964); Michael Futrell, *Northern Underground* (London, 1963); Z. A. B. Zeman and Wilfred Scharlau, *Merchant of Revolution* (London, 1964); G. A. Aleksinskii, "O provokatsii," *Sovremmenyi mir,* no. 3 (1915), pp. 50–63, and *Du tsarisme au communisme* (Paris, 1923).

of November 1918 so strongly colored the atmosphere of Swiss politics that even in the 1950s and 1960s debates on these two subjects could arise periodically in the Swiss press.[6] The works of Markus Mattmüller, Yves Collart, and Willi Gautschi have contributed a great deal toward putting the discussions on a more scholarly level.[7]

My own work, covering the war years of 1914 to 1917, contains several themes which cross at times but merge finally only at the time of revolution in Russia in 1917. I have attempted to give a general picture of the life of the emigrés—their discussions, their disputes, even their conditions of life. The Russians played an extremely important role in the development of the Zimmerwald movement, and in this context Lenin inevitably emerges as the single most important figure in this study.

I have also attempted to characterize the activities of the emigrés belonging to the minority nationalities of Russia. Historians have paid much less attention to these than to the socialists, but in many ways the two were closely linked. The great number of nationalities represented in Switzerland, however, precludes a comprehensive account of all of them; here I have had to settle for a more general picture.

My research has convinced me that the German intervention among the emigrés was largely restricted to contacting representatives of the minority nationalities. Therefore I have tended to link these two problems in my discussions. I have made no effort, however, to investigate the problem of military espionage or sabotage missions for which the Germans attempted to recruit emigrés. Such enterprises usually involved only one individual or at most a small conspiratorial group. Reliable documentation is usually lacking, and these episodes had little impact on the life of the emigrés in general.

Yet another strand to the study is attention to events within Russia. The military fortunes of the Tsarist government, reports of international developments, arrests and deportations—all these factors made an impact on emigré life. I have included a special chapter on the Russian parliamentary delegation in Western Europe in 1916 in order to point

6. See Maurice Pianzola, *Lénine en Suisse* (Geneva, 1952); the comment by Ernst Nobs, "Lenin und die Schweizer Sozialdemokraten," *Rote Revue* 33, 49–64; and Pianzola's response in his *Le Parti socialiste et l'ombre de Lénine* (offprint, Paris, 1954).

7. Markus Mattmüller, *Leonhard Ragaz*, 2 vols. (Zurich, 1957–68), vol. 2; Yves Collart, *Le Parti Socialiste Suisse et l'Internationale 1914–1915* (Geneva, 1969); Willi Gautschi, *Der Landesstreik 1918* (Zurich, 1968).

up the differences between the views of the official, legal opposition in Russia and the mood among the emigrés. This became a vital factor in the events of 1917.

The book falls rather naturally into two parts, divided by the Zimmerwald conference of September 1915 and the German military offensive into Russia in the summer and fall of 1915. Before these events, the socialists, the various minorities, and the Germans appeared to follow rather separate, though parallel, paths. They have accordingly been considered here in separate chapters.

The German offensive of 1915 opened up the question of the future of the territories of the Russian Empire which now fell under the occupation of the Central Powers. The nationalities question in Russia took on new urgency just as the socialist internationalists hesitantly began to organize themselves in opposition to the war. These developments, with sometimes complementary and sometimes antagonistic aims, also affected each other. The second half of the book, therefore, proceeds in a more strictly chronological order, following first one of these questions and then another.

THE RUSSIAN REVOLUTION IN SWITZERLAND

Russian Emigrés
and Swiss Asylum

From the middle of the nineteenth century on, Russians and Poles flocked to Switzerland for education or simply for refuge. Herzen, Bakunin, Lavrov, Nechaev, and Kropotkin had all left their impact on the alpine country, and such leading revolutionaries as Paul Axelrod, Vera Figner, and G. V. Plekhanov still lived there in the first years of the twentieth century. The very origins of the Russian Social Democratic movement lay in Geneva.

As the twentieth century grew older, Switzerland became less important to the Russians; educational opportunities had increased in other Western European countries and German and Austrian socialists showed increasing hospitality to Russian emigrés. The coming of World War I in 1914, however, reversed the trends, and an unusually heavy concentration of political emigrés soon established itself again in Switzerland. Refugees came first from Austria and Germany. Eventually others came from France, where they felt themselves too constricted by the demands of a warring government. In Switzerland the emigrés found both hospitality and distrust.

For the Swiss, the right of asylum represented a hallowed tradition. The government, it is true, reserved the right to deport foreigners who, in the words of the constitution of 1848, would "endanger the internal or external security of the Confederation," but because of Switzerland's federal structure, the central authorities had but limited power. The actual surveillance of foreigners, just as the right of granting citizenship, was a cantonal obligation. On the eve of World War I, as one writer noted, "the federal political police have not one policeman directly under their direction; nor do they have their own police agents in the cantons."[1]

The organization of the cantonal Fremdenpolizei (Alien Police) in Zurich at the end of the nineteenth century illustrated this relationship between the federal authorities and the cantonal authorities. By this time, the problem of asylum had taken on worrisome dimensions: the flow of foreigners was rapidly increasing, and these now included social revolutionaries, as hostile to the social structure of Switzerland as to that of their own countries.[2]

On October 22, 1889, aroused by a bombing incident in Zurich, the Bundesrat, the federal executive council in Bern, called upon the authorities of the city of Zurich to maintain a closer control over the issuing of identity papers to Russian students in Zurich. This request resulted in the establishment, in 1892, of a Fremdenbureau in the Zurich police administration, which centralized the granting of residence permits throughout the entire canton. The federal government agreed to pay the cantonal police 3,000 francs a year to underwrite the costs of the operation.[3]

The problem of dealing with foreigners was a far greater one in Switzerland than in any other European country. According to the 1910 census, 147 of every 1,000 residents of Switzerland were citizens of another country. This was to be compared with 2 of every 1,000 residents in Spain, 4 in Russia, 11 in Holland, 17 in Germany, 27 in France, and 31 in Belgium. One-fifth of the foreigners in Switzerland, moreover, lived in Zurich. Of the 25,282 industrial workers in Zurich, 14,081, or 53.6 percent, were foreigners.[4]

Foreigners with proper identification papers could receive either of two types of residence permits. An *Aufenthaltsbewilligung* (permission

---

1. J. Langhard, *Die politische Polizei der schweizerischen Eidgenossenschaft* (Bern, 1909), p. 330. See also Paul Siegfried Mutter, *Die schweizerische Bundesanwaltschaft als Behörde der politischen Fremdenpolizei* (Zurich, 1916).
2. In 1905 Great Britain altered its immigration laws, largely as a result of the growing influx from Eastern Europe, so as to give the government greater powers to exclude undesirables. See A. A. Geikinga, "Russkoe emigratsionnoe dvizhenie v Angliiu, cherez Angliiu i obratno v Rossiiu," *Izvestiia Ministerstva Inostrannykh Del* 1 (1912): 239–57.
3. ZStAr, P192.
4. See "Die Überfremdung Zürichs," *Neue Zürcher Zeitung*, Jan. 24, 1916; L. Hersch, "Les étrangers en Suisse," *Revue d'économie politique,* offprint (1919), p. 4.

to visit) granted permission to remain for a given period of time, while a *Niederlassungsbewilligung* (permission to settle) allowed the alien to stay indefinitely. Persons without proper identification papers could apply for a *Toleranz*, which, although renewable, was valid only for a specific period of time, usually a year. Another category of foreigners were the *Refraktäre*, persons who for one reason or another refused to answer the call to military service in their own countries. From the point of view of the Swiss authorities, only *Refraktäre* or persons in Switzerland with a *Toleranz* were considered political emigrés, that is, persons in Switzerland without legal identification papers.

According to the census of 1910, there were 4,607 residents of Switzerland whose native language was Russian, and another 2,047 listed Polish as their native language. In all, 8,458 persons had come from European Russia, of whom 3,933 were men and 4,525 women. The largest settlements included 2,155 persons in Zurich, 2,107 in Geneva, 865 in Lausanne, 720 in Bern, and 545 in Basel.[5]

After 1900, the Swiss political police seem to have paid relatively little attention to the Russian political emigrés, who were mostly socialists, and concerned themselves more with the activities of foreign anarchists, who were mostly Italians. Typical was their attitude toward the case of Henry Bint in 1903. Geneva police arrested Bint, a French citizen in the pay of the Okhrana, the Russian secret police, on the charge of attempting to bribe Swiss mailmen and of spying on Russian emigrés. The federal government ordered Bint deported to France but rejected a related appeal by Geneva authorities to close down a Russian printing press. The press, the government declared, was printing socialist literature, not anarchist, and therefore it represented no danger for Switzerland. Subsequent investigation, however, led to the expulsion of the Socialist Revolutionary terrorist Vladimir Burtsev.[6]

In 1905 the Swiss government faced another test when, on February 18, the Russian mission complained that Bern city officials had lent "moral and material concurrence" to collections on behalf of "fomenters of trouble in Russia." The Bundesrat rejected the complaint, declaring that the collections had no official character, and that in any case they aimed at helping not the fomenters of trouble but the victims.[7]

---

5. *Die Ergebnisse der Eidgenössischen Volkszählung vom 1. Dezember 1910,* 2 vols. (Bern, 1915), 1: 65, 74.
6. BBAr, Polizeidienst, Bd. 243.
7. BBAr, Polit. Dept., Russland, Varia, Sch. 528.

Of the Russians in Switzerland, one-fourth to one-third at any given time were students at Swiss universities, and this posed special problems for the Swiss authorities. In the winter semester of 1887–88, for example, Swiss medical schools had enrolled only a total of 95 Russian citizens, 65 of them women. In 1890, the Russian government had tried, in vain, to persuade the Swiss to accept only those Russian students who had official recommendations. By 1900, the number of Russians in medical schools had risen to 365, and the total number of Russian students at the seven universities of Switzerland to 805. By this time, the Swiss themselves had begun to worry at these numbers, and the universities tightened their entrance requirements. The shutting of three of the four women's medical schools in Russia in 1900, however, sent a flood of female students abroad. The universities at both Bern and Geneva experienced a great spurt in applications, beginning with the winter semester of 1900–1901.

In Zurich the number of women grew only in 1902, after the decision of the cantonal educational council, the Erziehungsrat, to admit women who could prove "attendance at a university for at least four semesters with at least twelve hours weekly," even if they had attended only as auditors. In the winter of 1901–2, 62 Russian women attended Zurich University; in the summer of 1902, 81; in the winter of 1902–3, 142; and in the summer of 1903, 162. In July 1903, the Erziehungsrat called on the rectorate of the university to reconsider this policy, and in the winter of 1903 Zurich rejected between 80 and 100 Russian applicants.[8]

Among the Russians were highly qualified as well as poorly prepared students. In 1898, Russians won twelve of the twenty seminar prizes awarded by Bern University. At the same time, many students came with an incomplete mastery of either German or French, and they often lacked the training in Greek and Latin required by the Swiss schools. Swiss students in turn complained that the Russians overcrowded the lecture halls of particularly popular professors; many did not even register for the courses. As the number of Russian women in Bern increased, eventually exceeding 400, critics referred to the medical school as a "Slavic girls' school."

By 1907, the number of Russian citizens enrolled at the seven Swiss universities had grown to 2,343, representing 34.2 percent of the total enrollment. The 1,311 Russians studying medicine constituted 70 per-

8. ZStAr, U98.4.

cent of the enrollment in Switzerland's five medical schools. Russian women, 1,454 of them in 1907, made up the majority of female students at the Swiss universities, with the result that many Swiss university graduates acquired Russian wives.

During the revolutionary turmoil of 1905–7 in Russia, the rector of Zurich University found it necessary to explain to the Erziehungsrat why so many Russians had come to Zurich. The renown of the university naturally provided the first reason, but the flow, he declared, would abate as soon as the situation in Russia had quieted down. He insisted that he required of Russian applicants "the highest preparation which they could receive in their own land." On the other hand, the university regularly admitted students expelled for political reasons from Russian universities.[9]

The rector also emphasized the "large sum of money" which the Russians brought to Zurich annually, without necessitating the hiring of any new faculty or the construction of any new buildings. In the fall of 1906, the Russians had paid registration fees amounting to 10,836 francs, about 57 percent of all fees collected; Russians, furthermore, had paid 2,450 of the 2,730 francs collected from auditors. Therefore, the rector pointed out, "the accusation that the foreign students only bring costs without contributing anything is . . . ungrounded." The rector rejected the idea of a quota for foreigners, and authorities in Zurich, like those in Bern, chose to restrict admissions mainly by raising fees for foreign students in general.[10]

Eventually the federal government entered the controversy. In January 1908, the *Bundesanwaltschaft*, the Federal Attorney General, issued a report complaining of the number of Russians studying medicine in Switzerland, "in part, persons with insufficient linguistic and scientific training." Asserting that in Lausanne and Geneva "there exists a mass of Russians who are strongly suspected of participating in common crimes," the report demanded still stricter controls on the admission of Russian students.[11] In the fall of 1908, the Bundesrat warned cantonal authorities, in the light of an outbreak of cholera in Russia, to maintain

9. In 1902, the university rejected an application from a Russian expelled from the technical school at Karlsruhe "wegen ungehörigen, die Achtung schwer verletztenden Benehmens gegenüber dem Rektor." In 1903 it reconsidered the case and admitted him.

10. Report of the rectorate, Nov. 5, 1906, ZStAr, U98.5.

11. BBAr, Polizeidienst, Russen in der Schweiz, 1908.

a special surveillance of Russian students in the university cities, "where they often live close together in unhygienic conditions."[12]

Still the Russians came. To be sure, the total number of Russian students declined after reaching a peak of 2,468 in the winter of 1907–8. Swiss authorities attributed the decline to more peaceful conditions in Russia and to the opening of German universities to Russian women.[13] Nevertheless, in 1909–10 at Bern, 262 of the 411 medical students were Russians. In Geneva in 1911–12, of 659 medical students 408 were Russians, including 282 women.

In 1913 and 1914 the number of Russians again began to rise. The rector of Zurich University explained this development by pointing to tighter conditions for admission to German universities and the establishment there of quotas for foreign students. In response, the rector, in agreement with the faculties of medicine and philosophy, established a quota, *numerus clausus*, for foreigners in the first and second semesters of medical school. "This will not be announced," he reported to the cantonal educational authorities, but, together with a new rule declaring that work in the natural science faculty could no longer count toward a medical degree, the measure should reduce the pressure of Russian students. The coming of war in 1914, however, proved a far more decisive factor in the subsequent decline in the number of Russian students in Switzerland.[14]

In general, the Russians in Switzerland kept to themselves, and few indicated any interest in acquiring Swiss citizenship. Many professed to find the ways and mores of the Swiss boring and stultifying, although some expressed grudging admiration for such Swiss institutions as the militia system. In turn, the alien ways, particularly of the Russian students, aroused antagonism on the part of the Swiss. Living conditions were difficult. Some emigrés opened businesses; some worked in the watch factories in La Chaux-de-Fonds. Others took more menial positions. A group of students in Geneva took a special three-month

---

12. ZStAr, U98.5.

13. "Jahresbericht des Akademischen Senates an die h. Direktion des Erziehungswesens der Universität," 1910, ZStAr, U101.

14. See ZStAr, U98.6. See also Ernst Gagliardi et al., *Die Universität Zürich 1833–1933 und Ihre Vorläufer* (Zurich, 1938); Richard Feller, *Die Universität Bern, 1834–1934* (Bern, 1935); Botho Brachmann, *Russische Sozialdemokraten in Berlin 1895–1914* (Berlin, 1962). Statistics on attendance at Swiss universities are taken from the records of the Eidgenössisches Statistisches Amt, Bern.

course at the university and qualified as masseurs at summer resorts in Germany. Working from the end of May to the end of September, they saved enough to support themselves through the academic year.[15]

The emigrés inevitably organized their own cultural centers. In Geneva, A. Kuklin established a Russian library, which he eventually turned over to the Bolsheviks. (V. A. Karpinsky became its director.) In 1906, on the outskirts of Geneva, I. I. Fidler organized a school for the children of political emigrés. The Bibliothèque Leon Tolstoy in Geneva had existed since 1875; in 1908, Russian students converted it into a circulating library.[16]

The largest Russian library in Switzerland belonged to Nikolai A. Rubakin, who fled the Tsarist Empire in 1907 and settled in Clarens. Formerly associated with the Socialist Revolutionary Party, he eschewed party activity in Switzerland. Beginning with about 8,000 volumes, he inherited the library of Alexander Herzen's daughter, and by 1920 his collection had grown to 48,000 volumes. At the time of his death in Lausanne in 1946, the library held about 100,000 volumes. A renowned bibliographer and popularizer, Rubakin carried on a voluminous correspondence—over 5,500 letters between 1911 and 1915—and drew emigré intellectuals in great numbers to his home. Among his regular visitors were V. I. Lenin, Anatole Lunacharsky, G. V. Plekhanov, and Vera Figner. Along with Paul Axelrod in Zurich, and Plekhanov in Geneva, Rubakin regularly received Russian intellectuals of all ideologies who travelled in Western Europe.[17]

In Bern, Professor Naum Reichesberg tended to attract Social Democratic emigrés. Reichesberg had left Russia in 1886 to attend the University of Vienna. In 1890 he came to Bern, where he received his doctorate the following year. After a further period of study in Berlin, combined with his last trip back to Russia in September 1891, he returned to Bern, where he became habilitated as a *Privat Dozent* in November 1892. In 1898 he achieved the rank of *Ausserordinarius*, but without salary. His most popular courses included "Social Relations

15. S. Assatiani, "Vospominaniia," MS, Columbia University Russian Archive, New York, pp. 86–87.

16. In 1918 the library, containing 4,000 books and 3,000 brochures, passed into the possession of the Bibliothèque publique et universitaire, Geneva.

17. See A. N. Rubakin, *Rubakin (Lotsman knizhnogo moria)* (Moscow, 1967), pp. 98, 105.

in the Nineteenth Century," "Socialistic and Communistic Theories," and "The Workers' Question Then and Now." In 1901 he established a seminar in statistics, and in 1903 the university began to pay him a regular salary. In 1906 he became *Professor Ordinarius* for Statistics and Political Economy.

Reichesberg belonged to no political party, although, in the words of the Okhrana, he and his twin brother Julian "maintained continued relations with various revolutionary groups in Switzerland, giving them material aid." The Okhrana considered him dangerous, but the Russian mission in Bern on occasion even issued passports on his recommendation.[18]

In Zurich, Fritz Brupbacher, a Swiss anarchist in the Kropotkin mold, gave aid to needy Russians. He was married to a Russian and had long shared the enthusiasm for Russian culture which marked many Swiss radicals at the beginning of the century. Willi Münzenberg, later a close collaborator of Lenin's, credited Brupbacher with first introducing him to Russian literature; other socialists however, decried Brupbacher's anarchist influence on young radicals.[19]

Russians in Zurich also enjoyed the opportunity of participating in the activities of the Verein Eintracht. Organized originally as a workingmen's educational society, Eintracht's membership consisted mainly of Germans and Austrians. According to one member, almost all the leaders of international socialism before 1914 had at one time or another belonged to it.[20] Through Eintracht, which officially belonged to the Social Democratic Party of the city of Zurich, foreigners received membership in the Swiss Socialist Party.

Among themselves, the revolutionary emigrés organized according to

18. See Okhrana report no. 1249, Oct. 23/Nov. 5, 1915, OAr, XIIIb(1), 1915; also BStAr, Hochschule, Juridische Fakultät, Lehrkörper. Reichesberg attended the International Socialist Congress in Basel in 1912 as a spectator, and during one session whispered to one of his students, "Ist das nicht hübsch?" The student, Pius Grigaitis, subsequently came to the United States with money borrowed from Reichesberg. Conversation with Grigaitis, Sept. 5, 1968.

19. Fritz Brupbacher, *60 Jahre Ketzer: Selbstbiographie* (Zurich, 1935), pp. 129, 190–91; V. Miuntsenberg, *S Libknekhtom i Leninym* (Moscow, 1930), pp. 34, 56; Georgij Chicherin, *Skizzen aus der Geschichte der Jugend-Internationale* (Berlin, 1921), pp. 63–64. See also Kurt Guggenheim's novel *Alles in allem* (Zurich, 1957), where Brupbacher appears as Franz Theodor Bluntschli.

20. M. Bronskii, "Uchastie Lenina v shveitsarskom rabochem dvizhenii," *Proletarskaia Revoliutsiia*, 1924, no. 4, p. 32.

party groups. Most major Russian parties maintained separate foreign sections, and many of these were centered in Switzerland. Many Russians, travelling abroad legally, hesitated to join regular party groups, however, and therefore there were also "cooperating groups" (*gruppy sodeistviia*) of one or another party. Most party organizations tended to locate in Geneva, partly because of the libraries there but also because of the printing facilities.

Representatives of the various non-Russian nationalities of the Tsarist Empire maintained separate national groups uniting all political parties, but the Russians worked almost exclusively through their party organizations. The emigré funds, *kassy*, organized in various Swiss cities to help comrades who could not find work, usually admitted to membership only regular members of party groups. The parties also attempted on occasion to organize cheap restaurants. (In 1909, the Union of Russian Political Emigrés in Geneva unsuccessfully sought to have its name inscribed in the city's business register.)

The emigrés received considerable help from their hosts. Throughout Switzerland, Germany, and Austria, organizations collected money for the aid of Russian political prisoners and exiles. Every March the Swiss Socialist Party solicited contributions for aid to the Russians. In the summer of 1914, the various organizations in Switzerland united to form the League of Swiss Relief Societies for Political Prisoners and Exiles of Russia, which had its headquarters on the premises of the Verein Eintracht.

The coming of the war forced new activities upon these various organizations, and at the same time, it threw them into great confusion and disorder. In many cases their original purposes were temporarily forgotten. In Switzerland, as in Russia and even in Paris, nationalist sympathies momentarily overwhelmed class, revolutionary feelings. Even the League of Swiss Relief Societies suddenly became an institution aiding all Russians in Switzerland, regardless of class or ideology.

With the outbreak of hostilities, Russians fled to Switzerland from Austria and Germany. As one emigré put it, "This small country with ancient revolutionary-emigré traditions fulfilled its last revolutionary service in the period of the imperialist war."[21] For the Swiss, the influx posed enormous problems. The government even feared the presence

21. *Ibid.*, p. 30.

of spies among the refugees. The *Journal de Genève* of August 22 reported that some 5,000 Russians were stranded in Switzerland without money. About 100 Russian students in Bern collectively asked landlords and grocers to extend credit. Students in Zurich publicly proclaimed that they "would not shy away from heavy physical labor" in order to raise money. Throughout Switzerland benefit concerts, literary evenings, and exhibitions collected money for refugee relief.

On August 2, Russians in Zurich, using the facilities of the league, organized a Committee of Social Salvation, which opened a kitchen in the quarters of the Union of Russian Students. On the first day, the kitchen had 15 customers; on August 14, the league requested Zurich authorities for permission to use a gymnasium, because the number of participants at dinner time had risen to 150. Of these, only 85 to 90 paid for their meals; the kitchen ran a daily deficit of 26 to 27 francs.[22]

When the Russian mission in Bern announced that Russian citizens would be able to return home on a steamer leaving Genoa, the league took over the task of handling reservations. The mission meanwhile proclaimed itself ready to help all nationals, but it urged all Russians in financial difficulty to take advantage of the opportunity to leave. The Swiss government also urged Russians to leave, even threatening deportation under certain circumstances.

Some 1,400 Russians indicated a desire to take the boat from Genoa, but on the day before departure a flood of cancellations came in as the emigrés apparently had second thoughts about returning home. Of a scheduled 600 passengers on a special train through Switzerland on September 9, only 250 made the trip. In the end, 566 Russians embarked on the steamer.[23]

The height of the cooperation among all Russians came on November 21 and 22, 1914, when representatives of various Russian colonies in Switzerland, including members of the league, met with officials of the Russian mission in Bern. The gathering, chaired by Professor Reichesberg, expressed gratitude to the Russian mission and to the Swiss people for the aid given to the refugees. The assemblage then established a

22. Archives of the league, IISH. See also *Neue Zürcher Zeitung*, Feb. 27, 1915, Feb. 17, 1916.

23. "Otchet o deiatel'nosti Imperatorskoi Missii v Shveitsarii," *Izvestiia Ministerstva Inostrannykh Del* 4 (1915): 174–76; *Neue Zürcher Zeitung*, Sept. 13, 1914.

Committee for Aid to Russian Citizens in Switzerland, with Reichesberg as president and Countess Sologub of Davos as vice-president.[24]
Both the government and the political emigrés were very embarrassed
later by this display of good feeling.[25]

The end of any cooperation was hastened by the Russian government's growing need for manpower. At the beginning of the war, the
Russian mission in Bern announced that for the time being only officers
need report home for military duty. On February 27, 1915, however,
the mission ordered all persons subject to mobilization to return home
within two weeks. Reports by the Okhrana, the Russian secret police,
spoke then of a wave of emigrés leaving France for Switzerland or the
United States; agents in Switzerland reported that the emigrés preferred service in the French army to service in the Russian. A meeting
of political emigrés in Zurich declared that those present had no
fatherland to defend; all refused to report.[26]

In the course of 1915 and 1916 the Russian government put considerable pressure on Russian emigrés in England and France, but the
Swiss government acted forcefully to protect the right of asylum. In
June 1915, when Zurich officials refused a request by the Russian
legation to deliver orders to two Russian citizens to appear for physical
examinations, the federal government confirmed that Swiss authorities
would not deliver communications concerning military service to
foreigners resident in Switzerland.[27]

Many Russian emigrés, of course, had preferred not to live it Switzerland. For some, Paris and London seemed more inviting, despite the
uncertainties of war, but Switzerland offered unique opportunities to
those who chose it. Old party lines lost much of their meaning; new
leaders and new issues arose. To a great extent, these emigrés, living
far from home, were unaware of developments in Russia. On the other

24. Countess Sologub, according to the Okhrana, "was known in revolutionary
circles as one of the big patrons for any kind of affair without exception." Report no. 1249, Oct. 23/Nov. 5, 1915, OAr, XIIIb(1), 1915.
25. Minutes of the meeting, in the archives of the league, IISH. See also
Golos, Nov. 29, 1914; Okhrana reports of Dec. 13/26, 1914, and Oct. 23/Nov.
5, 1915, OAr, XIIIb(1), 1914 and 1915; *Neue Zürcher Zeitung,* Dec. 20, 1914.
26. See Okhrana reports no. 279, Feb. 17/Mar. 2, 1915, no. 371, Mar. 6/19,
1915, no. 431, Mar. 20/Apr. 2, 1915, no. 492, Apr. 7/20, 1915, OAr, XIIIb(1),
1915.
27. BBAr, Polit. Dept., Russland, Varia, Sch. 528.

hand, the emigrés in Switzerland stood in the middle of the intellectual and political currents of wartime Europe. Switzerland quickly became a battleground of diplomacy and intrigue; the diplomatic corps in Bern grew from 71 in 1913 to 224 in 1919. Living in this mixed atmosphere of revolutionary politics, old diplomacy, and wartime intrigue, the Russian emigrés assumed a far greater role in international affairs during the war than they had ever enjoyed in time of peace.

2

The Crisis of
Internationalism

In the confusion of August 1914, Russian revolutionary leaders, scattered from Siberia to London, could present no unified front toward the war. The Second International had called upon socialists to oppose war: "Should war break out none the less, it is their duty to intervene in favor of its speedy termination and to do all in their power to utilize the economic and political crisis caused by the war to rouse the peoples and thereby to hasten the abolition of capitalist class rule." Two Russians and a member of the Social Democracy of the Kingdom of Poland and Lithuania—V. I. Lenin, Julius Martov, and Rosa Luxemburg—had written the statement, which had been adopted by the Stuttgart Congress of the Second International in 1907.[1]

In 1904–5, many Russian socialists had opposed the Tsarist war effort against Japan. The Second International had credited itself with having blocked the spread of the Balkan Wars in 1912, but as the holocaust of 1914 spread across Europe, the International in essence collapsed. Russia went to war on the side of the two Western democracies of England and France. The German socialists, the mainstay of the International, approved war credits for the Imperial government. French and Belgian socialists took cabinet posts. The Russian socialists watched in horror and struggled to comprehend the catastrophe.

Russian socialism itself had a long history of disputes and divisions.

1. Olga Hess Gankin and H. H. Fisher, *The Bolsheviks and the World War* (Stanford, 1960), p. 59.

The International Socialist Bureau, the executive organ of the Second International, included two representatives of the Marxist Russian Social Democratic Labor Party as well as a representative of the peasant-oriented Russian Socialist Revolutionary Party. The Socialist Revolutionaries, heirs of a dying terrorist tradition, had emerged from the revolutionary turmoil of 1905–7 in Russia with new, competing tendencies. One advocated "liquidating" underground activity and concentrating on working within the legal framework of Tsarist Russia. The other sought to maintain a revolutionary character, even while modifying the party's traditional idealization of the peasantry.

The Russian Social Democrats had split into two major factions in 1903—the Mensheviks, a group favoring the development of a mass party along Western lines, and the Bolsheviks, led by Lenin, who insisted on the formation of a more disciplined party of revolutionary activists. Over the succeeding years each group suffered its own internal crises. The Mensheviks, too, saw the development of a "liquidationist" faction eschewing illegal activity, and the Bolsheviks developed a "recall" faction which opposed participation in the Russian legislature, the State Duma, and demanded the recall of the elected Bolshevik deputies.

In 1912, representatives of a variety of factions met in Vienna to form the "August Bloc," a loose alliance backing the Menshevik Organizational Committee against the Bolshevik Central Committee. Even now, however, these two groups did not include all Russian Social Democrats: the *partiitsy,* an antiliquidationist group led by G. V. Plekhanov, and the *Vperëd* group, a Bolshevik faction, maintained their own freedom of action.

The August Bloc soon began to disintegrate into its constituent parts, but a new effort sponsored by the German Social Democrats and the International Socialist Bureau brought together representatives of the Central Committee, the Organizational Committee, the *Vperëd* group, the Plekhanovites, the Jewish Bund, the Social Democracy of the Latvian Region, the Lithuanian Social Democratic Party, two factions of the Social Democracy of the Kingdom of Poland and Lithuania, and the Polish Socialist Party (Left), in the hope of unifying the socialist movement in the Tsarist Empire. Lenin represented the target of the move, and he refused to attend the meeting, held in Brussels in July 1914. Instead, he sent his close friend Inessa Armand as his representative.

The participating groups, with the Bolsheviks and the Latvians abstaining, adopted a resolution in favor of unification. Lenin's opponents expected to carry their offensive to the next congress of the International, scheduled to meet in Vienna in August. Although Lenin enjoyed considerable support among the workers in St. Petersburg and Moscow, he now found himself isolated within the Second International.

The coming of the war in August 1914 made the resolutions of the Brussels meeting obsolete, but Lenin did not forget them. By the end of 1914, the Russian socialists had evolved a new alignment determined by new issues. The "defensists" favored supporting the Entente war effort; the "internationalists" opposed the war. Lenin, who came to dominate the wartime discussions among the Russians, would refer back repeatedly, however, to prewar controversies, justifying his earlier policies and identifying his wartime opponents with his prewar rivals.

Ironically, among the Russian revolutionary leaders who spoke out immediately in August 1914, those in Russia tended to oppose the war effort, while those in the emigration tended to support the Entente cause. Three of the founders of Russian Marxism—Plekhanov, Lev Deich, and Vera Zasulich—declared themselves for the Entente, as did Ilia Rubanovich, the Socialist Revolutionary representative in the International Socialist Bureau.

In St. Petersburg, now soon to be renamed Petrograd, the small Social Democratic faction in the Duma, including both Bolsheviks and Mensheviks, hastily drew up a manifesto denouncing the war as an imperialist struggle. When the Duma convened on August 8 in a special session, the faction presented its declaration and then left the chamber in a demonstration against the voting of war credits. The Tsarist government, however, would not long tolerate any open discussion of the war. The stenographic record of the Duma debate included the Social Democrats' declaration, but it made no mention of the walkout. In November, Tsarist authorities arrested the five Bolshevik deputies, and in December they closed down the socialist press.[2]

In contrast, Russian emigrés in Paris established the United Committee of the Russian Emigration with the avowed purpose of offering aid to France.[3] Some six hundred Bolsheviks, Mensheviks, and Socialist Revolutionaries volunteered for duty in the French Foreign Legion. One

---

2. See Gosudarstvennaia Duma, *Stenograficheskie otchety*, 4-yi sozyv, July 27, 1914, pp. 19ff; A. Badaev, *The Bolsheviks in the Tsarist Duma* (New York, 1932), pp. 199–200; *Berner Tagwacht*, Sept. 1, 1914; William English Walling, ed., *The Socialists and the War* (New York, 1915), pp. 189–93.

3. *Biulleten' ob"edinnenogo komiteta rossiiskoi emigratsii*, no. 1 (Aug. 15, 1914).

group, to emphasize its revolutionary aims, labelled itself the Russian Republican Detachment. The departure of the volunteers, however, left the political arena to emigrés who opposed the war.[4]

Among the most outspoken defensists were Plekhanov, the Socialist Revolutionaries Vladimir Burtsev and Boris Savinkov, and the anarchist Peter Kropotkin. Plekhanov spoke of the necessity of defending the French republic, and he accused the Germans of seeking to enslave Russia economically. Burtsev, who had won renown for his exposures of the Okhrana's penetration of revolutionary organizations, announced his support of the war effort in a letter to the London *Times*. When he dared to return to Russia, however, Tsarist authorities arrested him and deported him to Siberia. Kropotkin warned of the terrifying consequences of a German victory, and he insisted that an Entente victory would mean that this would be the "last European war."[5]

Only in September did the first voices rise publicly in Paris against the war, articulated in the newspaper *Golos* (*The Voice*). Many of these had taken defensist positions only a month earlier. The newspaper's founder, V. A. Antonov-Ovseenko, as head of the emigrés' Labor Bureau, had organized the recruitment office for military volunteers. D. Z. Manuilsky-Bezrabotny, Antonov's coeditor, confided to a friend that he too had almost succumbed to the "epidemic" of volunteering, "simply as if to suicide."[6]

Golos only gradually developed a comprehensive position toward the war, discussing it sorrowfully. The editorial board showed obvious regret at the action of the German socialists, and it apostrophized the Second International with the lament, "Where are you, beauty and pride of the earth?" *Golos* concentrated on countering the praise of Tsarist Russia put out by such erstwhile revolutionaries as Burtsev and Gustav Hervé in *La Guerre sociale* and Edouard Vaillant in *L'Humanité*. After printing an appeal for socialist support of the Entente, written by Emile Vandervelde, a Belgian who was president of the Second International, the editors of *Golos* warned that every blow against Germany "mag-

4. The Russian volunteers drew up a declaration denouncing Germany's threat to the Western democracies and concluding "Down with Tsarism!" Aline [pseud.], *Lénine à Paris* (Paris, n.d.), pp. 109–15.
5. See Samuel H. Baron, *Plekhanov: The Father of Russian Marxism* (Stanford, 1963), pp. 323–24; Angelica Balabanova, *Erinnerungen und Erlebnisse* (Berlin, 1927), p. 63; *Rech'*, Sept. 22, Oct. 15, 1914; Paul Avrich, *The Russian Anarchists* (Princeton, 1967).
6. Manuilskii to Aleksinskii, Oct. 20, 1914, Aleks. Ar., Varia Gr. 26.

nified the political weight of Tsarism in Europe." In response to Hervé's praise of prohibition in Russia, the newspaper declared, "Eh, Hervé, better that the Russian people drink even during war, while you stay silent."[7] On October 3, Julius Martov presented *Golos*'s program: "the quickest possible end to the war and the most radical step toward disarmament."[8]

Defensist and internationalist socialists debated the war in much sharper form in Switzerland. Although the Swiss government was concerned about possible violations of its neutrality—and Switzerland was itself torn by the passions of its German-speaking and French-speaking citizens—the Russian emigrés still found a considerable freedom of expression.[9]

The first reactions among the emigrés in Switzerland also had a defensist tone. Upon his arrival in Zurich, Leon Trotsky complained about the "unquestionable growth of nationalism and patriotism among Russian Social Democrats." Fritz Brupbacher wrote of Vera Figner, a revolutionary of long standing, "From the depression of a defeat she expects more than was possible in prewar conditions, but less than from a victory. She would also greet the defeat of the 'militaristic spirit' of Prussia. . . . These views run through these circles of intellectuals and, moreover, of revolutionaries of all shadings."[10]

The most active defensist was Gregory A. Alexinsky, who had once served as a Bolshevik deputy in the Second Russian State Duma. A veteran of the Bolshevik school in Capri, Alexinsky, together with Manuilsky, had been a member of the *Vperëd* faction from 1910 to 1914. In contrast to many defensists, Alexinsky did not put the need to defend France first; he argued for the defense of Russia, and travelled freely between Paris and Switzerland, delivering lectures urging support of the Russian war effort.

In the first two months of the war, the only emigré to call openly for

7. *Golos,* Sept. 18, 20, 1914.

8. According to Manuilsky, Martov had refused to be editor of *Golos,* arguing that it would be better to publish in Switzerland. Manuilskii to Aleksinskii, Oct. 27, 1914, Aleks. Ar., Voina, f. IX, 138.

9. On the reactions of Swiss socialists to the war, see Markus Mattmüller, *Leonhard Ragaz,* 2 vols. (Zurich, 1957–68), 2:53ff., and Yves Collart, *Le Parti Socialiste Suisse et l'Internationale 1914–15* (Geneva, 1969), pp. 33–85.

10. See Fritz Brupbacher, "Tagebuch," MS, ZSSAr, 1914, p. 117; *Ar. Monatte,* pp. 33–34; Vera Figner, *Nacht über Russland* (Berlin, 1928), pp. 577–79; L. Trotskii, *Voina i revoliutsiia,* 2 vols. (Moscow, 1918), 1:71.

the defeat of Russia was Vladimir Kosovsky, one of the founders of the Jewish Bund and a member of the Bund's Foreign Secretariat in Geneva. Long in semiretirement, Kosovsky gave speeches in Geneva, Bern, Basel, Zurich, and Lausanne. Although he was labelled a pro-German, he argued that he was an internationalist, not favoring either France or Germany. Nevertheless, he declared, "In comparison with Russia . . . Germany, with all her militarism, is a free land."[11]

On August 22, the emigré leadership of the Socialist Revolutionary Party met in Baugy, a small village on the Lake of Geneva. The meeting demonstrated the depth of wartime passions as the group split irreconcilably on the question of the war. I. I. Fondaminsky, a former liquidationist, argued that socialists must recognize the dangers for Europe in the event of a German victory; since Tsarist Russia had aligned itself with the democratic countries of Europe, Russian socialists should eschew any party activity which might weaken the war effort. Viktor Chernov, on the other hand, called for a vigorous campaign against war propaganda and for efforts to organize a "third force" of socialists from all countries to press for peace. He did not go so far as to advocate revolutionary activities, however, in the absence of a corresponding revolutionary movement in Germany. Chernov's only support came from Mark Natanson-Bobrov, who went on to support revolution, foreseeing the possibility of victory running from west to east—Germany defeating Russia but the Western powers defeating Germany. The meeting broke up without any sign of agreement.[12]

Chernov soon departed for Paris, where the Okhrana considered his arrival a major turning point in the emergence of an internationalist position among the socialist emigrés. On November 15, he began publication of his own newspaper, *Mysl'* *(Thought),* but like *Golos,* it had to operate in the shadow of the French censorship. In December, the military governor of Paris ordered both newspapers to avoid statements opposing France's war effort, not to discuss France's internal politics,

---

11. See *Informatsionnyi listok Bunda,* no. 7 (Jan. 1915), no. 10 (Dec. 1915). Kosovsky's own account of his lectures can be found in *Folkstseitung* (Warsaw), Nov. 6, 1931; see also his *Razgrom evreev v Rossii* (Geneva, 1905), reprinted in Switzerland during the war. For an interesting account of a clash between Kosovsky and Alexinsky, see J. S. Hertz, ed., *Doires Bundistn* (New York, 1956).

12. Protocol of the meeting, typescript, Hoover Institution, Stanford University. See also Oliver Radkey, *The Agrarian Foes of Bolshevism* (New York, 1957), pp. 91–94; V. Chernov, *Pered burei* (New York, 1953), pp. 295–306.

and to refrain from criticizing the foreign policy of the Triple Entente.[13]

Even Lenin's Bolsheviks proved no exception to the general picture of disorder and confusion among the Russian emigrés. Bolsheviks in Paris volunteered. In Switzerland, the Bolshevik groups generally showed less of a defensist tendency, but they too lacked decisive leadership. Lenin himself, living in Galicia, was arrested for a few days by Austrian officials on suspicion of being a spy, but after his release he obtained permission to travel to Switzerland.

Lenin formed his basic position on the war while still in Galicia. Persons with him at that time singled out his reaction to the German Social Democrats' approval of war credits on August 4 as decisive. According to one witness, Lenin, upon hearing the news, first expressed disbelief and then declared, "From this day on, I cease to be a Social Democrat and I become a Communist."[14] Others, however, have pointed out that Lenin, up to the outbreak of the war, had paid little attention to international affairs. He had not attended the Basel congress of 1912. His position on the war, therefore, represented a new line of policy for him.

Greeted at the Bahnhof in Bern by the local Bolsheviks on September 5, Lenin was full of questions about the war. Three days earlier, the Bern group had drawn up three theses: (1) the war meant the collapse of the Second International; (2) Germany would probably win the war; and (3) a German victory would mean the worst kind of reaction. Lenin agreed enthusiastically to the first point: "Right, absolutely right." To the other two points, however, he objected. On the question of who would win the war, he considered it still too early to tell. In response to the statement that a German victory would aid reaction, he accused his followers of Russian chauvinism. He only slowly defined his own defeatist views, but sternly objected to expressing a preference for any of the warring powers.[15]

On the following two days, Lenin presented his own theses on the war, which the Bern group readily accepted. Labelling the conflict a "bourgeois-imperialist and dynastic war," he criticized the German

13. Okhrana report, Dec. 11/24, 1914, OAr, XVIIr(1), f. 6.

14. Sergiusz Bagocki, *O vstrechakh s Leninym v Pol'she i Shveitsarii* (Moscow, 1958), p. 38.

15. G. L. Shklovskii, "Vladimir Il'ich nakanune konferentsii," *Proletarskaia Revoliutsiia*, 1925, no. 5, pp. 135–36.

Social Democrats for their "direct betrayal of socialism" and likewise criticized the leaders of the Belgian and the French Socialist Parties for having joined their governments. All this, he argued, represented "an ideological and political collapse of the International." Russian Social Democrats, therefore, should conduct a "merciless and ruthless struggle against Great Russian and Tsarist-monarchist chauvinism. . . . From the point of view of the laboring class and the toiling masses of all the people of Russia, the lesser evil would be the defeat of the Tsarist monarchy and its army."[16]

Although F. N. Samoilov, a Duma deputy, subsequently carried these theses back to Russia, Lenin's views did not immediately win wide notice; they circulated over the anonymous signature "A Group of Social Democrats," and Lenin even labelled them "copied from an appeal issued in Denmark." In Switzerland on a *Toleranz,* he feared the wrath of Swiss authorities.[17]

Lenin's declarations aroused considerable concern within the ranks of his party. The Bolshevik group in Geneva questioned his assertion that the defeat of the Tsarist monarchy would be the lesser evil. As V. A. Karpinsky warned, "Note here the possible connection: the German Social Democrats struggle against Russian Tsarism, and the Russian Social Democrats greet the victory of German arms." Karpinsky also objected to Lenin's vehement denunciation of the International: "It would be an exaggeration to define all that happened within the International as its 'ideological political collapse.' "[18]

Only in October did Lenin begin to speak in public, delivering a paper to a small gathering of Russians in Bern and on October 10 attending a lecture by Kosovsky. On October 11, Lenin put all other business aside in order to attend a lecture in Lausanne by Plekhanov. This historic confrontation between these two rivals constituted a major landmark in the development of the views of Russian Social Democracy towards World War I. It represented the first public meeting of major opponents on the issue of the war. Plekhanov, who spoke for an hour

16. Gankin and Fisher, *The Bolsheviks,* pp. 140–43; N. K. Krupskaya, *Reminiscences of Lenin* (Moscow, 1959), p. 283.

17. The Swiss decree on neutrality, issued in August 1914, provided: "Alle Personen, die sich nicht ruhig und der Neutralität gemäss verhalten, können in das Innere des Landes verwiesen werden; sind es Ausländer, so können sie ausgewiesen werden."

18. Gankin and Fisher, *The Bolsheviks,* pp. 146–49.

and a half, stood before a socialist audience for the first time since the beginning of the war. Lenin, who spoke for only ten or fifteen minutes, offered the first public presentation of his own position.

Plekhanov opened his talk by noting that neither technical conditions nor the psychological moment had permitted the opponents of war to block the outbreak of hostilities in the summer of 1914. The German Social Democrats, however, by voting for war credits, had failed to meet their elementary obligations. Since Social Democrats comprised one-third of the German army, they also had to share the blame for destruction in Louvain and Rheims. At the same time the French Socialists too were perhaps not entirely innocent, but they had to defend themselves. A nation which could claim in its history both the Great Revolution and the Paris Commune had the right to existence.

Plekhanov endorsed both the entry of French Socialists into the French cabinet and the decision of the Russian Social Democratic Duma faction to oppose war credits. The French action, he insisted, "responded to an extraordinary situation," while the Russians, alone among major European parties, had fulfilled their international obligations. He made clear, however, that he considered the French action the more realistic and the more meaningful: "It is easier for a five-year-old girl to keep her virginity than it is for a grown woman."

In response, Lenin agreed with Plekhanov's critique of the German Social Democrats. He disagreed, however, with the apologia for the French, who had shown "more chauvinism than socialism." The French position, he acknowledged, was "psychologically more understandable," but he insisted that the basic problem was not that of who had attacked whom. The task of Social Democracy was to struggle with chauvinism in its own land, not to "drift with the current." Rather than to enter the government, "it is better to go to a neutral country and from there to speak the truth."

In closing the meeting, Plekhanov countered by citing Marx on the right of a people to existence and therefore to self-defense. One must struggle with chauvinism, he agreed, but one must also calculate who is the aggressor in any given war.[19]

When Lenin returned to Bern on October 16, he received the news that the Bolshevik Duma delegation in Russia had endorsed his theses

---

19. The authoritative account of this meeting is in *Golos*, Oct. 18–21, 1914. See also Lenin's notes on Plekhanov's lecture, *Leninskii Sbornik*, 14:124–31.

on the war. He also learned of the response by Russian socialists to the appeal by Emile Vandervelde, president of the Second International, for support of the Entente war effort. The Bolsheviks had rejected it outright; the Menshevik leadership had remained silent; but one group, representing the Petrograd journal *Nasha Zaria (Our Dawn),* declared that while it could not support the war, it did not "oppose" the war.[20]

Lenin now decided to renew publication of the central organ of the Bolshevik party, *Sotsial'demokrat.* Although he had recently praised *Golos* as being the best socialist newspaper in Europe, he felt the need for a forum of his own. The text of his comments on the Bolshevik answer to Vandervelde has been lost, but he was undoubtedly as critical of it as he was of the socialist declaration to the Duma. He had objected first of all to the fact that the Bolsheviks had cooperated with the Mensheviks in writing the declaration, and the pacifist spirit of the statement conflicted with his own views. The answer to Vandervelde had discussed only the question of support of the Tsarist war effort and had offered no opinion, for instance, on the action of the French Socialists. *Sotsial'demokrat* was to be Lenin's vehicle for crystallizing socialist opinion.[21]

In any event, by late October Lenin was losing his enthusiasm for *Golos.* He had welcomed Martov's criticism of both the Germans and the French, but he despaired of Martov's refusal to condemn the International. *Golos* had long hesitated to comment on Plekhanov's position, on the grounds that the "patriotic" publications which had published his statements had possibly distorted them. Only in October did *Golos* finally turn on Plekhanov, but with obvious regret. When Anatole Lunacharsky lumped Plekhanov with Burtsev and Kropotkin, the editorial board objected, insisting that a qualitative difference still existed between the men.[22]

Martov, an old opponent of Lenin, was obviously embarrassed by the new alignment of Russian socialism. In a letter to Paul Axelrod on October 14, he noted that his position was closer to Lenin's than to Plekhanov's, but that he had "no desire to work together with him." On October 27, now fully acquainted with the reports of the Lausanne meeting, Martov still shied away from Lenin: "It is obvious that Lenin and Co. would compromise us more than they would help us."[23]

20. See Walling, *The Socialists and the War,* pp. 359–60; *Golos,* Dec. 23, 1914.
21. See Krupskaya, *Reminiscences,* pp. 388–89.
22. *Golos,* Nov. 1, 2, 1914.
23. *Pis'ma P. B. Aksel'roda i Iu. O. Martova* (Berlin, 1924), pp. 303, 305.

Nevertheless, Martov wanted to believe that Russian socialists were now divided only into two camps: for and against the war. *Sotsial'demokrat* appeared on November 1, and in *Golos* of November 12 Martov took note of the publication with the comment that old, useless disputes must be forgotten: "Leaving aside a few unfounded polemical attacks, we cannot but welcome this publication."

Lenin, however, had no intention of glossing over differences between himself and others. He complained that Martov yielded too easily to the men around him and that he had retreated from his original strong stand against the war. Lenin demanded not compromise and reconciliation but "splitting," "surgery," and the adoption of an uncompromising, revolutionary line. For the time being, however, Lenin restricted his appeal to the Russians. The emigré with the greatest international impact in the first months of the war was not Lenin, Plekhanov, or Martov, but rather Leon Trotsky.

Trotsky arrived in Zurich on August 4 from Vienna, which he had left immediately after being warned that the Austrian police had issued a warrant for his arrest. He plunged immediately into local politics, and in Fritz Brupbacher's words, "with Trotsky's arrival in Zurich, life returned to the labor movement, or at least to one sector of it." Together with Brupbacher, Leonhard Ragaz, and Willi Münzenberg, Trotsky worked to develop a radical socialist faction in Zurich.[24]

On October 7 the Eintracht Society, influenced by Trotsky, declared its position on the war, and because of Eintracht's reputation this document aroused discussion among socialists of all nationalities. The resolution proclaimed, "We denounce and decisively reject that antisocialist manner of action which divides the international proletariat under the flag of national defense and welds the proletariat to the war carts of the bourgeoisie." After asserting, "This is no war of aggression and no war of defense," the declaration went on to warn that a Russian victory would bring disaster to workers' organizations in Central Europe. In conclusion it demanded, "No forcible annexation of territory! No war indemnities! National self-determination as the basis for the formation of new states! A United States of Europe!"[25]

When the Social Democratic Party of the city of Zurich held a con-

---

24. See Fritz Brupbacher, *60 Jahre Ketzer: Selbstbiographie* (Zurich, 1935), pp. 188–89; Mattmüller, *Ragaz*, 2:97–113.
25. *Volksrecht*, Oct. 15, 1914.

ference on October 26 to debate the war, Trotsky and Fritz Platten, a Swiss socialist, spoke on behalf of the Eintracht resolution. To enthusiastic applause, Trotsky urged that problems of defense be left to those "who are masters over the armies and misuse them." The gathering went on to label the war a "crime," and "an unavoidable result of capitalist class rule." The conference demanded a quick end to the conflict.[26]

Trotsky systematized his views in a pamphlet entitled *The War and the International,* which represented the first Russian statement opposing the war addressed to an international audience. The work appeared late in November; Platten and other members of the Eintracht Society handled its distribution.[27]

Rejecting the idea that socialists could gain anything with the victory of either warring camp, Trotsky offered the "immediate ending of the war" as the "slogan under which Social Democracy can again gather its shattered ranks." The very struggle for peace would "not only free the workers of the hypnosis of nationalism, but [would] bring about a redeeming inner cleansing in the present official parties of the proletariat."[28]

Trotsky and Lenin confronted each other on October 27, when Lenin came to speak in Zurich. On this occasion Lenin declared, "It would not be bad if the Germans occupied Riga, Tiflis, and Helsinki." He later confided to his supporters that he had said this in order to test his audience, which consisted of several hundred Russians. The opposition rose to his challenge.

Trotsky led the attack, asserting that while he agreed with Lenin in regard to the character of the war, he still supported the Eintracht program: an immediate peace without annexations and without indemnities. "This very slogan," Trotsky insisted, "means a rising against governments . . . a revolution." In addition, Trotsky objected to Lenin's denunciation of the German socialist Karl Kautsky as a "traitor" to socialism. Another speaker, I. Kisilev, declared that only "German agents" could call for the defeat of Russia. The discussions extended over two evenings before Lenin returned to Bern.[29]

26. *Volksrecht,* Oct. 27, 1914.
27. See Leonhard Ragaz, *Mein Weg,* 2 vols. (Zurich, 1952), 2:78–79. The introduction appeared in Russian in *Golos,* Nov. 20, 1914. Reviews in *Volksrecht,* Dec. 4, 1914, and *Berner Tagwacht,* Dec. 28, 29, 1914.
28. Trotsky, *Krieg und Internationale* (Zurich, 1914), p. 81.
29. *Leninskii Sbornik,* 14:138–40; See also M. M. Kharitonov, "Iz vospominanii," *Zapiski Instituta Lenina,* 2:115–118; R. B. Kharitonova, "V. I. Lenin

Shortly thereafter Trotsky left Switzerland for Paris. His reasons for moving are not clear. In his memoirs, he spoke of having been named a correspondent for the liberal Russian newspaper *Kievskaia Mysl'*. On the other hand, he may have been drawn by the possibility of working on the staff of *Golos*. In any case, his decision came suddenly, for he had already applied for a *Toleranz* in Zurich, which was granted in December, after his departure. (According to a pencilled note in the Zurich city records, Trotsky had "departed without address.")

In December 1914 Martov came to Zurich to help organize the Foreign Secretariat of the Menshevik Organizational Committee. Lenin had praised Martov from a distance. Now he attacked him. Ironically, according to reports reaching the Okhrana, Martov, upon his arrival, had told his colleagues that he agreed basically with Lenin on the question of the war. Reportedly Martov, over Axelrod's opposition, considered forming a united front with the Bolshevik leader.[30]

Whatever the hopes Martov might have had, they vanished on December 16 when he addressed a gathering in Bern on the subject "The War and the Crisis of Socialism." Lenin labelled Martov's speech "a sociological introduction to eclectic politics." He criticized Martov for still clinging to the slogan of an immediate peace, even after the the German Social Democrats had just showed signs of splitting. Lenin also denounced Martov's failure to attack the "treachery" of the leaders of the Second International. Martov, in response, accused Lenin of demagogy.[31] Upon his return to Paris at the end of the month, Martov found more trouble as he immediately clashed with Trotsky over the editorial policies of *Golos*.

By the end of 1914, therefore, Lenin had made clear his program, and he had established himself on the left wing of the Russian socialist spectrum. His following was as yet minuscule. Many critics called him pro-German. Some pointed to the human costs involved in a military defeat, others to the support which Lenin now received from the anarchists. Nevertheless, using *Sotsial'demokrat* as his vehicle, he had passed from his defensive position at Brussels to a new offensive. His opponents

---

v tsiurikhskoi sektsii bol'shevikov," *O Vladimire Il'iche Lenine* (Moscow, 1963), pp. 148–49; S. V. Tiutiukin, "Leninskie referaty o voine (osen' 1914)," *Istoriia SSSR*, 1967, no. 2, pp. 39–41.

30. Reports dated Dec. 5/18, 10/23, 1914, OAr, XVIb(6) (b), f. 1.

31. *Sotsial'demokrat*, Dec. 12, 1914, Feb. 1, May 1, 1915; *Pis'ma Aksel'roda i Martova*, p. 307.

of old, he claimed, had now taken defensist postures, either openly or in disguised form, and had thereby shown themselves to be traitors to international socialism.

On the right wing of the socialist spectrum stood the defensists, ranging from the *Nasha Zaria* group through Plekhanov, Alexinsky, and Fondaminsky. Plekhanov laid out his position in a publication entitled *Social Democracy and the War*. The crux of his argument lay in his conviction that Belgium and France had been unjustly attacked. German militarism posed the greatest danger to Europe at the moment, and the international proletariat should unite to oppose it.

Plekhanov admitted that Russia's role in the war was ambiguous, and he hastened to assure his readers, "I am and remain an irreconcilable enemy of Tsarism." Yet a Russian defeat would only hinder revolution in Russia, and a Russian victory offered no serious threat to Europe, since no country "with a retarded economy" could dominate the continent. Although he denied that he had any pan-Slav sympathies, he characterized the war as a national struggle for existence on the part of the Russians.[32]

Alexinsky presented his position in a four-part essay entitled "The War and Socialism," beginning on November 15 in *Golos*. Socialists, he insisted, must not hesitate to assign guilt to any one party. Simply to blame the capitalist order was to evade the question. For his own part, Alexinsky declared that the German Social Democrats had failed in their obligations, while French and Belgian socialists had justifiedly responded to foreign attack: "We are not Tolstoyans." Speaking in Zurich on November 13, he had gone further, declaring that internationalism such as Lenin's played into German hands. Later he developed his views in still stronger terms, alleging that Lenin and Trotsky both were German agents.[33]

The majority of the emigré socialists stood in the broad middle of the political spectrum, opposing the war in principle but not sharing Lenin's desire for civil war and Russia's defeat. They advocated "no victories, no defeats." But even here vast differences existed; the old

32. *La social-démocratie et la guerre* (Paris, 1914). Reviewed in *Golos,* Dec. 26, 1914, and *Mysl'* Jan. 8–9, 1915.

33. See OAr XVIb(7), f. 8; Grégoire Alexinsky, *Du tsarisme au communisme* (Paris, 1923), pp. 24ff. The editors of *Golos* expunged Alexinsky's criticisms of Lenin in their publication. See Antonov to Aleksinskii, Nov. 24, 1914, Aleks. Ar., Voina, f. IX, 139.

organizations had shattered on the new issues, and no new ones had yet risen in their place.

Writing in December 1914, Lenin characterized the split among the socialists as representing three new tendencies: chauvinists who followed the policies of the opportunists, centrists who leaned toward the chauvinists, and internationalists, the opponents of opportunism. In 1916, from the other side of the fence, the Okhrana also saw three tendencies: "open defeatists," "disguised defeatists," and "defensists."[34] Pulled between the extremes, the mass of internationalists struggled desperately to establish their own identity.

34. *PSS,* 26:104; *Obzor,* p. 86. An Okhrana circular of December 26, 1914, had an entirely different picture, calling Alexinsky the left, advocating a policy "not to interfere with the war effort." Plekhanov, who wanted to "aid the war," was on the right. Lenin, who demanded "end the war" and "social revolution," constituted the center. OAr, IIe, f. 1, pp. 3–14.

3

The Leninist Offensive

In the confusion of the first months of the war, the Russian emigrés in Western Europe could speak for no one but themselves; old party affiliations meant little. In this vacuum, *Golos* had arisen as a rallying point for those opposed to the war, but its leadership deliberately chose not to turn the newspaper into either the organ of any existing socialist group or the seed of a new factional organization. As a result, the newspaper, while it represented radical tendencies, offered no systematic program. Its contributors differed widely in their respective views, and the editorial board found itself repeatedly divided on major issues.

Among the emigrés, only Lenin responded to the new conditions of wartime with a comprehensive program of action. To be sure, at first he worked just to consolidate his own party ranks; he made little effort to appeal to Western Europeans in the first months of the war. Nevertheless, by the winter and spring of 1915 he had developed a clear pattern: unyielding criticism of other Russian socialist leaders and violent denunciation of the leadership of the Second International, combined with a more flexible attitude toward dissident members of foreign socialist parties.

Although he chose to live in Bern, Lenin worked closely with V. A. Karpinsky in Geneva, from whom he received invaluable organizational assistance. With Lenin in Bern were G. E. Zinoviev and G. L. Shklovsky. Among his other important contacts were M. M. Kharitonov in Zurich and G. L. Belenky in Paris. Karl Radek eventually provided a channel for Germany and the Netherlands. Through Alexander Shliapnikov in

Stockholm and Maxim Litvinov in London, Lenin soon reestablished his communications with Petrograd as well as with socialists in England and Scandinavia. The Georgians and Armenians in Geneva served as a link with the Caucasus.[1]

According to Karpinsky, Lenin at this time addressed only restricted gatherings, open to party members or recommended persons. Fearing the Swiss police, he warned his followers to keep no incriminating evidence in their homes and to use invisible ink in their correspondence. Even so, Lenin's views soon became known throughout the emigration.[2]

Lenin had almost no following among the Swiss. On his very first evening in Bern, he visited the home of Robert Grimm, the editor of the Swiss Socialist Party organ *Berner Tagwacht*. Grimm at that time rejected what he viewed as a call to civil war in Switzerland, and he refused even to publish Lenin's theses on the war.[3] Although Soviet historians have insisted that Lenin strongly influenced the joint meeting of Swiss and Italian socialists held in Lugano in September, there is no evidence to support this claim.[4]

The confrontation with Plekhanov in October and the decision to resume publication of *Sotsial'demokrat* marked the real beginning of Lenin's public activity. The difficulties of publishing were frustrating. Since the party organ had been dormant for a year, Lenin had to ask Karpinsky to determine what number the issue should carry. The Bolshevik treasury held just 160 Swiss francs, a sum incapable of supporting the daily newspaper which Lenin desired.

The only printer with Russian characters whom Karpinsky could find

1. According to Shliapnikov, communications through Sweden tended to break down whenever he was not there. *Kanun semnatstogo goda*, 2 vols. (Petrograd, 1923), 1:88. See also G. B. Garibdzhanian, *V. I. Lenin i bol'shevistskie organizatsii Zakavkaz'ia (1893–1924)* (Erevan, 1967), pp. 219ff.

2. V. A. Karpinskii, "Vladimir Il'ich za granitsei v 1914–1917gg.," *Zapiski Instituta Lenina*, 2:75–76, suggested that Lenin had erred in evaluating the "class consciousness and acumen of his enemies." On the other hand, Lenin was probably influenced by the fact that Swiss police had raided G. L. Shklovsky's residence in the first days of the war.

3. Robert Grimm, "Lenin in der Schweiz," *Der öffentliche Dienst VPOD*, Apr. 13, 1956. Cf. the varying interpretations of this meeting in Arnold Reisberg, *Lenin und die Zimmerwalder Bewegung* (Berlin, 1966), p. 90; G. L. Shklovskii, "Tsimmerval'd," *Proletarskaia Revoliutsiia*, 1925, no. 9, pp. 77–78; Helmut König, *Lenin und der italienische Sozialismus* (Tübingen, 1967), pp. 13–14.

4. See Yves Collart, *Le Parti Socialiste Suisse et l'Internationale 1914–1915* (Geneva, 1969), pp. 103–5.

was Kuzma-Liakhotsky in Geneva, who besides working in the Ukrainian movement, handled the publications of most of the other Russian emigré groups in Switzerland. On top of all else, he worked only in the evenings. At one point, Krupskaya, Lenin's wife, complained, "The typesetter is nonparty and a positive man. He prints for all factions in turn." In any case, the Okhrana considered Kuzma's press incapable of publishing a daily, "even a small one."[5]

Despite these handicaps Lenin, together with Zinoviev and Karpinsky, managed to establish the form and content of the first issue of the newspaper within a week after the decision to publish, and issue no. 33 of *Sotsial'demokrat,* the central organ of the Bolshevik party, appeared on November 1, 1914. On November 14, Lenin announced that the newspaper "had been delivered at a point near the [Russian] frontier and would be forwarded on."[6]

Lenin laid out his program in a series of slogans, which he gradually refined during the fall and winter. In his September theses he had defined the war as a "bourgeois, imperialist and dynastic" conflict. As the slogan of the moment, he proposed, "first a thorough propaganda (to be spread also in the army and the area of military activity) for a socialist revolution and for the necessity of turning the weapons not against brothers, hired slaves of other countries, but against the reaction of the bourgeois governments and parties of all countries." The slogan appeared in finished form in a manifesto, published by *Sotsial'demokrat* in the name of the Central Committee: "The transformation of the contemporary imperialist war into a civil war is the only correct proletarian slogan, pointed out by the experience of the Commune, outlined in the Basel (1912) resolution, and derived from all the conditions of an imperialist war between highly developed bourgeois countries."[7] The manifesto also broadened the scope of Lenin's appeal. Although printed only in Russian, the manifesto posed tasks for all the Social Democrats of Europe, whereas the September theses had concentrated on Social Democracy in Russia.

5. Okhrana report, Feb. 2/15, 1915, OAr, XVIIr(1), f. 6; S. M. Levidova and S. A. Pavlotskaia, *Nadezhda Konstantinovna Krupskaia* (Leningrad, 1962), p. 106.
6. *PSS,* 49:28–31.
7. Olga Hess Gankin and H. H. Fisher, *The Bolsheviks and the World War* (Stanford, 1960), pp. 142, 156; D. Baevskii, "Partiia v gody imperialisticheskoi voiny," in M. N. Pokrovskii, ed., *Ocherki oktiabrskoi revoliutsii,* 2 vols. (Moscow, 1927), 1:377–78.

Lenin did not delude himself about the imminence of revolution and civil war. Writing to Shliapnikov on October 17, he warned, "We can neither 'promise' civil war nor 'decree' it, but we are obliged to work in this direction." The moment for civil war, he declared, was not yet clear; "We must allow this moment to ripen, we must systematically 'force it to ripen.' "[8]

Lenin scorned such individual actions as "refusal to serve in the army, strikes against the war, etc.," as being "simple stupidity, a miserable and craven dream about an unarmed struggle with an armed bourgeoisie, a yearning for the annihilation of capitalism without a desperate civil war or a series of wars." As for the slogan of "peace without annexations and without indemnities," Lenin wrote, "The *wise* bourgeoisie [of England] are *for* peace (of course, in order to *strengthen* capitalism). And we must not permit ourselves to be mistaken for petty bourgeoisie, sentimental liberals, etc. . . . We must stand for the slogan of the *revolutionary proletariat* which is capable of *struggling* for *its own* aims; and this means nothing but civil war."[9]

Upon his arrival in Bern, Lenin reportedly told Shklovsky, "He is not a socialist who does not, in time of imperialist war, desire the defeat of his own country."[10] In his theses, Lenin put this somewhat differently: "From the point of view of the working class and the toiling masses of all the peoples of Russia, the lesser evil would be the defeat of the Tsarist monarchy and its army." Lenin made his views clear to his intimates, but he apparently hesitated to make this point explicit in writing. Nevertheless, he added to the theses a call for "self-determination for the oppressed peoples of Russia," which implied the call for the defeat of the Tsarist government.

Lenin continued to couch this slogan in terms of the "lesser" or "least" evil in his manifesto of November 1. Orally, as he did in Zurich, he went further in discussing his "defeatism," but only after Karl Liebknecht's antiwar speech of December 2 in the German Reichstag did Lenin apparently feel free to write more openly. In an article entitled "On the National Pride of the Great Russians," published in December 1914, he declared that "we enlightened Great Russian proletarians" are "filled with national pride, and therefore we particularly hate our slavish

8. *PSS*, 49:14–15; Gankin and Fisher, *The Bolsheviks*, p. 158.
9. Gankin and Fisher, *The Bolsheviks*, p. 198.
10. G. L. Shklovskii, "Nakanune konferentsii," *Proletarskaia Revoliutsiia*, 1925, no. 5, p. 137.

past . . . and our slavish present." Because of this pride, Russian Social Democrats "cannot 'defend the fatherland' otherwise than by wishing defeat for Tsarism in every war." Even this statement, however, was buried deep in the article.[11]

Lenin's third major slogan concerned the fate of the International. His September theses had proclaimed the "ideological, political collapse" of the Second International. (A variant text, interestingly enough, read "the partial, ideological collapse.") The cause of the collapse was "petty-bourgeois opportunism." In his manifesto of November 1, Lenin emphasized the need to "construct a new and firmer socialist coalition of the workers of all countries." The "proletarian international," he explained, "did not perish and shall not perish. The working masses will create a new International in spite of all obstacles. The present triumph of opportunism is short-lived."[12]

As Lenin explained to Shliapnikov, "The slogan of 'simply' reestablishing the International is incorrect (because the danger of a spineless conciliatory resolution along the line of Kautsky and Vandervelde is very, very great!)."[13] Writing in *Sotsial'demokrat,* he went on to say, "The Second International is dead, conquered by opportunism. Down with opportunism and long live the Third International purified not only from 'deserters' (as *Golos* wishes) but from opportunism too!"[14]

Lenin was not alone, however, in calling for a Third International. At this point, the slogan represented a denunciation of the leadership of the Second International rather than a plan for a new organization. The Dutch socialist Anton Pannekoek had made this clear in the pages of the *Berner Tagwacht;* as he wrote to Grimm, "I view the attempts now being made to glue the old International together as humbug."[15]

Lenin also raised slogans which he subsequently abandoned. Such was his call in the September theses for the "transformation of all the separate states of Europe into a republican united states." He repeated this idea in the November manifesto as "the immediate political slogan of the Social Democrats of Europe."[16] Because of the difficulty in defining

11. See Baevskii, "Partiia v gody voiny," pp. 379ff.
12. *Ibid.,* p. 511; *PSS,* 26:2; Gankin and Fisher, *The Bolsheviks,* pp. 154, 156.
13. *PSS,* 49:13.
14. *Ibid.,* 26:41.
15. Robert Grimm Archive, 2. Teil IISH.
16. See Gankin and Fisher, *The Bolsheviks,* pp. 143, 155.

the specific tasks of the Social Democrats in each country, he eventually discarded this slogan.

A major part of Lenin's program called for criticism of his opponents: "We allow ourselves to think that internationalism consists only in an unequivocal internationalist policy pursued inside the party itself. . . . To seek refuge in silence or to wave away this bitter but unavoidable truth is, for a socialist, detrimental to the workers' movement."[17] The self-conscious socialist must make his program clear and explicitly distinguish his differences from his opponents and rivals.

For Lenin, his opponents fell into two categories, chauvinist and opportunist. In October, Lenin labelled Plekhanov a "French chauvinist," Alexinsky a "Francophile," and Kosovsky a "Germanophile." Chernov he freely linked with Boris Savinkov, an outspoken defensist. The German leader Karl Kautsky drew the brunt of Lenin's fire, but his attacks on other Russians gradually gained momentum. In January 1915, Lenin lumped together Plekhanov ("a continuous substitution of sophism for the dialectic"), the *Nasha Zaria* group ("it pours water on the mill of Great Russian, Tsarist-Purishkevichist chauvinism"), and Axelrod ("a model of 'Russian-Bundist' social chauvinism"). He charged Axelrod with a "double obeisance—one to the German social chauvinists, the other to the French." In Lenin's view, to explain the positions of the defensists, as Axelrod tried to do, constituted endorsing them: "One does not analyze arguments in favor of a pogrom; one only points them out so as to put their authors to shame in the sight of all class-conscious workers."[18]

Lenin posed as the rationale of his polemics, "Who with whom and who where?" The problem, he insisted, was "war on the opportunists and social-chauvinists" and not unity. The efforts of *Golos* and *Mysl'* to find a common ground for socialists were worse than useless: "The editorial board of *Golos* prefers unity with the social-chauvinists to a rapprochement with those persons who are unalterably opposed to social chauvinism."[19]

Lenin's first major opportunity to display his program came with the convening of an Entente socialist conference in London on February 14, 1915. Called at the initiative of Emile Vandervelde, the gathering was

17. *PSS*, 26:118.
18. *PSS*, 26:119–25, 157; 49:13, 101.
19. *PSS*, 26:117–18.

to serve as a private rather than an official meeting.[20] Since Vandervelde considered the Russian emigrés unrepresentative of the currents in Russia, he did not invite them. The Russians, however, insisted on their right to attend, and having won it, they entered into a bitter debate as to how or even whether they should exercise that right.

Some Socialist Revolutionaries and Social Democrats favored coordinating a Russian position before the conference. On January 29, *Mysl'* called for a "preliminary Russian all-socialist conference." On February 6, *Nashe Slovo (Our Word),* which had succeeded *Golos* after the latter's suppression on January 17, proposed to both the Central Committee and the Organizational Committee that internationalists unite to make a joint demonstration at the London meeting. On February 9, Lenin agreed, posing a nine-point program as the basis for a declaration. Repeating his slogans of civil war, class struggle, and a new International, Lenin went on to warn that the Organizational Committee and the Jewish Bund "will be on the side of 'official social patriotism' (in its Francophile form, its Germanophile form, or in the form reconciling these two tendencies)." Privately, Lenin expressed doubts about the possibility of agreement.[21]

The board of *Nashe Slovo* had trouble achieving an agreement even among its members. Martov won Trotsky's approval of a program of agitation for peace, opposition to the idea of a "national bloc," and a demand for the mobilization of international socialism against Tsarist reaction. Trotsky, however, rejected Martov's proposal that the two of them, together with Axelrod, represent the Organizational Committee in London.[22]

Martov seemed most concerned at this time by what he saw as an effort on the part of his opponents to picture him as an isolated man, separated from the main body of Mensheviks in Russia, who were considered defensist. He directed his own efforts, therefore, at publicizing the internationalist views of his friends—F. I. Dan, then in Siberia, and Axelrod. After Axelrod had refused to go to London for reasons of health, Martov resolved to go himself. The British government, however, frustrated this move by refusing visas to both Martov and his friend

20. Gankin and Fisher, *The Bolsheviks*, p. 273.
21. *PSS*, 49:62, 64.
22. Okhrana report, Feb. 24/Mar. 9, 1915, OAr, XVIc, f. 4; Martov to Axelrod, Jan. 21, 1915, *Pis'ma P. B. Aksel'roda i Iu. O. Martova* (Berlin, 1924), p. 315.

Stanislaw Łapiński (Pawel Lewinson), a representative of the Polish Socialist Party (Left).[23]

Both Bolsheviks and Mensheviks eventually had to rely on their sympathizers in London to represent them at the conference. Ivan Maisky agreed to take on this task for Martov and the Organizational Committee, and Maxim Litvinov for the Bolshevik Central Committee. Representing the Socialist Revolutionaries were Chernov, Natanson, Rubanovich, and A. A. Argunov. The Jewish Bund, the Latvian Social Democrats, and the Polish Socialist Party took no part.

The resolutions adopted by the conference denounced capitalism and criticized Tsarism, but at the same time the delegates made clear their support of the Entente cause. They declared that their aim was not to crush the German and the Austrian peoples, but that they were at war "only with the governments of those countries by which they are oppressed."[24] Some contemporary observers praised the conference as having reestablished the prestige of socialism. The French writer Romain Rolland welcomed "the first courageous word pronounced publicly by official socialism."[25] The Russian emigrés, however, had other views.

Two of the Socialist Revolutionary delegates supported the final resolution of the conference; Chernov and Natanson abstained. Chernov had suggested that the conference distinguish between the desirability of a French and English victory on the one hand and of a Russian victory on the other. The delegates refused to discuss the question. On February 23, *Mysl'* declared that the conference had accomplished nothing toward the reestablishment of an international socialist movement. Subsequently, Chernov found himself under attack for even having been present for the final vote.

Both Russian Social Democratic delegates left the conference before its conclusion. Maisky had plenipotentiary authority from Martov to make a statement in opposition to the war, but he simply handed Martov's written statement—which Chernov had brought to London—to the chairman and departed. Litvinov, on the other hand, virtually had to force his way into the meeting, despite the fact that he was the Central

---

23. Okhrana report, Feb. 13/26, 1915, OAr, XVIc, f. 4; Feliks Tych, *PPS-Lewica w latach wojny 1914–1918* (Warsaw, 1960), p. 73.

24. Gankin and Fisher, *The Bolsheviks*, pp. 278–79. See also *Ar. Monatte*, pp. 93, 113.

25. Romain Rolland, *Journal des années de guerre 1914–1919* (Paris, 1952), p. 261.

Committee's representative to the International Socialist Bureau. Silenced once by the chairman, who declared that his mandate was unclear, Litvinov subsequently made a second attempt to denounce the entire conference. When the chairman again interrupted, he left the hall in protest.[26]

In Paris, Martov publicly declared that both he and Łapiński would have voted against the final resolution. He criticized Chernov first for having remained in the meeting and then for having only abstained. The Bolsheviks added their own voices to the chorus attacking the conference, but more important, from Lenin's point of view, was Litvinov's dramatization of the idea of "splitting" with the Second International.[27]

At the end of February, Lenin convened members of the Bolshevik party to formalize his program on the war. He also wanted to reestablish the Bolshevik Committee for Organizations Abroad, KZO, which had disintegrated in August 1914 in Paris. At the same time, he had to deal with objections within his party to various of his slogans.

Most serious was the development of opposition on the part of Bolsheviks in Baugy. This group, headed by N. I. Bukharin, Elena Rozmirovich, and Nikolai V. Krylenko, opposed Lenin's defeatism and his call for civil war. Finding it impossible to express their views in *Sotsial'demokrat,* they were preparing to publish their own newspaper, to be called *Zvezda (The Star),* which would compete with Lenin's publications for both funds and readers. When Lenin objected, Bukharin argued that the group would remain loyal: "What can you have against another party newspaper which in its very first lead article declares that it shares the views of the central organ?"[28] This particular group was to cause Lenin trouble continually throughout the war, and the Bolshevik leader was undoubtedly disturbed by their youth. Bukharin, Rozmirovich, and Krylenko were all under thirty years of age; either they would accept the Leninist line or else they would lead a new divisive trend within the party.

Lenin had delayed the conference for some time because of his argument with the Baugy group. He had also awaited the arrival of two

26. Okhrana report no. 276, Feb. 17/Mar. 2, 1915, OAr, XIIIb(1), 1915; *Berner Tagwacht,* Feb. 20, 1915; Gankin and Fisher, *The Bolsheviks,* pp. 282–84.

27. See the account in Ia. G. Temkin, *Lenin i mezhdunarodnaia sotsial-demokratiia 1914–1917* (Moscow, 1968), pp. 115-20.

28. D. Baevskii, "Bor'ba Lenina protiv bukharinskikh 'shatanii mysli,' " *Proletarskaia Revoliutsiia,* 1930, no. 1, p. 23.

"Japanese" comrades, G. L. Piatakov and Eugenia Bosh, who had been making their way around the world after escaping from Siberia. (They had received their sobriquets after sending Lenin a postcard from Tokyo.) To Lenin's dismay, the two, upon arriving in Switzerland, went first to Baugy—Rozmirovich and Bosh were sisters. The Bolshevik leader decided to wait no longer, and when the conference opened on February 27, nine of the thirteen delegates present were residents of Bern. The other four, representing Paris, Zurich, Geneva, and Lausanne, were all regular correspondents of Lenin.[29]

The conference's image was obviously Lenin's greatest concern. As he declared to a friend a year later, in answer to a question as to how many delegates were necessary for an effective conference, "Just ten, even seven, maybe even five, but just that they are really true representatives of the masses, true revolutionaries, Bolsheviks, and underground workers. . . . Once we have correctly decided all questions, in accord with the movement of the toiling masses, of war and revolution, the number of delegates will not play such a great role, since each member of such a congress, even one of only ten real Bolsheviks or even less, will be more valuable than dozens and even hundreds of delegates of other congresses of another period."[30]

In the first phase of the meeting, Lenin met with serious opposition only on the question of his slogan "A United States of Europe." G. L. Shklovsky, the chairman of the conference, argued against it on economic grounds, but otherwise the assembled delegates accepted the proposal unanimously. The next day, Lenin himself discarded the slogan without any discussion.

On the question of the attitude toward the war, the conference endorsed the November manifesto as published in *Sotsial'demokrat.* The delegates went on to charge a commission of three members—Zinoviev, Lenin, and Inessa Armand—with elaborating "theses for a resolution within the limits set by the manifesto." After further discussion of such questions as the distribution of *Sotsial'demokrat,* the problem of cooperation with other emigré groups, and the formality of electing a new

---

29. Krupskaya claimed to have the proxy vote of the London Bolsheviks. Okhrana agents claimed that in naming the representatives, Lenin had antagonized Bolsheviks in London and in Zurich. Okhrana reports, May 26/June 8, 1915, and May 28/June 10, 1915, OAr, XVIb(2), f. 2.

30. M. Tskhakaia, "Vstrechi s Leninym," in *Takim byl Lenin* (Moscow, 1965), pp. 87–88.

Committee for Organizations Abroad, some of the delegates departed. The delegate from Zurich, Kharitonov, considered the conference to have ended, but after he had left the "Baugy group" arrived. A new phase of the conference's work ensued, as Bukharin and Lenin clashed on the question of the war.[31]

The final decisions of the conference represented a compromise. The Baugy group dropped its plans for a newspaper. The conference called for civil war, a new International, and a break with "social chauvinists," but Lenin yielded in accepting the more moderate defeatist formula: "the defeat of Russia under all conditions appears to be the lesser evil."[32]

Shortly after the ending of the Bern conference Lenin suffered a serious blow, as news came of the trial on February 23 in Petrograd of a group of Bolsheviks, including Duma deputies, who had been arrested three months earlier. Lenin's September theses had provided the basis of the government's case, and L. B. Kamenev, whom Lenin had personally sent to St. Petersburg in January 1914, denied that he subscribed to Lenin's defeatist position. In a letter of March 9, Lenin complained that the men on trial had "conducted themselves badly." In public, however, he emphasized the usefulness of the trial in publicizing the Bolshevik program.[33]

When an International Women's Socialist Conference met in Bern on March 26–28, Lenin greeted it with a well-prepared program. Organized by Klara Zetkin, chairman of the International Bureau of Women Socialists, the meeting brought together about twenty-seven women of whom at least eight were from Russia. Representing the Bolsheviks were Armand, Krupskaya, Zlata Lilina, Rozmirovich, and Olga Ravich. They had the cooperation of Anna Kamienska of the Social Democracy of the Kingdom of Poland and Lithuania. From the ranks of Mensheviks came Angelica Balabanova, now representing the Italian Socialists, and Irina Izolskaia, both from Zurich.[34]

31. See M. M. Kharitonov, "Iz vospominaniia," *Zapiski Instituta Lenina,* 2:120. The Okhrana interpreted the two sessions as constituting two separate conferences. See Alfred Erich Senn, "The Bolshevik Conference in Bern, 1915," *The Slavic Review* 25 (1966):676–78.

32. See Gankin and Fisher, *The Bolsheviks,* p. 190.

33. *PSS,* 26:168–76, 49:68. Cf. *Rech',* Feb. 13, 1915.

34. Olga Ravich, "Mezhdunarodnaia zhenskaia sotsialisticheskaia konferentsiia,

The prevailing atmosphere of the meeting was one which Lenin denounced as pacifist. The Bolsheviks had at first sought to limit the gathering to a more radical membership, but according to Armand, Zetkin decided to convene "an 'official conference' instead of a conference of the left."[35] The delegates spoke of seeking a "just peace." The Bolsheviks offered a resolution criticizing the socialist parties of the warring powers for having betrayed socialism, calling for an end to civil peace, and demanding a clear break with the Second International. By a vote of twenty-one to six, the meeting rejected the resolution, but in order to win unanimous support for the majority's resolution Zetkin agreed, after consulting Lenin, to publish the Bolshevik resolution in the official report of the conference. The Bolsheviks accordingly declared that while they still disagreed with the majority's resolution, they nevertheless accepted it as a first step in the revolutionary struggle. In turn, the *Berner Tagwacht* called the manifesto of the conference all the more important because it had been accepted unanimously, and it called the conference's work "fruitful in all ways."[36]

Speaking later in Zurich, Armand called the conference "a first step— a portent of greater things." A speaker in Geneva declared that while the conference had not done what should have been done, nevertheless it constituted an important move "toward the awakening of the masses and the first stone in the construction of a new international brotherhood of workers of all countries." Lenin criticized the majority's resolution sharply: "Not a word of censure for the traitors or a single word about opportunism."[37]

Lenin followed the same tactics at the beginning of April when an International Youth Conference, under the direction of Willi Münzenberg, opened in Bern. Represented by Armand and G. I. Safarov, Lenin remained outside, communicating by telephone. The political currents of the youth conference resembled those of the women's conference, and

1915g.," *Proletarskaia Revoliutsiia*, 1925, no. 10, p. 169; Okhrana report, Apr. 8/21, 1915, OAr, XVIIs, f. 3; *Nashe Slovo*, Apr. 13, 1915. Temkin, *Lenin*, p. 128n, has indicated that a protocol of the meeting exists in Russian archives.

35. Temkin, *Lenin*, pp. 122ff.; Pavel I. Podliashuk, *Tovarishch Inessa* (Moscow, 1965), pp. 143ff.

36. *Berner Tagwacht*, Apr. 3, 1915; N. K. Krupskaya, *Reminiscences of Lenin* (Moscow, 1959), pp. 301–2; *Sotsial'demokrat*, June 1, 1915; Angelica Balabanova, *My Life as a Rebel* (London, 1938), pp. 148–51.

37. Temkin, *Lenin*, pp. 132–33; *PSS*, 26:204.

when their resolution was defeated by fourteen to four, the Bolshevik delegation staged a walkout. The majority of the conference refused to pass judgment on the Second International. Lenin then received a delegation from the meeting, and another compromise resulted.[38]

One of the most significant results of the youth conference was Lenin's meeting with Münzenberg, who was impressed by his "stubbornness." When the leadership of the conference subsequently established a permanent international youth secretariat in Zurich, Münzenberg, its director, drew Lenin's special attention. By 1916, the two were co-operating closely.[39]

Balabanova later wrote that Lenin apparently had some sort of master plan of revolutionary strategy in mind. While advocating a split with the Second International, he was showing a certain spirit of compromise toward internationalists from various Western European countries. On the other hand, he showed no such tolerance or spirit of compromise in dealing with his Russian opponents, whom he labelled either open or disguised defensists.

In the aftermath of Vandervelde's London conference, *Nashe Slovo* had called for a conference of all Russian internationalists. The Mensheviks hoped for an even broader conference than *Nashe Slovo* had proposed. During the month of March, Viktor Chernov travelled through Switzerland to confer with representatives of both the Organizational Committee and the Central Committee, as well as with Socialist Revolutionary groups. Lecturing in the Eintracht House on March 12, he called for greater pressure by workers' groups on the governments of Europe. On March 15 in Lausanne, he called for peace, to be contracted not by the present government of Russia but by a constituent assembly.[40]

On March 23, Lenin issued his response to the proposal for unity among Russian internationalists, and he thereby essentially killed the idea of a conference. Agreeing in principle that unity was a nice idea, he questioned just who might be considered an internationalist. He

38. See Temkin, *Lenin*, pp. 133–36; *Berner Tagwacht*, Apr. 17, 1915; Balabanova, *My Life*, p. 152; Maurice Pianzola, *Lénine en Suisse* (Geneva, 1965), p. 112; Krupskaya, *Reminiscences*, p. 303.

39. See Babette Gross, *Willi Münzenberg: Eine politische Biographie* (Stuttgart, 1967), pp. 33ff.

40. Okhrana reports, Mar. 13/26, 1915, and Apr. 7/20, 1915, OAr, XVIIg, f. 2, and Apr. 23/May 6, 1915, OAr, XVId, f. 2. See also *Zhizn'*, Apr. 15, 21, 1915.

twitted his opponents with the point that they had stood with Plekhanov against the Bolsheviks in Brussels in 1914. He declared that the Bund "breathes an unideological eclecticism" and that its organ "undoubtedly adheres to the Germanophile chauvinist point of view." The Organizational Committee in Russia was defensist; its Foreign Secretariat in Zurich at best represented five members. Axelrod, in any case, held an "obviously chauvinist (almost Plekhanovist) position."[41]

In response, *Nashe Slovo* deplored the Bolsheviks' tendency "to turn a partial disagreement in viewpoint into a reason for counting Social Democrats among the social chauvinists." Trotsky later added his own voice more explicitly, publicly complaining that the Bolsheviks sought allies within Western socialist parties while attacking or ignoring other Russian organizations and groups: "Either the British Independent Socialists, Nicod, and Merrheim are your allies, and so is *Nashe Slovo* (yet you pass over it in silence, for considerations which are not of a fundamental nature), or you have no allies at all in the International."[42]

Now, for the first time, Lenin began to collect an international following. "No matter that we are so few," he declared, "we shall have millions with us." He considered his work "already different, closer to action."[43] In contrast, other Russian internationalists proved incapable of developing strong organizations, and a drift into Lenin's camp was already visible in the spring of 1915.

Nashe Slovo itself gave evidence of the problem as it published analyses of the new alignment among Russian socialists. On March 5, Kazimierz Zalewski asserted that persons who hoped to "avoid" the split which Lenin was demanding had to recognize that the split in fact already existed. On March 6 and 7, Lunacharsky spoke of "new watersheds" among Russian Social Democrats; a new "high ridge" ran through the party. Unity was essential, to be sure, but only a unity which excluded all those persons compromised by nationalist, chauvinist feelings.

Lunacharsky's article stemmed from the revival of the *Vperëd* group in Geneva. Organized in 1908, it had proclaimed as its purpose "uniting comrade Bolsheviks without distinction of shade." In 1913 and 1914, the group had split as G. A. Alexinsky and D. Z. Manuilsky, both in

41. Gankin and Fisher, *The Bolsheviks*, pp. 164–67.
42. *Ibid.*, pp. 168, 173.
43. Krupskaya, *Reminiscences*, p. 303; *PSS*, 26:190.

Paris, had sought a stronger anti-Leninist stand. Lunacharsky had maintained his conception of the organization not as a faction but as a means of uniting all Bolsheviks.

The war added to the group's troubles, as Alexinsky became a defensist and Manuilsky participated in the founding of *Golos*. In August, Lunacharsky himself adopted a defensist position, but in November 1914 he publicly attacked Plekhanov. Although he at first praised Martov, he soon turned against him, particularly on the question of splitting.[44]

In December 1914, the *Vperëd* group in Geneva held its first meeting in six months, criticizing those socialists who had worked with the Russian mission in Bern during the fall. Lunacharsky came to Switzerland to participate in the group's next meeting, held on January 30, 1915, at which it declared itself in favor of the organization of a new, third International. Lunacharsky assumed the task of formulating a definite program.

Back again in Paris, Lunacharsky pressed the editorial board of *Nashe Slovo* for a strong declaration favoring a conference of internationalists and criticizing the defensists. Martov opposed any attack on the *Nasha Zaria* group, despite pressure from most of the other members of the board. The majority itself could reach no agreement, as Manuilsky went so far as to propose limiting the conference to "those elements believing that the war is the immediate prologue to social revolution." In a compromise decision, Lunacharsky's position appeared in the newspaper over his own name. The *Vperëd* group in turn issued its first public statement as an endorsement of Lunacharsky's article.[45]

Martov and Axelrod set themselves against formally recognizing the new divisions among Russian Social Democrats. Martov could enthusiastically join Lunacharsky in criticizing the Socialist Revolutionaries for not denouncing such a defensist as Rubanovich, but he was hesitant to condemn Social Democrats. Paul Axelrod declared that at the end of the war he expected to be able to work again with Plekhanov, but not with

44. Okhrana report, Oct. 29, 1914/Nov. 11, 1914, OAr, XVIIg, f. 1; A. V. Lunacharskii, *Vospominaniia i vpechatleniia* (Moscow, 1968), pp. 134–48; *Golos*, Nov. 1, 1914.

45. *Nashe Slovo*, May 28, 1915; Yves Collart, "A propos de deux lettres d'Anatole Lounatcharski," in *Contributions à l'histoire du Comintern*, ed. Jacques Freymond (Geneva, 1965), p. 126; undated letter from Lunacharsky to the Geneva group, probably written at the beginning of March 1915, in the Vperiod Ar.

Lenin. The new divisions, he argued, had little in common with the old struggles between "revisionists" and "Marxists." It was unwise to emphasize the differences between some camps and at the same time to remain silent about "the defects in the position of Lenin's journal." Axelrod consistently opposed all tendencies to reach agreement with Lenin.[46]

Lenin had now established his position on the left wing of the socialist movement among Russians as well as internationally. Socialists who still rejected him gradually found that as their own positions became more radical, they were actually nearing Lenin's program on one or another point. As Trotsky said in reply to Axelrod, the new divisions would not only prove long-lasting, but they would in fact dominate the political scene for many years.[47]

46. "Iz besedy s P. B. Aksel'rodom," *Nashe Slovo*, May 12, 16, 1915; Temkin, *Lenin*, p. 135n.

47. *Nashe Slovo*, May 16, 1915; Trotskii, *Voina i revoliutsiia*, 2 vols. (Moscow, 1918), 2:123–25.

4

The Nationalities

For the Tsarist government, the problem of the national minorities of the Empire posed as great a threat as the socialist movement. Foremost among these minorities stood the Poles, who even before 1914 had well-developed hopes and ambitions of national independence. Others, nurturing hopes of eventual independence, proposed more moderate programs of national autonomy within the framework of the Empire. Although the Tsarist government tended to encourage rivalries and antagonisms between national groups, it feared the developing strength of the national movements, and as a result, many leaders of the nationalities found their places beside socialists in prison, in Siberia, and in the emigration.

The Russian liberals, who were concerned for the greatness of Russia, and the socialists, who were concerned for Russia's economic unity and development, also watched the national movements carefully, debating the expediency of supporting one or another of them. In turn, the politics of each nationality contained a variety of contending factions, including conservatives who favored the Russian monarchy and socialists who argued in favor of the establishment of an all-Russian republic. On the whole, however, the leaders of the minorities tended to associate themselves with the Russian left, liberal or socialist, even though they themselves were more conservative in their own social philosophies.

At the Duma's special session on war credits, held on August 8, 1914, the Duma deputies from the minority nationalities rose one after another to proclaim their loyalty to the Russian government. Other minority leaders who held no positions in the official order, to the contrary, tended to favor the defeat of the Tsarist government. In their opposition to the government, many felt no loyalty to the state.

The Jews in Russia held an anomalous position among the nationalities. Unable to claim any given territory as ethnically Jewish, they had representatives in almost all camps. Epitomizing the crosscurrents of nationalism and social revolution was the Jewish Bund, the Allgemeyne jüdische Arbeiterbund (General Jewish Workers' Alliance), founded in Vilna in the early 1890s. It was an integral part of the Russian socialist movement, yet it had difficulty in defining its own relationship to the other socialist parties.

The members of the Bund had a strong consciousness as Jews, especially as a persecuted minority in Russia, and although the Bund took part in the debate on the war among Russian socialists, the basically defeatist attitude of its Foreign Secretariat reflected the politics of Russia's national minorities more than it did the attitudes of the other socialist parties. At the same time, the Bundists opposed the breakup of Russia into national states, which would only divide up the Jewish population. They favored a democratic state guaranteeing cultural autonomy to national groups.[1]

The Poles constituted the most numerous element, after the Russians, among the Tsarist emigrés in Switzerland. They had long flocked, both legally and illegally, to Swiss institutions of higher learning, even preceding the Russians in many places, particularly the university and the ETH (Eidgenössische Technische Hochschule) in Zurich and the Catholic university in Fribourg, founded in 1889. In Zurich the Polish students had established a Verein polnischer Studierender in 1887. Other organizations of varying duration followed; the Polnische fortschrittliche Studentenverein, founded in 1910, sought to unite "students of both institutions of higher learning, as well as academics of Polish nationality in general, who support the 'economic, political, and national freedom of peoples.' "[2]

Fribourg, which included three Poles on its faculty, even attracted

---

1. In March 1915 the Foreign Secretariat of the Bund denounced Zionist "Palestinophile agitation" as another wartime illusion. *Nashe Slovo,* Mar. 7, 1915.

2. Hans Erb, *Geschichte der Studentschaft an der Universität Zürich 1833–1936* (Zurich, 1937), p. 381. See also Jan Hulewicz, "Les études des Polonais dans les universités suisses, 1864–1918," in *Pologne–Suisse* (Warsaw, 1938), pp. 118–31.

the attention of the German government, both because of its religious character and because of its role in educating Polish nationalists. The Reich had long refused to recognize academic degrees earned in Fribourg. Not all the students, however, were revolutionaries. In 1913, for example, the Russian legation in Bern challenged Swiss police treatment of two Polish students in Fribourg who belonged to "families of high Polish nobility."[3]

Since Poland was the first battlefield between Russia and the Central Powers, the loyalty of the Poles became a major issue in the very first days of the war. Grand Duke Nikolai Nikolaevich, Commander in Chief of the Russian armed forces, promised the Poles autonomy; the Austrian army proclaimed that it was advancing into Russian Poland, "and we will nevermore leave this land"; the German press reported large-scale risings in Poland against Russian rule.[4]

Long divided in their political loyalties as a result of the partition of Poland between Austria, Russia, and Prussia, Polish leaders carried their old alignments into the war. The only Pole present at the Duma's special session of August 8, a National Democrat, supported the Russian cause. The Party of Political Realism and Roman Dmowski's National Democratic Party welcomed the manifesto of the Russian Commander in Chief. In contrast, Józef Piłsudski, a leader of the Polish Socialist Party, favored the Central Powers against Russia, and on August 6 he led a small force, to be called the Polish Legion, into Russian Poland and seized Kielce "in the name of free and independent Poland." Behind this initiative arose a Supreme National Committee, organized in Cracow and pro-Austrian in orientation.[5]

The socialist emigrés were themselves deeply split on the Polish question. In *Golos,* Kazimierz Zalewski (Stanislaw Trusiewicz) published several articles calling for the establishment of Poland as an "independent, neutral country."[6] On the other hand, several Polish socialist

---

3. The Swiss police charged the students with having mutilated a Swiss army uniform and having mixed up shoes outside hotel room doors. BBAr, Polit. Dept., Russland, Varia, Sch. 528.

4. See Alexander Dallin, "The Future of Poland," in *Russian Diplomacy and Eastern Europe, 1914–1917* (New York, 1963), pp. 1–77.

5. See R. Dyboski, "Military Efforts and Political Activities of the Poles," in *The Cambridge History of Poland,* 2 vols. (Cambridge, 1950–51), 2:463.

6. *Golos,* Sept. 24, Nov. 7, 1914; Okhrana report no. 10, Jan. 3/16, 1915, OAr, XIIIb(1), 1915. On Zalewski, see Georg W. Strobel, *Quellen zur Geschichte des Kommunismus in Polen, 1878–1918* (Cologne, 1968), pp. 122–23.

groups opposed the idea of independence. In the first days of the war, representatives of the SDKPiL (Social Democracy of the Kingdom of Poland and Lithuania), the PPS-Lewica (Polish Socialist Party–Left) and the Bund met in Warsaw to denounce the war and to declare their opposition to Piłsudski. Representatives of these groups in the West echoed their sentiments.

The SDKPiL had long distinguished itself for its opposition to Polish nationalism. Rosa Luxemburg, one of the party's founders, had engaged Lenin in a polemic on just this point. Luxemburg, who held posts in both the SDKPiL and the German Social Democratic Party, insisted that nationalism obscured the common interests of workers of all nations; socialists could not support the principle of national self-determination. Lenin, who bore no sympathy for bourgeois nationalism, nevertheless argued that the failure to recognize the strength of national feeling only played into the hands of the ruling classes. In any case, Lenin continued, the socialist revolution would not occur in all countries at once. It would take place over a period of time. The principle of national self-determination therefore could be a progressive force in national liberation movements against colonial and imperial powers. Despite Lenin's arguments, the SDKPiL maintained its position, and it attracted many Jewish activists who opposed both Polish nationalism and the nationalist elements in the program of the Bund.

The SDKPiL split into two groups in 1911, and in 1914 the division took definite form. On the one side stood the Central Committee (Zarząd Główny) and on the other, an amalgam of dissident local groups, the National Committee (Zarząd Krajowy). Although the insistence of the "dissidents" on working with Lenin was a major factor in the split, in their opposition to the war and their denial of the principle of national self-determination the two groups were virtually indistinguishable. Personal factors had probably contributed most to the split.[7]

The leadership of the Central Committee included Leo Jogiches, Rosa Luxemburg, and Adolf Warski. The National Committee included the brothers Stein (Stein-Dąbrowski and Stein-Kamieński), Jakob Fürstenburg-Hanecki, and Karl Radek. Kazimierz Zalewski hung uncertainly suspended between the factions.

7. See J. P. Nettl, *Rosa Luxemburg*, 2 vols. (London, 1966), 2:548–600; Strobel, *Quellen*, pp. 62–83; Georges Haupt, ed., *Correspondance entre Lénine et Camille Huysmans 1905–1914* (Paris, 1963), pp. 100–103.

The PPS-Lewica had broken off from the Polish Socialist Party in 1907. Although objecting to the nationalistic spirit of PPS leaders such as Piłsudski, the group did not go so far as the SDKPiL, instead accepting the idea of autonomy for Poland. Its chief representative in the emigration, Pawel Lewinson-Łapiński, was a close friend of Julius Martov.[8]

All the Polish socialist groups cooperated in the Krakowski Związek Pomocy dla Więźniów Politicznych (The Cracow Union for Aid to Political Prisoners), often referred to by its German name, the Krakauer Verband. Formally organized in 1911, although its origins dated back to 1895, this group gave aid to both Russian and Polish political prisoners and exiles. At the beginning of the war, Sergiusz Bagocki, an old friend and medical consultant of Lenin and Krupskaya, moved the secretariat of the group to Zurich. With him came Feliks Kon and Alexander Bucewicz. Bagocki himself lived in Wil, but the Krakauer Verband came under the supervision of the League of Swiss Relief Societies. In relief work, as in their political disputes, the radical Polish socialists were more closely tied to the Russian socialists than to the Polish nationalists.[9]

Polish emigrés in Switzerland enjoyed easy access to both liberal and socialist publications. As the *Journal de Genève* of May 16, 1915, noted, "sympathies for Poland are a Swiss tradition." The Poles, of course, had their opponents too. In the *Neue Zürcher Zeitung* of August 13, 1914, Solomon Grumbach (Homo) declared that the idea of a Polish rising against the Tsar was illusory, that Poland's economy was inextricably linked to Russia's, and that the Poles as a people were "incapable of self-government." On August 17, a Polish writer answered that independence would in fact prove an economic boon for Poland, and he declared that party strife would give way to the higher cause of "freedom and independence." On August 26, the newspaper commented that the Russian Poles were "ripe for revolt—overripe."[10]

Polish groups in Switzerland split along all the lines of their compatriots

8. On Łapiński, see Strobel, *Quellen,* pp. 111–12; Janina Kasprzakowa, "Pawel Lewinson-Łapiński (1879–1937)," *Z pola walki,* 1965, no. 3, p. 101.

9. In a speech in Zurich on January 23, 1915, Felix Kon spoke of a unified revolutionary movement: "Die frühere Gegensätze zwischen Russen, Polen, u.s.w., sind nicht mehr vorhanden." *Volksrecht,* Jan. 25, 1915.

10. Grumbach, an Alsatian member of the French Socialist Party, attempted to prove the solidarity of all the peoples of Russia by claiming that members of the nationalist Union of the Russian People were known to have kissed Jews. *Neue Zürcher Zeitung,* Sept. 7, 1914.

at home. The Supreme National Committee in Cracow sent representatives to Switzerland to collect funds and recruit volunteers for the Polish Legion. What support the Central Powers enjoyed, however, was largely pro-Austrian. There were no pro-German Polish organizations; Berlin had the cooperation only of individuals. The pro-Austrian elements centered their activities in Rapperswil, a picturesque city on the Lake of Zurich and the site of a Polish national museum, where they operated an information agency. They also collected funds for war relief through a Swiss bank in Rapperswil.[11]

The librarian of the Polish museum, Stanislaw Zielinski, was arrested in the fall of 1914 on the charge of having violated Swiss neutrality by assisting in the recruitment of seventy-six volunteers for the legion. Although a Swiss court acquitted him, the Russian government, among others, henceforth kept a close eye on his activities.

On January 19, 1915, Swiss President Guiseppe Motta received a delegation of Poles, including the novelist Henryk Sienkiewicz, the pianist Ignacy Jan Paderewski, Professor Jósef Wierusz-Kowalski of the University of Fribourg, and Antoni Osuchowski, a lawyer originally from Warsaw. The delegation announced the creation of the Comité général des victimes de la guerre en Pologne, which, in Sienkiewicz's words, was to be "purely philanthropic and nonpolitical." Motta in turn approved of its aims and assured the Poles that the Swiss government sympathized with them.[12]

The new organization, which soon established its headquarters in Vevey, named Sienkiewicz its honorary president and Paderewski honorary vice-president. Osuchowski served as president of the executive committee. Using Sienkiewicz's name prominently, the group issued a public appeal for funds, sponsored concerts throughout Switzerland, and generally sought out the support of foreign intellectuals resident in Switzerland. Sienkiewicz also won the support of the papacy. In all, the committee established 174 "Pro Prolonia" branches throughout the world, of which 117 were located in the United States. By March 31, 1917, it had collected 15,827,500 Swiss francs, over half of which came from America.[13]

---

11. On the Polish museum, see Helmut Neubach, "Das Polenmuseum in Rapperswil," *Zeitschrift für Ostforschung* 13:721–28.

12. See Marcel Handelsman et al., *La Pologne: Sa vie économique et sociale pendant la guerre* (Paris, 1932), 1:566–68.

13. *Ibid.*, p. 568.

The committee sought to avoid connection with any one belligerent, but its members felt free to follow their own paths. Sienkiewicz considered disputes over orientation to be "sterile and even harmful." Germany, he considered, was in the better strategic position at the moment, but he did not believe that the Central Powers would win the war. Neither the Entente nor the Central Powers could promise Poland anything substantial. In Kielce at the beginning of the war, he had reacted coldly in his contacts with the Polish Legion. Soon thereafter, having received permission to travel to Cracow, he had chosen to move on to Switzerland, where his first interest was the relief of war suffering. In the summer of 1915, he welcomed the fall of Warsaw to the Germans because the battle line had now moved on eastward, giving Poland respite.[14]

Erasmus Piltz, the committee's secretary general, worked openly for the Entente cause. The Austrian minister in Bern characterized Piltz as "undoubtedly the *spiritus rector* and political head" of pro-Russian Poles in Switzerland. He apparently cooperated with the Russian mission in Bern, while at the same time maintaining contact with the Austrian mission. In the view of the Austrian minister, Piltz would be found on the side of the winner. At the end of February 1915, Piltz called upon Poles in Paris to abstain from advocating independence in order not to antagonize the Russian government.[15]

Piltz also worked on compiling a Polish encyclopedia aimed at informing the Western European public about Polish affairs. He himself undertook the direction of a single-volume edition, and Professor Kowalski began organizing a three-volume work. (Jan Żółtowski later replaced Kowalski.) The first results of the project appeared in 1916 and served as a major instrument of Polish nationalist propaganda.

The most widely travelled member of the relief committee was Paderewski, who made his way to the United States. Not all were happy

14. Both the Austrian police and the Okhrana affirmed Sienkiewicz's neutrality. See the Okhrana reports of Nov. 1/14, 1914, Jan. 5/18, 1915, July 21/Aug. 3, 1915, Aug. 28/Sept. 10, 1916, OAr, XIX, ff. 5, 11, 12B; Austrian police report, July 1915, HHSAr, PA, 904/8e/61; Roman Dmowski, *Polityka polska i odbudowanie państwa* (Warsaw, 1926), p. 168; Janusz Pajewski, *Wokół sprawy polskiej: Paryż-Lozanna-Londyn 1914–1918* (Poznan, 1970), pp. 111–15.

15. See Gagern to Vienna, June 15, 1915, HHSAr, PA, 904/8e/8; Austrian police report of September 30, 1915, HHSAr, PA, 904/8e/79; Marian Leczyk, *Komitet Narodowy Polski a Ententa i Stany Zjednoczone 1917–1919* (Warsaw, 1966), pp. 29–30, 32.

with his work, however, especially with his decision to include Russian diplomats in the Pro Polonia branches. In Paris, the Russian ambassador, Alexander Izvolsky, together with Madame Bertie, the wife of the British ambassador, was named honorary president of the local committee, arousing strong protests among the emigrés.[16]

On January 22, 1915, the *Gazette de Lausanne* published a long article entitled "La Pologne et la Guerre," which argued the need of an independent Poland for the stability and peace of Europe. The author of the anonymous work, Jan Kucharzewski, subsequently organized a society bearing the same name, Pologne et la Guerre. His purpose was to publicize the cause of Polish independence without attaching the fate of the country to one or another of the belligerents. The society opened a public reading room in Lausanne and embarked on an ambitious program of publication.

The society wanted to develop an image of Poland as a viable political and national entity. Writing in 1915, Kucharzewski argued simply for the existence of a Polish nation; by 1916, he had progressed to the point of discussing Poland's role as a European state. Other writers undertook to present Poland's economic life, its culture, and its politics. More than anything else, the group emphasized Poland's role as a buffer between the great powers. On the other hand, as one writer noted, the Poles had to maintain their independence of action; "The enemy of today can become the ally of tomorrow and vice versa."[17]

The relationship between Kucharzewski and Sienkiewicz's committee was uneasy. Many Poles feared to strike out on such a vague path as Kucharzewski proposed. It could in fact antagonize either the Austrians or the Russians. Sienkiewicz and Paderewski, however, apparently blocked a move within the committee to denounce Kucharzewski's stand, and they reportedly ordered several thousand copies of his article from the *Gazette* when it appeared as a brochure.[18]

To a certain degree, the various Polish organizations complemented each other even as they competed. The relations between La Pologne

16. Undated memorandum, OAr, XIX, f. 5.

17. Charles Potulicki, "La Pologne d'hier et de demain," *La Revue politique internationale*, no. 18 (1915), p. 273. See also Kucharzewski's *Reflexions sur le problème polonais* (Lausanne, 1915) and *L'Europe et le problème polonais* (Lausanne, 1916); Pajewski, *Wokół sprawy polskiej*, pp. 115–20.

18. Henry Korybut-Woroniecki, "Stowarzyszenie 'La Pologne et la Guerre' w Szwajcarii," *Niepodległość*, no. 41, p. 396.

et la Guerre and the Supreme National Committee's press bureau in Rapperswil, for example, were cool. Kucharzewski, a former National Democrat, gave only "cautious and conditional support" to the policy of the Polish Legion. Nevertheless, as on of Kucharzewski's supporters said of the Rapperswil group, "that sector had to be occupied by someone."[19] In a period when the possibilities of a really active policy were limited, the various organizations kept a number of channels open.

The German offensive of the summer of 1915 gave great encouragement to the Austrophiles among the emigrés in Switzerland. The occupation of Przemysl and Lvov during the month of June offered the first stimulus. The news of the fall of Lvov reached Bakherakht, the Russian minister in Bern, just as he was entertaining a delegation of Poles from Fribourg and Lausanne, and the minister excused himself from the gathering, complaining of a "sudden indisposition." The German mission in Bern cheerfully reported that Russophiles among the Poles were dismayed by the events on the front.[20]

The advance into the Ukraine nevertheless posed a dilemma for the Central Powers. Among the recipients of Austrian aid had been the Ukrainians, who had long maintained a sort of Piedmont in the Austrian crownland of Galicia. In August 1914 in Vienna, a group of emigrés from the Russian Ukraine organized the Alliance for the Liberation of the Ukraine, Bund zur Befreiung der Ukraine, which received considerable financial aid from the Central Powers. Calling for a "democratic socialist" Ukraine, the organization proposed a program of land reform together with nationalist revolution. It claimed to represent an alliance of Ukrainian parties, but in September it underwent a split. Dmytro Dontsov, one of its founders, broke with it on personal grounds. Several others, led by Mykola Zalizniak, broke away as the Ukrainian Socialist Revolutionary Party. Both Dontsov and the Socialist Revolutionaries maintained connections with Austrian and German officials; Zalizniak in particular enjoyed the personal patronage of several important Ukrainian politicians in Vienna. As a result, the Austrians found themselves buried under conflicting reports, full of mutual recriminations between the Ukrainian factions. Nevertheless, Vienna continued for a time to give some aid to each.[21]

---

19. *Ibid.,* p. 427. See also Michał Sokolnicki, *Rok czternasty* (London, 1961), pp. 355–58.
20. See Bethmann-Hollweg to Stockholm, July 31, 1915, *All. et la paix,* pp. 148–49; Gagern to Vienna, June 28, 1915, *HHSAr,* PA, 904/8e/12.
21. Copies of documents concerning Ukrainian affairs in the Haus-, Hof-,

The Ukrainian Alliance sought to influence the press in neutral countries and also to recruit support among other emigrés from Tsarist Russia. To this end, it sent a delegation into Switzerland, but the group met with a generally hostile reception. All regular emigré party groups in Switzerland rejected its overtures. The Georgian Social Democrats in Geneva made their position public in an open letter which they published in the emigré press. Trotsky and Manuilsky added their voices in attacks published in *Golos*. In its reports to the Austrian authorities, the Alliance vaguely claimed successes for its mission; in fact, it was a failure.[22]

One group with which the Alliance did briefly maintain relations was Lenin's Bolshevik Party. From his days in Galicia, Lenin seems to have had extensive contacts among Ukrainian groups, and in December 1914 the Alliance claimed to have aided Lenin "with money and through help in the reestablishment of traffic with Russia."[23] This apparently meant, in particular, help in the distribution of *Sotsial'demokrat*. In January 1915, however, Lenin notified the leader of the Alliance, Marjan Bassok-Melenevsky, that he would have nothing more to do with it.[24]

The Alliance suffered further defeats when the Austrian government began to reconsider the consequences of supporting both Polish and Ukrainian ambitions. The pro-Polish elements expressed considerable opposition to the Ukrainians, and Vienna eventually chose the Poles. In 1915, the Alliance moved its headquarters to Constantinople, and by the summer of that year, support of the Ukrainian movement had devolved upon the Germans, who had no significant Polish support which could embarrass them.[25]

The successes of the Central Powers in the summer of 1915 also forced the emigrés to reevaluate their positions. On July 31, the Austrians took Lublin. To the north, the Germans took Ventspils

und Staatsarchiv, as well as police records, can be found in the W. K. Lypynsky East European Research Institute, Philadelphia, Pa. See also *Ereig. Ukr.*

22. See *Golos,* Nov. 21, 24, 25, 1914. The Okhrana reported that Trotsky's attack had had a "very profitable effect on the whole colony" in Paris. No. 1651, Dec. 5/18, 1914, OAr, XIIIb(1), 1914.

23. ". . . mit Geld und durch Hilfe zur Herstellung des Verkehrs mit Russland unterstützt." *Ereig. Ukr.,* 1:183.

24. *PSS,* 49:50; *V. I. Lenin ob Ukraine* (Kiev, 1957), pp. 447–48.

25. On July 22, 1915, a German diplomat in Bern wrote, "Die Österreicher haben es uns überlassen, die ukrainische Sache selbst in die Hand zu nehmen." AAM, T120/5224/K489055.

(Windau) and Mitava (Mitau) in July. On August 18, they took the key fortress of Kaunas (Kovno). In the center of the advance, German forces entered Warsaw on August 5, Brest-Litovsk on August 25, and Grodno on September 2. The fall of Vilna to the Germans on September 19 marked the end of the offensive, which left Poland, Lithuania, and a good part of the Ukraine in German and Austrian hands, thereby depriving Russia of about one-fourth of its prewar industrial plant and raising questions about the future of the occupied territories.

In the first months of war, the German government, through intermediaries in Denmark, had sounded out the Russian court about the possibilities of a separate peace. By August 1915, the peace feelers had failed, and the German authorities turned more decidedly toward revolutionary endeavors. The Auswärtiges Amt, the German Foreign Office, moreover, entered into serious discussions with the Austrians over the specific fate of Poland, which was to serve as the key issue in the nationalities question.

The concern of the Russian government for Poland was demonstrated by Prime Minister Goremykin's promise of autonomy, made to the Duma on August 1 and followed by a directive from the Tsar ordering the working out of a specific program. On the other hand, questions arose in the West, possibly stimulated by German interests, of Russia's willingness and ability to continue the war. On September 9, 1915, the Russian mission in Bern complained to the Swiss government about an article entitled "Russia's Distress" which had appeared in the *Neue Zürcher Zeitung*. Complaining that there had been no corresponding article on troubles in the Central Powers, the Russians demanded legal action against the newspaper for this violation of the neutrality of the Swiss press.[26] The mission later considered it necessary to insert an item in the *Journal de Genève* of January 27, 1916, labelling that newspaper's discussions of the possibilities of Russia's signing a separate peace the work of "malevolent and clearly tendentious raconteurs."

The Poles manifested great concern about the developments in the East. Sienkiewicz, despite his public reserve, privately denounced the Russian army's policy of devastating areas which it was abandoning

---

26. BBAr, Polit. Dept., Russland, Varia, Sch. 528.

as "barbaric and absurd."[27] When the Germans occupied Warsaw, one Polish deputy to the Russian Duma, Michael Lempicki, chose to remain there; in the fall of 1915, he visited Rapperswil to encourage the pro-Austrian camp.

In September, the Agence polonaise centrale en Suisse came into being in Lausanne as a result of the work of a committee headed by Professor Sigismond Laskowski. Its purpose was to inform European opinion "competently and impartially" about Poland. Originally non-party, the agency gradually came under the domination of the National Democrats.[28] In November the rival, pro-Austrian press agency moved its headquarters to Bern, declaring that Rapperswil had been a sentimental choice, but that it now needed a more central location.[29]

Confusion about Polish affairs increased when Roman Dmowski chose to leave Russia and work in Western Europe. The Russian retreat had convinced him that only a victory of the Western powers could deliver Poland from the Germans; he, like Erasmus Piltz, now considered Russia essentially beaten.[30] The tactics of the Russian army, he declared, had alienated all sympathy for the Russians among the Polish population. His plan now was to establish unofficial Polish representations in each Allied capital.[31]

Dmowski's mission centered on London and Paris, but he visited Switzerland twice in the early stages of his work. He apparently talked even with Austrian and German officials, but his major concern on both occasions was to consult with his sympathizers in Lausanne, who had organized a secret "Political Circle."

At a meeting in February 1916, the circle drew up a formal program for Polish independence under the aegis of the Entente. "The interest of Poland in the present war," the declaration stated, "demands the defeat of Germany." Polish leaders should work for Polish independence in an understanding with the Entente powers; they should seek good relations between Russians and Poles; leaders in Austria and Germany should maintain contact with their governments, but they should not

---

27. Romain Rolland, *Journal des années de guerre 1914–1919* (Paris, 1952), p. 523.
28. See Okhrana report, Sept. 22/Oct. 5, 1915, OAr, XIX, f. 8.
29. *Polen*, 4:279. Reports of both press agencies can be found in the archive of Edmond Privat, La Bibliothèque de la Ville, La Chaux-de-Fonds. See also Pajewski, *Wokół sprawy polskiej*, pp. 120–26.
30. Dmowski, *Polityka polska*, p. 164; AAM, T120/5224/K489125.
31. Dmowski, *Polityka polska*, p. 169.

join in the work of the pro-Austrian group in Cracow and Vienna. In neutral countries such as Switzerland, Poles should publicize the Polish cause, support relief work, and serve as a channel of communications between Poles at home and abroad.[32]

Dmowski's presence in the West worried both Russian officials and Polish socialists. In *Nashe Slovo* of February 2, 1916, Zalewski called Dmowski the "symbol of the Polish counter-revolution." Although Dmowski now supported independence for Poland, Zalewski warned, the only permanent aspects of Dmowski's ideological outlook were his anti-socialist and anti-Jewish views. Dmowski's support could only compromise the idea of Polish independence; other bourgeois Polish leaders must dissociate themselves from him.[33]

The Okhrana attributed the National Democrats' growing disillusionment in the Russian cause to the Tsarist government's administrative practices in Galicia, to rumors that Nicholas II had refused an audience to a Polish delegation, to continual postponement of promised reforms, and, of course, to military defeats.[34] In Paris, Izvolsky eventually prevailed upon the French government to ban any commentary on the Polish question in the French press. Poland was to be considered an internal problem of the Russian empire.

Among the persons directly affected by the French government's interdiction was Edmond Privat, a French-Swiss journalist who contributed to *Le Temps* and *L'Humanité*. At the beginning of the war, Privat had taken up the cause of autonomy for Poland, but in the course of 1915 he came to support independence. A man of great energy in advocating a cause, he organized a French Committee for the Independence of Poland. Philip Berthelot of the Quai d'Orsay personally notified Privat of the press ban, calling Polish independence "an unrealizable thing," a "utopia." Privat responded by moving his campaign to Switzerland, where he organized the International Committee for the Independence of Poland. In the *Journal de Genève* of

---

32. See Leczyk, *Komitet Narodowy*, pp. 50–53; Paul Roth, *Die Entstehung des polnischen Staates* (Berlin, 1926), pp. 36–38; Titus Komarnicki, *Rebirth of the Polish Republic* (London, 1957), pp. 49–51; Pajewski, *Wokół sprawy polskiej*, p. 131.

33. Russian and Polish emigrés claimed credit for forcing cancellation of a lecture planned by Dmowski at the Sorbonne in March 1916. *Nashe Slovo*, Feb. 26, Mar. 19, 1916.

34. Report no. 1469, Dec. 28, 1915/Jan. 10, 1916, OAr, XIX, f. 11.

March 23, 1916, he urged the Entente to make an unequivocal statement in favor of Polish independence lest the Central Powers win Polish loyalties by default.[35]

In the midst of these changing circumstances, the Germans began to step up their activity among the nationalities and among the emigrés. On September 9, 1914, the German Chancellor had envisaged exploiting the nationalities question in Russia, proclaiming that Russia must be "pushed back as far as possible from the German border and that its domination over the non-Russian subject peoples be broken."[36] In their first tentative moves among the emigrés, the Germans had met with but limited success. In Scandinavia, German diplomats became very active in the Finnish question. The German embassy in Constantinople played an important role in the Ukrainian movement. In the summer of 1915, the mission in Bern plunged deeply into the fray.

35. "Edmond Privat, 1889–1962," *Revue neuchateloise,* no. 43/44, pp. 38–39; Rolland, *Journal,* pp. 328–29, 798, 835; Okhrana report no. 123, Feb. 3/16, 1916, OAr, XIIIb(1), 1916.

36. See Fritz Fischer, *Griff nach der Weltmacht* (Dusseldorf, 1964), pp. 155–56; also his "Deutsche Kriegsziele: Revolutionierung und Separatfrieden im Osten 1914–1918," *Historische Zeitschrift* 188:259–310.

5

Romberg's Friends

Freiherr Gisbert von Romberg, Germany's minister in Bern from 1912 to 1919, had a deep interest in the affairs of Russia. He had served as Consul General in Sofia and then for a time in the Auswärtiges Amt in Berlin. In a letter to the Foreign Ministry, written in 1916, he explained his boldness in making a recommendation for Germany's policies in Eastern Europe by declaring that "we Russians" were gravely concerned.

Allowed a certain latitude in the recruitment and support of agents, he became the chief of a rather sizable intelligence network. At times his interest in Russia led him to contradict the official policies of the Auswärtiges Amt; at other times, where no policy had been established, he had a strong influence on the formation of new trends. Together with his councillor, Carl von Schubert, Romberg represented an important part of German policy toward Eastern Europe during the war.

Certain characteristics emerged to mark Romberg's activities. He represented the idea of revolutionizing Russia along national lines. Closely following the activities of the socialists, he distrusted them, especially Lenin, whom he saw as attempting to forge a common front of revolutionaries in both Russia and Germany. Among the nationalities, he distrusted the Poles, with whom he had almost no contact.[1] Furthermore, he and Schubert evidenced a marked preference for dealing with

1. In a report written at the end of August 1915, Schubert spoke of the necessity "das geplante Reich Polen nach Möglichkeit einzuengen." AAM, T120/5224/K489091.

persons of noble title. What they collected, however, was a group of enterprising adventurers and opportunists who had ambitions far beyond serving as agents of the German Empire. The most important of these were an Estonian, Alexander Kesküla, a Ukrainian, Wolodimir Stepankowski, and a Lithuanian, Juozas Gabrys.

Alexander Kesküla visited Romberg in September 1914 to inquire about German intentions toward Russian revolutionaries in general and toward Estonia in particular. Kesküla had emigrated from Estonia, where he had participated in the revolution of 1905 as a member of the Bolshevik party. After studying in Germany, he came to Zurich in 1911, where he joined the Eintracht Society. Beginning in 1912 he studied at the University of Bern, and for the last three semesters before the war he studied political economy with Reichesberg.[2]

Although Romberg knew nothing of his background, Kesküla obtained a permit to travel through Germany to Sweden. Late in December, on his return trip, he visited the Auswärtiges Amt, where he obtained an initial grant of 10,000 marks for the development of his plans for national revolution in Russia. His cover name in working with the Germans was Alexander Stein.

Once back in Switzerland, Kesküla plunged enthusiastically into his new work. His relations with Lenin have attracted a great deal of attention and speculation, but Kesküla cast his eyes primarily in other directions. His first concern remained always the fate of his native Estonia. He did not hesitate to complain about German ambitions in the Baltic, and he informed Romberg that he expected "no help for the nationalities" from the Russian socialists. He viewed Tsarist Russia as a multinational state, and he favored its disintegration.[3]

According to Kesküla, he met Lenin personally only once during the war. If so, the meeting probably took place in the spring of 1915. The relationship between the two men was at the most a limited one. Through the person of another Estonian, Arthur Siefeld, Kesküla claimed to have penetrated Lenin's organization in Switzerland, anonymously transmitting German money into the Bolshevik coffers and at the same time obtaining information on Lenin's activities and programs.[4]

---

2. Kesküla's student records are among his papers held by the Yale University Library. On Kesküla's life, see Adolf Gasser, "Der schlafende Tiger," *Nationalzeitung* (Basel), July 5, 1964.
3. See AAM, T120/4824/L248639, L248642, L248677, L248729.
4. See Michael Futrell, *Northern Underground* (London, 1963), pp. 145–46.

Siefeld's activities still remain unclear. He lived in Zurich from 1913 but joined the local Bolshevik group only in 1915. In 1916 he served as his party's representative to the control commission of the Zurich emigré fund. Lenin relied on him as a contact with Italian circles. In April 1915, he sent *Nashe Slovo* ten francs in the name of the Swiss Union of the Social Democratic Emigration of the Estonian Region. At about the same time, *Sotsial'demokrat* recorded the receipt of five francs from "an Estonian." On the occasion of its fiftieth issue in February 1916, *Sotsial'demokrat* received an unusually large contribution of seventy-five francs from Zurich. Such contributions, however, constituted only a pittance in the total budget of both newspapers. The Estonian Union publicly declared its support of the cause of "revolutionary socialism" and its rejection of a German "orientation."[5] While Siefeld may well have given Keskküla information about Lenin's activities, there is no evidence that he affected Lenin's policies in any way.

The major evidence of Keskküla's relationship with Lenin consists of a report, written by Romberg in September 1915, announcing that Keskküla "had succeeded in discovering the conditions on which the Russian revolutionaries would be prepared to conclude peace with us in the event of the revolution being successful." On the basis of this single document, a number of writers have proceeded to the assumption that Keskküla had enlisted Lenin for the German cause.[6] In actual fact, the situation seems to have been quite different.

Keskküla exploited the tactic of name-dropping. He used his acquaintance with Lenin to impress Romberg, and despite warnings by Bolshevik leaders against dealing with him, Keskküla penetrated Bolshevik organizations in Scandinavia simply by using Lenin's name.[7] The evidence does not support his exalted claims of having "discovered" Lenin. He seems rather to have seized upon a few pieces of information to impress first the Germans and subsequently a variety of historians.

5. See the series of articles by A. Virolainen of Zurich in *Nashe Slovo*, July 1915.

6. See Futrell, *Northern Underground,* pp. 121, 150; Stefan Possony, *Lenin: The Compulsive Revolutionary* (Chicago, 1964); Fritz Fischer, *Griff nach der Weltmacht* (Dusseldorf, 1964), pp. 178–79. The text of Romberg's report is reprinted in Z. A. B. Zeman, *Germany and the Revolution in Russia 1915–1918* (London, 1958), pp. 6–8.

7. See A. Shliapnikov, *Kanun semnadtsatogo goda,* 2 vols. (Moscow, 1923), 1:204–5, 2:100–102; Futrell, *Northern Underground,* p. 121.

Throughout the summer of 1915, Lenin was pressed by opponents and supporters alike for a more precise definition of his conception of the "defeat of one's own government." Kesküla's celebrated report of September 1915 constituted nothing more than a prepublication summary, selectively edited, of an article which Lenin published in *Sotsial'-demokrat* of October 13, 1915.[8] Had Romberg read Russian, he could have easily obtained a much more thorough presentation. At any rate, even Romberg's garbled version did not constitute an exposé of "the conditions on which the Russian revolutionaries would be prepared to conclude peace"; Kesküla had simply repeated the revolutionary program which Lenin openly offered his Russian supporters.

Kesküla's own program focussed on the preparation of a mass rising of nationalities in Russia. At the end of January 1915 he travelled to Vienna to establish contacts with the Ukrainians, whom both he and Romberg considered to be the nationality ripest for revolt. Out of this visit came an idea to organize a preparatory conference and subsequently a congress "with the aim of establishing a bloc of nationalities" of Imperial Russia.[9] He fully realized, however, the tensions existing between the nationalities. Like many others, for instance, he opposed the idea of a large Poland.

By the spring of 1915, Kesküla had so convinced the German authorities of his usefulness that he received a pass, dated May 14, 1915, and valid for six months, allowing him to travel at will back and forth between Sweden and Switzerland by way of Germany. Eventually he came to spend more and more time in Scandinavia, and his cooperation with Romberg waned. The German minister, in turn, came to lean more on other agents among the emigrés.

Wolodimir Stepankowski (Stepankivski), a Ukrainian, represented a different type of contact. A Russian citizen, he had lived in England before the war and had published a brochure, *The Russian Plot to Seize Galicia*. Although he claimed to be pro-Entente, he soon left for Vienna, where he unsuccessfully offered his services to the Austrian Foreign Ministry. He remained in Austria until the spring of 1915, apparently working with the Ukrainian Socialist Revolutionary Zalizniak. Since the

8. *PSS,* 27:48–51. Although Lenin's editors declare that he wrote these theses between October 6 and October 9, the tone of the essay indicates that he had been repeating his arguments for some time.
9. Romberg to Berlin, Feb. 25, 1915, AAM, T120/4824/L248678–79.

Okhrana in 1916 still considered him to be pro-Entente, Stepankowski probably maintained his connections with Entente sources even while working with the Central Powers.

Stepankowski first wrote to Romberg from Montreux on May 15, 1915, reporting that he had asked various persons in Austria for letters of recommendation on his behalf to the German legation in Bern. On June 7 he wrote again, declaring that he had "some special projects" which he wanted to discuss. Among these was the publication of a journal, *L'Ukraine,* in Lausanne beginning in June, for which he would request German subvention.[10]

Romberg met Stepankowski on July 15 and was offered a variety of proposals, ranging from a request for money to a plan for sending agents into the Ukraine. Romberg required little persuasion. Working in Stepankowski's favor was the fact that he had made Schubert's acquaintance in London. (Schubert, on the other hand, warned, "One can never know what all goes on in a Ukrainian head.")[11]

Berlin advised Romberg to act cautiously. Secretary of State Arthur Zimmermann warned that propaganda for the Ukrainian cause had "only a limited interest" for Germany. The Ukrainians seemed to be deeply divided among themselves, and Stepankowski had "absolutely no relations any more with Ukrainians in Russia and in his time has been excluded from a number of parties." Romberg should therefore respond in a "friendly but negative fashion." To this, Diego von Bergen, an Auswärtiges Amt specialist in Russian revolutionary affairs, added that he considered a Ukrainian revolution "a utopia," since the Ukrainians "would only rise in the event we march in; all elements are lacking for a rising on their own." The Austrians, too, advised that Stepankowski should be treated "politely but with a certain reserve."[12]

The negative reports from Berlin and Vienna apparently stemmed from sources within the Alliance for the Liberation of the Ukraine. Stepankowski personally hated Bassok-Melenevsky, who had once used a whip against him. To Schubert, Stepankowski repeatedly insisted that

10. AAM, T120/5224/K489017, K489019.
11. Schubert to Bergen, Sept. 8, 1915, AAM, T120/5224/K489168.
12. Zimmermann to Romberg, June 7, 1915, Bergen to Schubert, Aug. 16, 1915, Austrian report, July 15, 1915, in AAM, T120/5224/K489036, K489070, K489038. On Bergen, see Fischer, *Griff nach der Weltmacht,* p. 145.

the leaders of the Alliance were "little men" of "no standing" and with "shady backgrounds."

Despite the unfavorable reports, Romberg was obviously impressed by Stepankowski's ideas and by his acquaintances. For one, Stepankowski proposed the formation of a Ukrainian National Committee, to be headed by Count Michael Tyszkiewicz, a resident of Lausanne. He also indicated that he had his own contacts in Vienna. From Romberg's point of view, Tyszkiewicz represented a conservative alternative to the more democratic Ukrainian Alliance.[13]

Even Zimmermann, in his first premonitory message, had considered it worthwhile to develop Stepankowski's acquaintance, since he had promised to bring new contacts to Romberg. Stepankowski's circle included Englishmen, a few French, a wide variety of socialists, and even political agents of other powers. In September, Berlin authorized the payment of 3,000 francs monthly to him, and Stepankowski quickly came to replace Kesküla in Romberg's operations, when the Estonian chose to remain in Scandinavia.[14]

Besides indirect contacts through Kesküla or Stepankowski, Romberg had little to do with Russian socialists in Switzerland. He agreed with Kesküla that nationalist revolution in Russia held out better prospects for Germany than did socialist revolution. He had almost nothing to do with Alexander Helphand, "Parvus," the best known of the German agents among the Russian socialist emigrés in Western Europe.

Parvus's only appearance in Switzerland during the war came in May and June of 1915, and aside from sowing seeds of confusion and doubt among the emigrés, he had little lasting impact there. Nonetheless, his brief visit offered a vivid contrast to Romberg's quiet mode of operation.

After participating in the Russian revolution of 1905, Parvus had made his way to Turkey, where in the years before the war he had accumulated a small fortune through rather obscure means. In January 1915, after supporting the efforts of the Alliance for the Liberation of the Ukraine, he presented to the German embassy a plan for revolu-

---

13. See Schubert's memorandum, AAM, T120/5224/K489086.

14. Kesküla called Stepankowski an "ideal political agent," but one to be handled carefully: "St. will politische Kombinationen ausnützen, mit den Diplomaten aller möglichen Länder junglieren, sie gegen einander ausspielen." Stepankowski also "plays the aristocrat too much, without being one." AAM, T120/5224/K489183–86.

tionizing Russia. German interests were identical with those of the Russian revolutionaries, he asserted, and he combined socialism with the national question by calling for the destruction of Tsarist rule and for the division of Russia into smaller states.

On March 9 in Berlin, Parvus produced a more detailed account of his program. Proposing a conference of emigré Social Democratic leaders, he planned to build his organization upon the foundation of a united Russian Social Democratic Party, which would include Jewish, Ukrainian, Lithuanian, and Finnish Social Democrats. (He was apparently familiar with *Nashe Slovo*'s attempts to call a socialist conference.) He considered the Socialist Revolutionary Party less useful: "Its members are more inclined to nationalism." The whole endeavor should receive the broadest possible publicity, exploiting the emigré press as well as the publications of neutral states. He then went on to speak of independence for the Ukraine, possible independence for Finland and the Caucasian nationalities, and the need to give aid to the Bolsheviks and the Bund. The German government put one million marks at Parvus's disposal in the neutral cities of Copenhagen, Zurich, and Bucharest.[15]

Parvus's public speeches in support of the German war effort earned him much abuse. A Tsarist victory, he insisted, would open "a new era of boundless capitalist exploitation." In *Nashe Slovo* of February 14, 1915, Trotsky wrote an ironic obituary for his erstwhile friend, announcing that the revolutionary Parvus had died and that the Germanophile using that name had to be an imposter. Opposition to the German war effort, Parvus countered, could not help the cause of revolution in Russia because Social Democracy there was still too weak.[16]

Up to the time of Parvus's arrival in Zurich, only Alexinsky had publicly accused him of being in the pay of the Central Powers, and for the internationalists in Switzerland, an attack by Alexinsky constituted an encouraging credential. Parvus was obviously well financed. Setting himself up in a good hotel in Zurich, he proceeded to indulge himself

15. See Zeman, *Germany and the Revolution,* pp. 1–2, 140–52; Z. A. B. Zeman and Wilfred Scharlau, *Merchant of Revolution* (London, 1964), pp. 145–50; Leo van Rossum, "A propos d'une biographie de Parvus," *Cahiers du monde russe et soviétique* 8 (1967): 244–63.

16. See Parvus's "Für die Demokratie gegen den Zarismus" (written in October 1914), *Die Glocke* 1:83, and "Offener Brief an Nasche Slowo" (written April 11, 1915), *Die Glocke* 1:157.

in food, drink, and women. His generosity with money won him easy access to emigré circles, and he met privately with many individuals, including Lenin, Rubakin, and Stepankowski. His meeting with Lenin took place in Bern at the end of May, but it came to naught. Lenin reportedly accused him of being an agent of the German Social Democrats and ordered him to leave.[17]

Lenin warned Bukharin against working with Parvus, but he apparently raised no objection when Jakob Fürstenburg-Hanecki, a member of the National Committee of the SDKPiL, joined Parvus's staff in Copenhagen. Although some writers have insisted that Hanecki's activities represented cooperation between Lenin and Parvus, it can also be argued that Hanecki was Lenin's agent in keeping an eye on Parvus.[18]

At the end of June, Parvus left Switzerland for Denmark. According to the Okhrana, he had planned to establish a base in Switzerland, but Italy's entry into the war had forced him to move to Scandinavia. He had, however, recruited several emigrés to work for him in Copenhagen in a new scientific institute for the statistical study of the consequences of the war. He made no further effort to work in Switzerland, and his visit constituted hardly more than an episode in the life and activities of the emigrés. Occasional scandals still cropped up; on November 10, 1915, for example, the Russian emigré fund in Bern debated what it should do with a 500-franc note which Parvus had donated. V. Kasparov, a Bolshevik, insisted that the money be returned. The Mensheviks and the Bundists argued that they had accepted it in good faith, that they had not requested it. In the end, the fund kept it.[19]

Romberg had no direct contact with Parvus. The latter's open, even blatant tactics were in marked contrast to the conspiratorial meetings between Romberg, Schubert, Keskula, and Stepankowski. Romberg continued, after as before the visit, his own work among the nationalities, work which at times bore signs of directly contradicting that of the Auswärtiges Amt or of the War Ministry in Berlin.

Working with the emigrés had its pitfalls. Both Romberg and his

17. See Zeman and Scharlau, *Merchant of Revolution*, pp. 156–59, and Parvus's account in *Pravda glaza kolet!* (Stockholm, 1918), pp. 51–52.

18. Soviet writers have presented Hanecki as one of Lenin's most faithful supporters during World War I. See also Futrell, *Northern Underground*, pp. 152ff.

19. Iosif Bazian to Alexinsky, Nov. 11, 1915; Aleks. Ar., Voina, f. III, 71.

Austrian colleagues in Bern constantly received visitors of all classes, ranging from Russian nobility to Georgian musicians. In June 1915, the Austrian minister reported that a visitor had proposed sending thousands of publications to Russian prisoners of war. The man had previously been in America, the minister noted wryly, "and therefore he did not shy away from large numbers." Another visitor proposed to publish a collection of "important and as yet unknown, sensational documents" about Russia. Since he expected large sales in America, he requested only "modest financial help," together with a guarantee of asylum in either Germany or Austria-Hungary.[20]

Sometimes the working agents also proved to be careless. In September 1915, Schubert complained several times about Dr. Max Zimmer, a collaborator of Parvus and a specialist in Ukrainian affairs. Introduced to Romberg by Stepankowski, Zimmer was a landowner from Anatolia who had ties with the War Ministry as a result of his work among Ukrainian prisoners of war. When he spoke to Stepankowski about recruiting agents for sabotage behind the Russian lines, Romberg and Schubert, who wanted to know nothing of such "illegal" work, protested to Berlin. Schubert also complained that Zimmer had sent an open telegram referring to "payments in Lausanne" and linking Stepankowski's name with Romberg. The legation therefore asked the Auswärtiges Amt to keep Zimmer out of Switzerland altogether.[21]

Well within the limits of Romberg's interests and preferences was Juozas Gabrys, whose name Stepankowski first mentioned on August 9, 1915. Romberg had never heard of Gabrys before, but in subsequent years the two worked closely together. From the beginning, Romberg was intrigued by Stepankowski's glowing account of Gabrys's contacts in Paris, as well as by the prospect that this man, a Lithuanian, would provide another link in the chain limiting the Poles. A few days later, Gabrys himself came to Romberg.

20. Gagern to Vienna, June 26, 1915, HHSAr, PA, XXVII, 53/Berichte, 76; Romberg to Berlin, June 15, 1915, AAM, T120/4818/L244208. N. A. Rubakin may have been behind both these proposals.
21. Schubert to Bergen, Sept. 8, 1915, AAM, T120/5224/K489165. It was the German practice to leave espionage and "illegal" work to the attachés. Major Herbert von Bismark, the German military attaché in Bern, apparently concentrated his efforts on the war against England and France. See Z. V. Gempp, *Geheimer Nachrichtendienst und Spionageabwehr des Heeres* (Berlin, 1940), IX (2), 120–23, VIII, 165–69 (Microfilm Series T177/1440); V. K. Agafonov, *Zagranichnaia okhranka* (Petrograd, 1918), pp. 177–82.

A resident of Paris since 1907, Gabrys had achieved a certain renown for his work in the founding of the Union of Nationalities and for editing the union's organ, *Les Annales des nationalités.* He enjoyed extensive contacts in French intellectual and political circles. With considerable financial support from Lithuanian Catholic organizations in the United States, he had founded a Lithuanian Information Bureau in Paris, but in the summer of 1915, he announced that he was transferring the bureau, together with the editorial offices of *Les Annales des nationalités,* to Lausanne, ostensibly because of the pressures of censorship in wartime Paris. The real reason, however, was Gabrys's calculation of the fortunes of war: ". . . it was necessary to find a tie with the government of Germany, since the Germans were advancing ever further into Lithuania. Therefore it was necessary to move."[22]

Gabrys's decision was not a sudden one. In the fall of 1914, while on a fund-raising tour of the United States, he had asked the German ambassador in Washington for a letter of introduction to the German representative in either Bern or Rome.[23] Stepankowski was obviously exaggerating when he informed Romberg that he, personally, had persuaded Gabrys to moderate his pro-Entente position. Gabrys had come to Switzerland with the express purpose of seeking contact with the Germans.

Gabrys also brought new life to the small Lithuanian colony in Switzerland. Up to this time, the Lithuanian students, mainly in Fribourg, had cooperated with the Poles. One of Gabrys's first actions was to summon the three members of the Fribourg group "Lituania" to Bern for a conference with a Latvian. This gathering denounced Russian policies in the Baltic and spoke out in favor of some sort of Latvian-Lithuanian federation. The most striking feature of the conference, however, was the publicity which Gabrys won for it in the Swiss press. *Der Bund* (Bern) of September 4 reported the gathering as having had an anti-Russian character, and the *Basler Nachrichten* of September 21 described it as anti-German.[24]

22. Juozas Gabrys, "Tautos sargyboje," MS memoirs in the possession of Dr. Albertas Gerutis, Bern, 2:29. See also *Pro Lituania* 1:101–2.

23. Here, as elsewhere, Gabrys's published memoirs, *Vers l'independance lituanienne* (Lausanne, 1920), p. 56, are less than honest. His unpublished memoirs, "Tautos sargyboje," 1:141ff., are much franker and more reliable.

24. The Okhrana was at a loss to explain the meeting, which Latvian socialists denounced as a Russian provocation. One report, however, surmised

In speaking with Romberg, Gabrys expressed his undying opposition to Russia and indicated that he even favored the incorporation of Lithuania into the German Empire. Because of his contacts in Paris, he also requested that the Germans not use his name in their communications. Instead he suggested the pseudonym Peter G. Comte de Garlawa.[25]

Like Stepankowski, Gabrys had to await a formal decision from Berlin before joining Romberg's payroll. Romberg, moreover, received conflicting testimony about his new recruit. Keskula, for one, took an immediate dislike to him, and on September 17 told Schubert that Gabrys was a "worthless person, without backbone," a *Dummkopf*: "He lies." Keskula claimed that Gabrys had created his international standing by intrigue: in Lithuania claiming to have influence in Paris, and in Paris claiming influence in Lithuania. Keskula even recommended another Lithuanian, Abbé Antoine Visconte (Antanas Viskontas), as an alternative, if Romberg really wanted a Lithuanian.[26]

Gabrys forced the issue on September 2, when he requested permission to travel through Germany to attend a meeting of Lithuanians scheduled for Stockholm. Among the participants was to be Martynas Yčas, a Lithuanian deputy in the Fourth Duma and an important member of the Russian Constitutional Democratic Party. Gabrys hoped also to be empowered to organize a Lithuanian National Committee in Switzerland. (Schubert himself had encouraged Gabrys to think of organizing a national committee.) Although Schubert admitted, "To be sure, we don't know too much about him," the mission recommended that the German government grant Gabrys a visa. On September 14 the Auswärtiges Amt complied, and Romberg said nothing about Keskula's uncomplimentary comments.

that the meeting represented the "activity of a single person." Okhrana report no. 258, Mar. 12/25, 1916, OAr, XXII, f. 1B. See also *Berner Tagwacht*, Oct. 2, 26, 1915, and *Gazette de Lausanne*, Oct. 18, 1915. Gabrys also succeeded in misleading historians. See Werner Basler, *Deutsche Annevionspolitik in Polen und im Baltikum* (Berlin, 1962), p. 265; Malbone W. Graham, Jr., *New Governments of Eastern Europe* (New York, 1927), p. 360n; Edgars Andersons, *Latvijas vesture* (Stockholm, 1967), p. 141.

25. Garliava was the name of the village where Gabrys was born. "Gabrys" was itself a pseudonym; his real name was Paršaitis. See AAM, T120/5224/K489060, K489073.

26. AAM, T120/5224/K489183. Keskula's reports indicate clearly that he understood little of Lithuanian politics.

For Kesküla, the possibility of meeting Yčas, who at the beginning of the war had hailed the Russian "crusade" against Germany, outweighed his personal reservations about Gabrys. Kesküla hoped to use Yčas to develop contacts with other nationalist leaders, especially Moslems, and he dreamed of persuading Yčas to resign his seat in the Duma as a demonstrative action against the Tsarist regime. In any case, Yčas could contribute so much to Kesküla's hopes of fostering national revolution in Russia that, in spite of himself, Kesküla endorsed Gabrys's proposed trip. He undertook, moreover, to accompany Gabrys.

The two left for Sweden on October 2. For Kesküla, the meeting with Yčas had no significant result, although he thought at first that he had successfully won Yčas's cooperation. He called the Duma deputy a "clever but in any case serious politician" and insisted to Romberg that Yčas had warned him against Gabrys. Yčas in fact remained loyal to the Russian cause until 1917, although he was to speak with German agents several times more. In March 1917, Yčas assumed the post of Deputy Minister of Education in the postrevolutionary cabinet of Prince G. E. Lvov.

For Gabrys, the meeting with Yčas was far more profitable, despite the personal hostility between the two men. Yčas accepted a number of letters for Ukrainians which Gabrys had carried at Stepankowski's request. The two men established a Swedish-Lithuanian relief society, headed by the mayor of Stockholm, and Yčas agreed to the formation of a Lithuanian National Committee in Switzerland.

At the end of October, Gabrys returned to Switzerland alone; Kesküla chose to remain in Scandinavia for the time being. On November 2, he appeared at the German mission in Bern to return the passport which Romberg had given him and to report on his trip. The conference, he announced, had empowered him "to represent Lithuania abroad for the time of the duration of the war." Upon the war's end, four other Lithuanians would join him in establishing a "regular delegation of the Lithuanian nation."[27]

With Kesküla absent, Stepankowski pressed the Germans to give Gabrys their formal support. At one point, he suggested that he, Gabrys,

27. Stepankowski summarized Gabry's report in a memorandum, handwritten in English, AAM, T120/5224/K489334. See also Kesküla's letter of Oct. 30, 1915, AAM, T120/5224/K489324; and the conflicting accounts in Gabrys, *Vers l'independance lituanienne,* pp. 81–92, and Martynas Yčas, *Atsiminimai nepriklausomybes keliais,* 3 vols. (Kaunas, 1935), 2: 171–72.

and Keskula should organize a "triumvirate" for the purpose of collecting information. Gabrys would work on France, Keskula Germany, and Stepankowski England. This idea was stillborn, but Stepankowski and Gabrys offered still other projects.

In the fall of 1915, the Union of Nationalities was planning the compilation of a map of the nationalities of Europe, to be published in an edition of 10,000 copies. In hopes of avoiding reference to Alsace-Lorraine, Schubert attempted to persuade Stepankowski to limit the map to Russia. Stepankowski responded that if the Union of Nationalities was the sponsor, the map had to show all of Europe. A compromise decision proposed to publish the map in sections, depicting Russia first.[28]

To increase the pressure for a quick and favorable decision in Gabrys's case, Stepankowski reported that the Lithuanian's Parisian "friends" were urging him to return to France. There, Stepankowski warned, Entente pressures might undo all his efforts to win Gabrys for the Germans. Gabrys in turn asked that the Auswärtiges Amt allow several representative Lithuanians to come to Switzerland for consultation.

Schubert and Romberg urged Berlin to make some concession. Schubert, who declared that he had told Gabrys "all sorts of nice things about Lithuania," insisted that while he did not mean to exaggerate the man's significance, he could "perform very useful services." Romberg opined, "I would consider it useful to win Gabrys for us on a continuing basis." From Berlin, however, Diego von Bergen warned, "I don't consider it practical to encourage the Lithuanian nationalist aspirations too much."[29]

In consultation with Ober Ost, the military authorities on the eastern front, the Auswärtiges Amt finally offered to send Rittmeister Steputat (Steputaitis), a Prussian Lithuanian, to meet Gabrys. Since Steputat was a German officer, the meeting had to take place in Stuttgart. On January 9–11, 1916, the two men reached a formal agreement whereby Gabrys promised to produce pro-German and anti-Russian propaganda and to publish a German counterpart to his periodical *Pro Lituania*. He would in return receive a monthly subsidy of 1,000 marks.[30]

Romberg's agents rendered valuable service. When Emile Vander-

28. AAM, T120/5224/K489239.
29. Schubert to Bergen, Dec. 8, 1915, Romberg to Berlin, Nov. 29, 1915, and Bergen to Schubert, Dec. 15, 1915, in AAM, T120/5224/K489489, K489427, K489496.
30. See Alfred Erich Senn, "Garlawa: A Study in Emigré Intrigue, 1915–1917," *Slavonic and East European Review* 45:414–15.

velde of Belgium visited Geneva in January 1916, for example, Gabrys spoke with him at length, and immediately reported to the Germans. Stepankowski transmitted the gossip of English and French newspapermen, and even obtained first-hand information on the work of the socialists of all countries. In turn, when General Erich Ludendorff later complained that the Lithuanian national movement in 1916 was directed from Switzerland, he was in fact testifying to the pressure which Gabrys had been able to exert through his cooperation with Romberg.[31]

Romberg, of course, had his rivals. Besides the seemingly ubiquitous Okhrana agents, other Russian agencies had their representatives in Switzerland. The chief Russian political agent, Vsevolod Sviatkovsky, brought himself to Romberg's attention by walking into the publishing office of Stepankowski's *L'Ukraine,* ostensibly to acquaint himself with the Ukrainian question. Criticizing Russian policies in the Ukraine, Sviatkovsky offered to help the Ukrainians by writing directly to Russian Foreign Minister Sazonov. Stepankowski reported the visit to Romberg the very next day, and Romberg requested advice from Berlin. The Auswärtiges Amt replied that there could be "no doubt that Sviatkovsky is not only the representative of the Petersburg Telegraph Agency but also a Russian secret agent."[32]

Thereafter Stepankowski and Sviatkovsky sparred regularly in discussions of the war. At one point, Sviatkovsky characterized the members of the Russian mission in Bern as all incompetent, with the exception of M. M. Bibikov, to whom Sviatkovsky in fact was reporting. On another occasion, he warned Stepankowski that someone had seen him visit the German mission in Bern. Stepankowski reciprocated by telling him of the national aspirations of Ukrainians and Lithuanians.

In all, Romberg was probably better informed about the political realities among the Russian emigrés, and in fact about events in Switzerland generally, than were the various Entente observers. Russian and Western agents seemingly believed that every German-speaking Swiss and every Russian socialist was actually a German agent. As one British diplomat wrote in 1916, "The basis of all the Swiss trouble, even before the war, is that a German-Swiss is a German first and a Swiss after-

31. Erich Ludendorff, *Meine Kriegserinnerungen 1914–1918* (Berlin, 1921), p. 374. Yčas complained, "The Germans reckoned more with emigré Lithuanians than with Lithuania itself." *Atsiminimai,* 3:19.

32. AAM, T120/5224/K489173, K489273. See also J. F. N. Bradley, "The Russian Secret Service in the First World War," *Soviet Studies* 20:245–46.

wards. Zurich is even worse than Bern in this respect."[33] Although the English paid little attention to the Russian emigrés, Tsarist officials, and to a lesser degree the French, held the corollary view that every Russian opposing the Tsarist regime was a German agent. German diplomats and intelligence officers held much more balanced views of the motivations of the Russian emigrés.

Schubert and Romberg believed that the loyalty of various of their informants, such as Gabrys, was not to be bought; it was not determined by money. In 1915 and 1916, this was probably true. The German mission profited by Germany's successes on the battlefield. Kesküla, Stepankowski, and Gabrys, while working with Romberg, thought first of their own roles in their respective national movements. On the other hand, Romberg conceived of his activity as simply contributing to the disintegration of Russia; he held no strong sympathies for any particular national movement. As time went by, however, these original intentions became confused.

33. PRO, F.O. 371/vol. 2766A/63810.

6

Toward a Renewed International

Romberg's growing activity testified to the part which Switzerland came to play in the First World War as a center of intrigue and diplomacy, particularly after Italy's entry into the war, in May 1915, had completed the ring of belligerents around the country. At the same time, some Swiss became more active as peacemakers; Robert Grimm took the initiative of pressing for renewed international cooperation between socialists of all nations. Russian emigrés in Switzerland, cut off from their homeland, now found themselves thrust into major roles in an entirely new political drama.

In the winter of 1914–15, the Russian socialists had evolved a new political alignment, determined in general by their attitudes toward the war and in particular by their reactions to the explicit alternatives of Lenin's "defeatism" and Plekhanov's "defensism." In their debates and disputes they actually became a model for socialists of other countries, and as Grimm struggled to bring internationalist elements together, the Russians stood all around him—encouraging, criticizing, and at the same time competing.

The periodic Okhrana report for the third quarter of 1915 declared that the activity of Russian revolutionaries in Paris had lagged during the summer. Following their national custom they had chosen to travel, many going to Switzerland. *Nashe Slovo*, it reported, had featured almost no polemical articles. A report from Switzerland, dated July 15, spoke on the other hand of the new influx of emigrés coming from

France as a sign of stepped-up activity. The emigrés, moreover, were allegedly becoming more and more Germanophile.[1]

Below the quiet which the Okhrana saw in Paris lay not passivity but rather ferment, culminating in the formation of new factions. A bitter debate within the *Nashe Slovo* editorial board epitomized the struggle going on within the Russian emigration and, to a certain degree, within all European socialist parties.

One of *Nashe Slovo*'s major problems had always been its own identity. United by their general opposition to the war, the members of the editorial board split sharply over their actual program and over the specific role to which they should aspire among the emigrés. On May 9, the board issued a declaration rejecting the idea of forming a new faction, and calling for comradely relations with all party factions supporting "revolutionary internationalism." This represented a victory of sorts for Martov, who considered Trotsky's ambitions an even greater threat than Leninism.[2] The declaration, in the long run, failed to satisfy anyone.

Although Martov complained that he had had to make many compromises in hammering out the final text, Manuilsky and Antonov-Ovseenko, who used the name Anton Gallsky, refused to sign it, stating that they would yet offer their own manifesto. For some time, Trotsky and Manuilsky had accused the "Zurich Mensheviks" of seeking to control the newspaper through Martov. According to Lunacharsky, Manuilsky was in fact considering aligning himself openly with Lenin; Trotsky, on the other hand, reportedly favored organizing a separate faction. The other members of the editorial board feared Trotsky's personal motives, but, as Lunacharsky noted, to act without him would be "nonsense."[3]

In a series of editorials entitled "Our Position," Trotsky now declared that the old divisions of Russian socialism had been liquidated. The paramount issue dividing factions was now the attitude toward the war. *Nashe Slovo* refused to support either the Menshevik Organizational Committee or the Bolshevik Central Committee; it rejected both

1. See OAr, XVIb(2), f. 6, and XVIb(6)(a).
2. *Pis'ma P. B. Aksel'roda i Iu. O. Martova* (Berlin, 1924), p. 332.
3. Lunacharskii to the *Vperëd* group in Geneva, undated letter probably written in the first days of March 1915, Vperiod Ar.

the Menshevik charge that it was contributing to a split and the Bolshevik charge that it was guilty of "a halfway policy" *(polovinchatost')* or of "pacifism."[4]

On June 6, Manuilsky and Antonov, supported by Lunacharsky and Zalewski, published their own manifesto demanding a clearer, more definite policy. Unity could not be realized through the old factions; what was necessary was "rallying all Social Democratic internationalist elements" and working first of all with *Sotsial'demokrat.*[5] On August 8, Manuilsky retired as editor of *Nashe Slovo* and departed for Switzerland. Solomon Dridzo-Lozovsky, a Bolshevik who had lived in Paris since 1909, replaced him.

The Mensheviks, too, had their complaints, even criticizing Martov for making too many concessions to Trotsky. The Menshevik Foreign Secretariat in Zurich now began the publication of its own irregular periodical, *Izvestiia,* and in the second issue its secretary, S. Iu. Semkovsky, attacked both *Nashe Slovo* and *Sotsial'demokrat.* The "defeatists" of *Sotsial'demokrat* were in fact taking a nationalist position; "universal defeat" was a hopeless dream. Those who complained of treason to socialism on the part of socialist leaders were appealing to an "idealized" mass. Both *Golos* and *Nashe Slovo,* moreover, had not thought the matter through and had slipped too easily into the Leninist line. Trotsky and his supporters "apparently have the goal of forming a separate third faction of 'nonfactionalists.' " Writing to Axelrod, Semkovsky complained, "It is completely incomprehensible how [Martov] can remain silent."[6]

At one point Axelrod considered resigning from the Foreign Secretariat in protest against Martov's continued association with Trotsky. Critics questioned whether Martov's presence on the staff of *Nashe Slovo* signified a split on his part with the Foreign Secretariat. In answer to Semkovsky and Axelrod, Martov insisted that secondary conflicts should not be allowed to force a split with *Nashe Slovo;* to others, he responded that he was serving on the board with the approval of his sympathizers.[7]

4. *Nashe Slovo,* May 15, 29, June 5, 1915.
5. See Ia. G. Temkin, *Tsimmerval'd-Kintal'* (Moscow, 1967), p. 14n.
6. *Pis'ma Aksel'roda i Martova,* p. 339n; *Izvestiia,* June 14, 1915. Cf. *PSS,* 26:292–97.
7. See *Nashe Slovo,* July 11, 21, 1915; *Pis'ma Aksel'roda i Martova,* p. 342.

Trotsky and others on the editorial board regarded Semkovsky's attacks as a violation of the truce implicit in the declaration of May 9. Manuilsky complained that Semkovsky was conducting a "systematic agitation against our internationalist newspaper," and he declared that "all internationalists" should rally to the support of *Nashe Slovo*.[8]

A new polemic in July made Martov's position still more insecure. In a letter published in *Nashe Slovo* of July 11, a Menshevik, Rafail Grigoriev, questioned why the newspaper directed so many more attacks against the Menshevik Organizational Committee than against the Bolshevik Central Committee. Trotsky responded that the Mensheviks were tolerating a higher degree of defensist opinion within their ranks than was Lenin. On July 23 and 24, Trotsky renewed his series "Our Position," asserting that *Nashe Slovo* did in fact represent a third position, between the "sectarianism" of *Sotsial'demokrat* and the spirit of "unity" advocated by the Organizational Committee.

The controversy lapsed at the beginning of August as Martov departed for Switzerland. To his friends, Martov referred to Trotsky's public statements as "stupid." He also expressed the hope that "sooner or later [Trotsky's] inadequacy as 'chief' of a faction and organizer will become obvious," and he warned that Trotsky's "bankruptcy" might destroy *Nashe Slovo*. Trotsky in turn had only scorn for Martov: fate had placed Martov "in a time of revolution without endowing him with the necessary resources of willpower." Martov's departure only postponed an open split between the two; it did not avert it.[9]

Preceding Martov to Switzerland was Viktor Chernov. French authorities had closed down *Mysl'* on March 3 and then had put new pressures on its successor, *Zhizn' (Life)*. In April, Parisian officials forbade meetings, reports, and lectures aimed at raising money for the newspaper. When the editorial board discussed the possibility of transferring its offices to Switzerland, the printers warned that the French government would undoubtedly block its circulation.

8. Manuilskii to *Vperëd* group, undated letter, Vperiod Ar.

9. See *Pis'ma Aksel'roda i Martova*, p. 347; Trotsky, *My Life* (New York, 1960), p. 246. Ia. G. Temkin, in *Lenin i mezhdunarodnaia demokratiia 1914–1917* (Moscow, 1968), p. 44, insisted that "the differences between [Martov and Trotsky] retreated to the background before their joint attacks on the tactics of the Bolsheviks and their common statements against splitting with the social traitors."

The newspaper nevertheless moved to Geneva in the latter part of June. Chernov hoped for more freedom; with all its blank, censored spots, he declared, *Zhizn'* had come to look like a map of unexplored Africa. In Switzerland, he converted the newspaper into a weekly, but his hopes for additional funds from Swiss sources proved vain. The Russian Socialist Revolutionary groups in Lausanne and Geneva were small and weak; Chernov's publication withered for lack of readers. Eventually the Okhrana persuaded the French government to forbid its importation into France, and *Zhizn'* ceased publication in December 1915.[10]

Anatole Lunacharsky, on the other hand, left Paris on May 28 to renew publication of *Vperëd* in Geneva. On August 25, 1915, the first issue appeared, taking issue with all the major internationalist positions: the Leninist view of treason on the part of the leaders of the Second International, the Menshevik argument that the war and the breakdown of the International had been a matter of chance, and even the position of *Nashe Slovo,* which it called the wisest, that the roots of the catastrophe lay in the history of the working class. Lunacharsky instead pointed to the low cultural level of the proletariat, stressing the "need to educate and unite all the revolutionary internationalist elements."

During the spring and summer of 1915, a number of other emigré organizations in Switzerland also showed signs of revival. Perhaps typical was the meeting in Geneva, on June 13, of the Central Committee of the West European Union of Students from Russia, which had been inactive since the beginning of the war. Present were representatives from Bern, Geneva, Lausanne, and Zurich, who all spoke of the necessity of renewing their work in cooperation with socialist emigrés.[11]

The old divisions nevertheless persisted. In March 1915 the Russian anarchist group in Lausanne, led by Alexander Ghe (Heinrich Goldberg), began publication of a journal *Rabochee znamia (The Workers' Banner)*, which criticized *Golos* and Kropotkin but praised Lenin:

10. An undated and unsigned memorandum in OAr, XVIIr(1), f. 6, recorded, "I have taken measures to prevent the importation of *Zhizn'*." An Okhrana memorandum dated December 1915 declared that *Zhizn'* was no longer so influential in Paris after its editorial offices had moved. OAr, XVIb(6)(a), f. 4.

11. Okhrana report, Sept. 12/25, 1915, OAr, XVIb(7), f. 3. See also *Golos zarubezhnogo studenchestva,* 1915–16.

"Only the Leninists gave the correct slogan." The Second, Socialist, International, it declared, was dead; the anarchists had long before pointed out the weaknesses of its "bourgeois-reformist character." The publication went on to call for social revolution and the formation of a new workers' International.

D. Z. Manuilsky responded to this attack with the comment that the anarchists, who could not really understand the course of events, were nevertheless trying to describe them. Referring to Kropotkin, he noted that the war had brought confusion not only to the International but also to the "romantic illusions of yesterday's partisans of sabotage and the general strike." The anarchists, however, dismissed Manuilsky's comments by characterizing the International as a destroyed Catholic Church and *Nashe Slovo* as a bishop surveying the wreckage. The International, they insisted, had fallen because of its "class amorality."[12]

For all their disputes, the internationalist emigré organizations in Switzerland took an active part in the efforts to revive socialism as an international movement. About a third of the delegates to the women's conference in March had been emigrés from the Tsarist Empire. In the summer of 1915, Russians were to be found in the center of almost all efforts to hold international meetings in Switzerland.

In April 1915, the Swiss Socialist Party issued an invitation for a conference of socialist parties of neutral states, to meet in Zurich on May 30. Following the example of the Lugano conference of the Swiss and the Italians in September 1914, the gathering would consider "action by Social Democracy of neutral states on behalf of peace." A number of events intervened to block this plan—a meeting in Vienna of the socialist parties of Germany and Austria-Hungary, the sinking of the *Lusitania,* and the entry of Italy into the war. Nevertheless, the Swiss invitation planted the seed for the calling of a broader conference.

Upon hearing of the planned conference, Martov, still in Paris, warned Grimm that such a meeting would be useless. He urged the Swiss to enlarge the base of the meeting by inviting socialists from belligerent countries; only such a gathering could produce meaningful results. Axelrod, who transmitted Martov's communication to Grimm, suggested that there be a conference of official parties with the opposition invited as

12. *Rabochee znamia,* Mar., Apr. 1915; *Nashe Slovo,* Mar. 20, 1915. An anarchist manifesto declared that anarchist propaganda must "logically seek the weakening and destruction of all governments." *Nabat,* May-June 1915, pp. 3–4.

"guests"; the guests could exert pressure on the official delegates and produce some sort of understanding.[13]

Grimm responded that "there is almost nothing to be done with the official parties" and that the Swiss party would probably refuse to sponsor such a meeting. If nothing should come of the conference of neutrals, "representatives of the opposition in all lands should gather." This must not, however, mean a split, but rather only the "establishment of a line of action for the struggle against the war." Toward that end, a small international committee must be formed, to include Germans, English, Russians, and "above all" a French representative. Although Axelrod agreed that Grimm's idea was the only practical one, he nevertheless expressed reservations about any possibility of success. At least six weeks would be necessary for a representative to come from Russia.[14]

On May 21, the leadership of the Swiss Socialist Party decided to drop plans for the conference of neutrals. Grimm then pushed ahead with his proposal for a conference of the left, even though the Swiss party, as he had expected, refused to sponsor it. Grimm's basic network was made up of Angelica Balabanova for communication with the Italians, Morgari with the English, and Martov with the French. His contact in the United States was another Russian, Moses Aronson, the brother-in-law of the German Socialist Eduard Bernstein. His chief advisor on Russian affairs was apparently Axelrod, and for Polish affairs Maximilian Walecki, a member of the PPS-Lewica.

As late as the end of June, Grimm still hoped that the preparatory meeting for the conference of the left would include representatives of England, France, and Germany. For the full conference, tentatively planned for the middle of August, he wanted to add delegates from the United States and Russia. He did not want to be limited to the emigrés living in Switzerland. The English, however, found it impossible to travel, and prospective French representatives considered the risks too great for two trips into Switzerland, once for a preparatory meeting and then again for the general conference. Grimm therefore found that he simply could not escape the influence of the Russian emigrés.

At the same time, the Russians could not agree on a single course of action themselves. According to the Okhrana, a meeting of Russian

13. See *Zimm. Bew.*, 2:50–54, 61–62; *Pis'ma Aksel'roda i Martova*, pp. 329–30; Temkin, *Tsimmerval'd–Kintal'*, pp. 26–27; *Nashe Slovo*, May 11, 1915.
14. *Zimm. Bew.*, 2:64–67.

socialist leaders, including Axelrod, Semkovsky, Kosovsky, and Kon, tried unsuccessfully, on June 20, to formulate a mutually acceptable internationalist program.[15]

When the preparatory conference met on July 11, 1915, the seven participants claimed to represent four countries. Five of them, however, were natives of Russia. Besides Axelrod, Zinoviev, and Balabanova (representing Italy), there were two Polish socialists, Adolf Warski of the SDKPiL Central Committee and Walecki of the PPS-Lewica. The other two participants were Grimm and Morgari. The group recognized its own limited constituency by scheduling a second preparatory conference for August 8, at which representatives from at least England, France, and Germany should be present.

Grimm, Morgari, and Balabanova prevailed with their view that the invitation list for the conference of internationalists should be as broad as possible. Zinoviev stood alone in opposition on several points, insisting that yet a third Polish group, the National Committee of the SDKPiL, as well as the Social Democracy of the Latvian Region, should be included in the preparatory work, and opposing any invitation to "centrists" such as Hugo Haase in Germany. His proposal to invite a Latvian and an additional Pole failed by a vote of one favoring, five against, and one abstaining, and his effort to allow the German left to decide whether Haase should be invited failed by a vote of one to six.[16]

As the basis for the invitation of groups to the conference of internationalists, the preparatory meeting adopted a recommendation of the Italian Socialist Party, made a week before Italy's entry into the war: the conference should include "all socialist parties, or their sections, and all labor organizations which are against any civil peace, which adhere to the basis of the class struggle, and which are willing, through simultaneous international action, to struggle for immediate peace." Those parties which supported the war effort were thereby to be excluded. Inviting the centrists remained an open question.[17]

Grimm soon found that the wrangling among the Russian socialists —much of which he apparently did not understand—would continue to plague him no matter what he did. The SDKPiL National Committee

---

15. Report of July 2/15, 1915, OAr, XVIb(2), f. 6b.
16. See Olga Hess Gankin and H. H. Fisher, *The Bolsheviks and the World War* (Stanford, 1960), pp. 312–15; *Zimm. Bew.*, 1:39.
17. Gankin and Fisher, *The Bolsheviks*, pp. 312–13; Julius Braunthal, *History of the International*, 2 vols. (London, 1967), 2:41.

complained bitterly because it had not been invited to the preparatory meeting; its representative insisted that it had been the only Polish group to take "a clear, anti-social-patriotic position." The Bolsheviks protested that Grimm had surrounded himself with centrists and Mensheviks: "It is clear that no one cares seriously about the calling of the so-called left conference." Axelrod, on the other hand, repeatedly warned Grimm against trusting Karl Radek, of the National Committee, and Lenin. Lenin, he wrote, "seeks to transfer his beloved methods of factional struggle into the International."[18]

Grimm pressed ahead. By the end of July, it became clear that the second preliminary conference had to be postponed. Grimm tentatively set the new date for August 20. Even that proved impossible, and on August 19 he announced that the "whole affair is definitively put off to the fifth of September." Furthermore, the meeting would now constitute the full conference; there would be no more preliminary gatherings.[19] This decision brought new problems.

On August 22, Zinoviev renewed his demand that the conference invite, among others, the Polish National Committee and the Latvians. Grimm hoped to limit the Russian representation to three or four delegates, but Axelrod, for one, warned against excluding any party factions of either the Russians or the Poles. Even the Socialist Revolutionaries, as well as the representatives of *Nashe Slovo* and *Zhizn'*, must be included.[20]

In a circular letter of August 26, Grimm sought to resolve the issue. Declaring that the general attendance at the conference had to be limited, he insisted that the Russian and Polish representations had to be limited: "Every appearance must be avoided from which one could conclude that this is merely a demonstration by the Russian emigration." Each group —the Central Committee, the Organizational Committee, the Central Committee of the SDKPiL and the National Committee, the PPS-Lewica, the newspapers *Nashe Slovo* and *Zhizn'*, and the Bund—could send one delegate. "Thereby the Russian and Polish delegation would have eight mandates, definitely more than the delegations of other lands."[21] Nevertheless, despite Grimm's efforts, the Russians sent more delegates than their quota.

18. *Zimm. Bew.*, 2:70–74, 87–88; Temkin, *Lenin*, pp. 172–73.
19. *Zimm. Bew.*, 2:94.
20. Axelrod to Grimm, Aug. 23, 1915, Grimm Archive, 2. Teil, IISH.
21. *Zimm. Bew.*, 2:97–99.

Grimm had complete charge of the conference. He was in fact acting on his own responsibility, for he did not even have the backing of his own party. He signed his official letters simply with the title "National Councillor" *(Nationalrat)*. His arrangements for the meeting were a secret apparently shared only by Balabanova. In his note of August 26 to the Russians, he repeatedly emphasized the need to keep everything "strictly confidential." The participants were to gather at the Volkshaus in Bern on Sunday morning, September 5, at 10 A.M. The conference would then take place "in the environs of Bern, in the country." He took charge, himself, of all the problems of housing and feeding the delegates.

However justifiable, the tight control of preparations irritated Lenin, who argued that Grimm was trying "to close the door to the left." Lenin had left Bern at the beginning of July for the remote resort of Sörenberg, located at the foot of the Brienzer Rothorn in the canton of Lucerne. He kept in touch with a few of his followers, instructing them to telephone him at 8:30 in the morning if they wished to speak with him. Since Zinoviev was spending the summer at the resort of Hertenstein, on the Lake of Lucerne, Lenin relied on Karl Radek for his information about Grimm's work.[22]

Radek, whom Axelrod denounced as "one of Lenin's channels or instruments," was gradually assuming a greater role in Lenin's program. A member of the National Committee of the SDKPiL and also active with the radical German socialists in Bremen, he had been expelled—at Rosa Luxemburg's insistence—from both the SDKPiL Central Committee and the German Social Democratic Party. When he had first come to Switzerland in the fall of 1914 he had lived in Zurich, where he seemed to be closest to Axelrod.

At the end of November 1914, Radek returned to Germany, but by the spring he was again in Switzerland. He now split with Axelrod, charging that the Mensheviks had not come out strongly enough against the defensists, and he openly joined Lenin. (Some authors have maintained that he also had contacts with Parvus-Helphand.) According to Radek himself, "daily contact with Lenin, and discussion with him, definitively persuaded me that the Bolsheviks constituted the only revo-

---

22. See Temkin, *Lenin,* p. 183; *PSS,* 49:78. Krupskaia's ill health had necessitated a vacation in the mountains. See Leonhard Haas, "Lenins Frau als Patientin bei Schweizer Ärtzten," *Jahrbücher für die Geschichte Osteuropa* 17:420–36.

lutionary party of Russia."[23] His cooperation with Lenin was facilitated by the decision of the National Committee of the SDKPiL, taken in June 1915, to support Lenin. The Bolshevik leader welcomed them, despite his reservations about parts of their program.[24]

Radek, an Austrian citizen by birth, entered enthusiastically into the polemics of the Russian emigrés. When a Menshevik writer noted that he had refused to support the idea of a split in the German Social Democratic Party, Radek responded that while the observation was "objectively" correct, he objected to its having been made by a Menshevik, whose own Organizational Committee had criticized Lenin. Martov then insisted that Radek, who advocated one thing for Germany and another for Russia, could hardly be the mentor of the Russian socialists. Lenin also objected to Radek's distinction between opposition in Germany to the war, and the position of the Bolsheviks, to calling one "the product of ferment among the masses" and the other the "orientation of a small group of revolutionaries." Klara Zetkin once urged Grimm to censor Radek's articles in the *Berner Tagwacht,* which appeared over the pseudonym Parabellum: "His explanations are often so imprudent that they border on provocations."[25]

Despite these polemics, Radek quickly assumed an important position among the emigrés. A conference of foreign socialists in Zurich on June 30 elected him to serve with Feliks Kon and Fritz Platten on a standing executive committee charged with publishing information about proletarian opposition to the war. (Balabanova was chairman of the group.) For Lenin, he served as a channel of communications with both the Dutch and the Germans; he also helped in translating manuscripts into German.[26]

Radek's relationship with Lenin, to be sure, had its full share of conflict. When Radek suggested that Lenin return to Bern from Sörenberg to make his influence felt in the planning for the conference of interna-

23. See Karl Radek, *Lenin: Sein Leben und Werk* (Berlin, 1924), pp. 15–24; Georges Haupt and Jean-Jacques Marie, *Les Bolcheviks par eux-mêmes* (Paris, 1969), p. 332; Lyman Legters, "Karl Radek als Sprachrohr des Bolschewismus," *Forschungen zur osteuropäischen Geschichte* 7:196–322; Warren Lerner, *Karl Radek: The Last Internationalist* (Stanford, 1970), pp. 31–53.

24. Temkin, *Lenin,* pp. 160–61.

25. See *Nashe Slovo,* May 8, June 10, 11, 12, 1915; Temkin, *Lenin,* p. 198; Zetkin to Grimm, Jan. 28, 1915, Grimm Archive, 2. Teil, IISH.

26. See Okhrana report, Aug. 22/Sept. 4, 1915, OAr, XVIc, f. 5. Radek apparently supplanted G. L. Shklovsky as Lenin's German-language specialist.

tionalists, Lenin refused, questioning whether Grimm was attempting to avoid consulting the Central Committee. Lenin charged Radek with being too pliant and unsuspecting in dealing with the Swiss leader. It was Grimm's obligation to send a formal invitation to the Central Committee, or "possibly, naturally, also to my address; this is more direct." When Radek produced a draft declaration for the leftist faction to present to the conference of internationalists, Lenin criticized it sharply. Radek's statement was "too academic . . . Not a word about social chauvinism and opportunism and the struggle with them!!" Even Radek's second draft underwent considerable revision at Lenin's hands.[27]

With the experience of the women's conference and the youth conference behind him, Lenin prepared carefully for the upcoming conference. His program provided: "(1) to go when they summon it; (2) to unite the left, i.e., the supporters of *revolutionary activities,* in advance against *their own* governments; (3) to present to the Kautskyite trash *our* draft resolution (the Dutch + us + left Germans + 0, and that is not bad, *later* it will be not zero but all!); (4) to put forth 2–3 speakers at the conference."[28] Charging Radek with the task of preparing a resolution or a manifesto, he turned his own efforts to the preparation of a pamphlet to be called *Socialism and the War* and to be distributed to the conference.

After Grimm's announcement that the full conference would take place on September 5, Lenin became still more active. He urged his potential allies to come. He welcomed the mandate sent him by the Latvian J. A. Berzin (Winter). He directed Alexandra Kollontai to insist that Swedish radicals come. He even offered to defray part of the costs of the Dutch if they would but come to the conference. (If they could not, he urged them to give their mandate to Radek.) In order to coordinate the efforts of the left, he scheduled preliminary meetings for September 2 and 3 in Bern.

On the level of theory, Lenin now enunciated one of his most important pronouncements on the development of revolutionary conditions. Rejecting the idea of a "United States of Europe," he argued that under

27. See Lenin's letters to Radek, *PSS,* 49; Temkin, *Lenin,* p. 193. In his *Tsimmerval'd–Kintal',* p. 38, Temkin insisted that Radek agreed with Lenin only in form, not in substance. The significant fact about Lenin's correspondence with Radek, however, would really seem to have been Lenin's willingness to rely on him.
28. *PSS,* 49:82.

capitalism such a slogan was "either impossible or reactionary." Any arrangement could only be temporary: "Uneven economic and political development is an absolute law of capitalism. Hence, the victory of socialism is possible first in several or even in one capitalist country alone." While an important part of Lenin's view of imperialism, this observation would later serve to justify the experience of Bolshevik rule in Russia.[29]

In response to a variety of attacks on his views, he wrote another article, "The Defeat of One's Own Government in an Imperialist War." Trotsky, he charged, had used "inflated phraseology" and had completely "lost his way among three trees," in that he had interpreted Lenin's position as favoring a German victory. In this " 'thought' or rather want of thought," Lenin claimed to see no difference between Trotsky, Semkovsky, and "Bukvoed" (D. B. Riazanov).[30] "The opponents of the slogan of defeat simply fear themselves, refusing to recognize the obvious fact of the inseparable link between revolutionary agitation against the government and helping bring about its defeat." Without this slogan, one's "revolutionary ardor" degenerates "into an empty phrase, or sheer hypocrisy."[31]

Lenin also did what he could to weaken his opponents. In August, he waged an unsuccessful campaign to block an invitation to the conference for the *Nashe Slovo* group, which he insisted was indistinguishable from the Menshevik Organizational Committee. The group, in any case, had not been a political party in Russia and should be ineligible on that score. The Foreign Secretariat of the Organizational Committee had abandoned its own claims to internationalism, according to him, by failing to denounce "defensist" statements by Mensheviks in Russia. At one point, Lenin criticized Zinoviev for not having attacked *Nashe Slovo*'s program of "peace" sharply enough. As he wrote to the Dutch Socialist Wijnkoop, "The clever statesmen of both warring groups" would probably support "the idiotic 'program of peace' in order to stifle the growing revolutionary ferment."[32]

29. *PSS*, 26:351–55.

30. In the summer of 1915 Riazanov, a leading Social Democratic writer, came to Switzerland from Vienna, where he had headed the Russian colony. He was a member of no faction, and associated himself with *Nashe Slovo*. See the report on his work in Vienna in OAr, VIIIb, f. 14; also, Ernst Nobs, "Lenin und die Schweizer Sozialdemokraten," *Rote Revue* 33:50–52.

31. *PSS*, 26:286–91.

32. *PSS*, 26:292–97, 49:83, 93, 115; Temkin, *Lenin*, pp. 181–82.

At the beginning of September, Lenin finally departed Sörenberg for Bern. For the delegates of the upcoming conference he had a battery of publications and declarations. He and Zinoviev together had prepared the pamphlet *Socialism and the War,* translated into German by Radek. For those who read Russian, he had the first and only issue of a new journal, *Kommunist,* edited by Bukharin, Piatakov, and Bosh. In addition, he had prepared his own "left manifesto," which, together with Radek's, he would present to his sympathizers for their approval.

Writing in *Kommunist,* Lenin apparently felt no particular need to denounce his Russian opponents, apart from Plekhanov. His article, entitled "Collapse of the Second International," concentrated on educating his Russian readers on the causes and significance of the phenomenon of social chauvinism, which he equated with "Kautskyism."[33] Zinoviev supplemented the article with one of his own, recounting and criticizing the development of Russian "bourgeois" nationalism and also the attitudes toward the war on the part of other Russian socialist groups.[34]

Socialism and the War represented a synthesis of Zinoviev's and Lenin's *Kommunist* articles. The thrust of the essay lay in its effort to distinguish Lenin's views from those of the defensists and of other internationalists: "The protagonists of victory for one's own government in a given war, just as the protagonists of the slogan 'neither victory nor defeat,' take the point of view of social chauvinism. The revolutionary class in a reactionary war can only desire the defeat of its own government." All the previous international conferences in Switzerland had been "imbued with the best intentions, but they did not at all see the specific danger."[35] Reasserting the Bolshevik slogans, the essay concluded that there was no real difference in the entire socialist spectrum from Plekhanov to Trotsky.

Lenin arrived in Bern intending to force the conference of internationalists to take a radical position on the war. He had never challenged Grimm's initiative in calling the meeting, but neither did he praise Grimm; rather, he bitterly criticized him for his relatively moderate views. Lenin chose to exploit Grimm's efforts by organizing his own faction within Grimm's movement.

33. *PSS,* 26:209–65.
34. G. E. Zinoviev and V. I. Lenin, *Protiv techeniia* (Petrograd, 1918), pp. 178–269.
35. *PSS,* 26:327, 337.

7

The Russians at Zimmerwald

At the beginning of September 1915, the tempo of activity at the Volks-haus in Bern picked up with the arrival of delegates for the conference of internationalists. The time of letter-writing receded into the past, and the time of formal and informal meetings began. Grimm had drawn up the broad plans for the holding of the conference; Lenin took the initiative in defining the substance of the discussions.

On September 2, Lenin and Zinoviev met in Bern with three members of the dissident faction of the SDKPiL: Radek, Mieczyslaw Bronski, and Henryk Kamienski. Although the Polish group were probably Lenin's closest allies, he still was far from satisfied with their views. (Writing from Copenhagen, Fürstenburg-Hanecki urged Kamienski to hew to Lenin's position.) Lenin and Radek had as yet failed to produce a mutually agreeable text for a draft resolution. The Poles were not so ready to lump together all the centrists as social chauvinists, and true to their own history, they refused to endorse the idea of national self-determination which Lenin now espoused. Needing their support and faced by a solid front, Lenin on this occasion decided to compromise. He agreed to use Radek's draft resolution, with his own corrections added.[1]

Lenin's demands for a left resolution called for a general ideological statement "(1) absolutely condemning the social chauvinists and oppor-

---

1. See Ia. G. Temkin, *Tsimmerval'd-Kintal'* (Moscow, 1967), pp. 46–47; N. E. Korolev, *Lenin i mezhdunarodnoe rabochee dvizhenie* (Moscow, 1968), pp. 67–68.

tunists; (2) containing a program of revolutionary actions (whether to say civil war or revolutionary mass action is not so important after all); (3) against the 'defense of the fatherland' slogan, etc."[2] Accordingly, his own draft had labelled imperialism "the highest stage of capitalism" and had stressed the slogan of "defeat of one's own country." The final draft adopted at the meeting of September 2 either totally ignored or significantly modified these statements.

At Lenin's insistence, Radek had agreed to insert sharper criticism of the centrists and the "social-patriots." Nevertheless, Radek's text lacked Lenin's declaration that defense of the fatherland meant treason to socialism. Lenin had warned that the call for a quick peace constituted deceit. The final resolution called for "a struggle for the quickest possible ending of the human slaughter." Lenin had written of the oppression of nations. The final resolution criticized calls for national independence. The resolution also indicated that "the socialist organization of the advanced capitalist lands" was the "only possible slogan" for socialists opposing the war. The text concluded with the Leninist call, "Our slogan is not civil peace between classes, but civil war."[3]

Two days later, on September 4, a somewhat larger group met, including Lenin, Zinoviev, Jan Berzin of the Latvian Social Democracy, J. Borchardt from Germany, Platten, Radek, E. Höglund from Sweden, and Ture Nerman from Sweden. The appearance of several uninvited persons, including Trotsky, added to the acerbity of the discussions. When Trotsky, who had arrived in Switzerland only the day before, declared, "I don't know what is meant by massive revolutionary activities," Radek replied that in Germany, "opportunists who oppose revolutionary activities also usually 'don't know' what is meant thereby." Trotsky, on the other hand, claimed to have blocked a new move by Lenin to deny a vote to the *Nashe Slovo* group. In the end, the gathering again endorsed Radek's resolution in preference to Lenin's text, albeit with extensive changes.[4]

As the delegates arrived, many other private meetings took place. Even the representatives of the three Polish delegations—the PPS-

2. Lenin to Kollontai, after July 11, 1915, *PSS*, 49:95; Olga Hess Gankin and H. H. Fisher, *The Bolsheviks and the World War* (Stanford, 1940), p. 315.
3. Radek's original text lies in Soviet archives. See Temkin, *Tsimmerval'd-Kintal'*, pp. 47–48, and *Lenin i mezhdunarodnaia sotsial-demokratiia* (Moscow, 1968), pp. 200–202. See also *PSS*, 26:282–85, 383–85.
4. *Sotsial'demokrat*, Oct. 11, 1915; *Nashe Slovo*, Oct. 6, 9, Nov. 5, 1915.

Lewica and both factions of the SDKPiL—conferred, at the suggestion of the PPS. On this occasion, Walecki proposed that the three groups stand "as solidly as possible" at the conference.[5] Full unity, however, still eluded the Poles.

On September 3, the Menshevik Foreign Secretariat issued its own manifesto, "A Letter to the Comrades in Russia." Russia was in the throes of a greater crisis than that facing any of the other warring great powers, the document asserted. Only a popular revolution could save the country from German imperialism. The Russian proletariat, which desired peace and not annexations, should advance the slogan: "An all-national constituent assembly to liquidate the autocratic (June 3) structure." French money had saved the monarchy in 1906; now the European proletariat must help the Russian people.[6]

On the morning of September 5, the delegates gathered as Grimm had ordered. Seated in four carriages, they then set out for the Bernese Oberland, the uplands south of Bern. According to Trotsky, "the delegates themselves joked about the fact that half a century after the founding of the First International, it was still possible to seat all the internationalists in four coaches."[7]

Grimm's entourage travelled some two hours up the steep, winding road overlooking the Emmental. Their destination, the Calvinist village of Zimmerwald, had just twenty-one houses and one hundred forty-five inhabitants. The arrival of more than thirty delegates to the socialist conference, coming on a Sunday afternoon, must have caused a great commotion, but Grimm had chosen the site with the aim of avoiding the French and German newspaper correspondents who infested the Volkshaus in Bern. He prohibited the delegates from sending letters for the duration of the meeting, and they received no news from the outside world. For recreation they could take mountain walks, or else listen to Grimm's yodeling and Viktor Chernov's rendition of Russian folk songs.[8]

At four o'clock in the afternoon of the fifth, Grimm called the con-

5. See Temkin, *Lenin,* pp. 205–6; Feliks Tych, *PSS-Lewica w latach wojny 1914–1918* (Warsaw, 1960), pp. 77–78.

6. See *Zadacha rossiiskogo proletariata (pis'mo k tovarishcham v Rossii)* (Geneva, 1915); *Obzor,* pp. 41–42.

7. Leon Trotsky, *My Life* (New York, 1960), p. 249.

8. See Jules Humbert-Droz, *Der Krieg und die Internationale* (Vienna, 1964), pp. 129–32; L. Trotskii, *Voina i revoliutsiia,* 2 vols. (Moscow, 1918), 2:44.

ference to order. He again vainly attempted to limit the role of the Russian emigrés: "above all the Russians should get together and shorten the discussions, that is, just *one* speaker."[9] Of the thirty-eight delegates, twelve represented Russian and Polish socialist groups: Zinoviev and Lenin of the Central Committee; Jan Berzin-Winter of the Social Democracy of the Latvian Region; Trotsky of *Nashe Slovo;* Martov and Axelrod of the Organizational Committee; P. L. Girš-Lemansky of the Bund; Mark Natanson-Bobrov of the Socialist Revolutionary Central Committee and Chernov of *Zhizn';* Warski of the SDKPiL; Pawel Lewinson-Łapiński of the PPS-Lewica; Radek, listed simply as "Poland." In addition, Balabanova, the conference's interpreter, represented the Italian Socialist Party. In the preliminary reports on the activities of the internationalists in the various countries, eight Russians and Poles spoke.

In the longest of the speeches, Axelrod defended the role of the emigrés: "What happens in the emigration is just as important as what happens among other parties even within their own land." In contrast to his own earlier warnings to Grimm about the necessity of bringing representatives from Russia, he argued that the Russian delegates at the conference did not represent "just the refugees, but their parties in their entirety." Russian emigré organizations maintained official ties with their domestic organizations; Western socialists, he argued, did not properly understand the Russian situation.

Axelrod had prepared his own ground for the conference with the publication, in German, of *The Crisis and the Tasks of International Social Democracy,* wherein he argued that a French-German understanding must be the first step toward international reconciliation and that this should be easier for the Germans than for the French. The longer the civil peace in the warring countries lasted, the more susceptible the Western socialist parties would be to Leninist influences. Only the Russian emigration and the anarcho-syndicalists had taken a fully leftist position in regard to the war.[10]

In his opening speech at Zimmerwald, Axelrod refrained from attacking Lenin directly, and instead presented the call of the Menshevik Organizational Committee for a constituent assembly as the program

---

9. *Zimm. Bew.,* 1:57. Unless otherwise cited, all references to the debates at Zimmerwald have been taken from the protocol as published in vol. 1 of this work.

10. P. B. Axelrod, *Die Krise und die Aufgaben der Internationalen Sozialdemokratie* (Zurich, 1915). See also *PSS,* 27:52–58.

of all Russian internationalists. The Russians were divided in two, he declared, those favoring a defensist posture until a constituent assembly could meet, and those demanding the immediate formation of a constituent assembly. When later challenged in his estimate of the demand for a constituent assembly, Axelrod explained that he had meant his declaration only as an expression of hope. He obviously could not say that all internationalists were actually calling for an assembly. His purpose in ignoring the defeatists, he insisted, had been to "point out the relationship of forces which exist among us, between internationalists as a whole, represented at the conference, and their opponents."[11]

The Bund's representative, acting under Kosovsky's orders, contrasted his own position to Axelrod's, declaring that the emigration had never played a really significant part in the direction of the Bund's activities. Therefore the Foreign Secretariat of the Bund had chosen to limit his mandate to that of an observer at the conference. Lemansky subsequently refrained from signing any declarations made by the conference.

Speaking for the three Polish groups, Łapiński asserted that "the situation in our land is a thousand times worse than in Belgium." Berzin of Latvia reported that the revolutionary movement in the Baltic area was growing. Chernov affirmed this view for Russia as a whole and declaimed, "The New International will be an International of deed or else it will not be."[12]

Neither Trotsky nor Zinoviev felt it necessary to justify the role of the emigration as Axelrod had done. Trotsky in fact declared that the work of *Nashe Slovo* was so well known that he had nothing to say. A French speaker, indeed, had already praised the support which the French opposition had received from "the Russian comrades with *Nashe Slovo*."[13] Zinoviev, on the other hand, indicated that Axelrod, in his concern for party unity, was in fact consorting with social patriots; the Bolsheviks too hoped for unity, "but on the basis of internationalism. We cannot struggle together with the social patriots."

Despite their numbers, the Russians did not dominate the conference

11. *Nashe Slovo,* Oct. 27, 1915.

12. Charles Rappoport, a Russian emigré living in Paris, had made the same statement—"Die dritte Internationale müsse zur Internationale der Tat werden" —in a speech to the Eintracht Society on August 25, 1915. *Volksrecht,* Aug. 26, 1915.

13. Cf. the interpretation in Temkin, *Lenin,* p. 219.

so much as form its character. Apart from the very fact of meeting together, few of the delegates seemed to have any clear purpose in mind.[14] In this context, Lenin's preparations forced the discussions to take the form of reactions to his proposals. He stood in the very center of the deliberations, and from the beginning, the delegates differentiated according to their support of or opposition to the Leninist program.

On September 7, the third day of the conference, Radek came forth with a resolution and a manifesto in his own and in Lenin's name. Arguing that revolutionary action constituted the only true action for peace, he insisted that the slogan "struggle for peace" was inadequate. All talk about national independence and defending democracy, moreover, only served to mislead the proletariat. The task of all socialists lay in arousing the working masses to "revolutionary struggle against capitalist governments." This included the denial of war credits, refusing to serve in ministerial cabinets, street demonstrations, and strikes: "Civil War, not civil peace, is the answer."

The manifesto went on to address itself to the working masses, urging them to demand that their socialist leaders oppose war credits and resign from cabinet posts. "But that is not enough." The masses must also themselves act: "You must go into the streets; let your call ring in the ears of the rulers: Enough of this butchery!" The masses must set as their goal the "overthrow of the capitalist governments."

Two competing manifestos came forth, one the product of the German delegation and the other a joint production by Trotsky and the Dutch socialist Henriette Roland-Holst. The Germans also joined with the French delegation in a ceremonial reconciliation to offer a declaration, "This war is not our war." Condemning the violation of Belgium's neutrality, the declaration called for a "peace which ravishes no people and no nation . . . No annexation, either open or disguised, and no forced economic attachment."

Trotsky and Roland-Holst had acted at the suggestion of the latter. Meeting in Trotsky's room, they wrote what Trotsky laughingly called "my first German text."[15] Their manifesto, like the others, condemned the imperialistic character of the war. Noting the growing "mighty mass

---

14. In his notes, Lenin complained at one point, "only words here, no action." *Leninskii Sbornik,* 14:179.

15. Cited in *Zimm. Bew.,* 1:134n.

struggle against the war in all countries," the manifesto repeated the call of the Germans and the French: "This war is not our war. It brings us only ruin and double chains to our children." Condemning civil peace, it called the working classes "into the great street of the class struggle . . . For peace, against war! Through our pressure, through our revolutionary strength to peace!"

Most speakers accepted the general lines of the resolution offered by Radek, but they expressed reservations about the manifesto. Was it wise, questioned Grimm, to "reveal our tactical measures to the enemy"? Should the manifesto be addressed to the socialist leaders or to the working masses? Modigliani of Italy challenged the necessity of issuing a manifesto. Trotsky thought that Lenin had made too "sectarian" an impression. Chernov declared his agreement "in principle with the Radek resolution, but not with his manifesto." Bertha Thalheimer of Germany thought it unwise, "for strategic reasons," to publish Radek's manifesto.

In the course of the discussion, several deputies called for a limit on debate because of the growing heat of the exchanges. The chairman, Christian Rakovsky, insisted on continuing, declaring, "Polemics are inevitable." The most pointed exchanges came between Lenin and his opponents. The Germans, led by Georg Ledebour, attacked him more bitterly than the Russians did. (After his opening speech, Axelrod, probably Lenin's greatest critic, spoke no more.) The Germans, to be sure, felt themselves on the defensive throughout the conference.

In commenting on Radek's call to street demonstrations and revolutionary actions, Ledebour insisted, "Whoever signs such a manifesto has himself the obligation to take the lead. From here we should not direct such a call to other people, and people who find themselves in safety, as do some of the signers, should not do it." Any signer from a warring country would be a marked man. Adolph Hoffmann later echoed this view: "Zinoviev said, 'If you do it, you must say it.' They, however, say it since they are out of the country."

Lenin alone among the Russian emigrés reacted to these statements: "It was inevitable that it should come here to a struggle of views between Ledebour and us." He complained, "It is unheard of, to assert that our manifesto is underwritten just by people who live in safety." This was an "old, shabby argument." The passive revolutionism of the Germans was one of the worst qualities of the Second International.

The manifesto, he argued, could even be issued without signatures: "The problem is this—either real revolutionary struggle or only empty babbling."[16]

Arthur Merrheim, a French representative, took a different tack, arguing that a revolutionary movement could arise "only out of the struggle for peace." (Lenin had reportedly spent some eight hours attempting to recruit Merrheim's support.) Turning to the Bolshevik leader, he stated, "You, Comrade Lenin, are dominated not by the desire for peace but by the wish to erect the foundation pillars of a new International. This is what divides us. We want a manifesto which promotes peace; we don't want to emphasize what divides us but what unites us."

In his opening speech, Grimm had already emphasized that the conference was "in no way to serve for the formation of a new International." Modigliani of Italy repeated the thought that the conference could not be "the point of departure to a third International." Ledebour too insisted that his Berlin comrades had not given him a mandate to found a Third International. Rakovsky expressed the view that one could not say that the International no longer lived: "It lives on to a degree as a political idea."

The various Russian speakers, after their introductory comments, tended to avoid direct attacks on each other. Although at least one Soviet historian has insisted that Lenin's work was hindered by the "endless intrigues of Martov, Axelrod, and Trotsky,"[17] publicly Trotsky and Martov took relatively conciliatory positions. In presenting his own draft of a manifesto, Trotsky declared, "Generally speaking, I am in agreement with the Radek resolution." He opposed the resolution only on the grounds that such an extensive revolutionary program could not yet be put into effect.

Martov directed his comments mainly at the Germans. Since the Germans had been leaders and models before the war, they had to bear special criticism for their support of their government. "We are against

16. The protocol of the conference, as written by Grimm and Balabanova, did not repeat the complete text of all statements. See the varying accounts of this exchange in Temkin, *Lenin,* p. 231; Alfred Rosmer, *Le Mouvement ouvrier pendant la guerre,* 2 vols. (Paris, 1936–53), 1:384; Henri Guilbeaux, *Wladimir Iljitsch Lenin* (Berlin, 1923), p. 40; Maurice Pianzola, *Lénine en Suisse* (Geneva, 1965); G. E. Zinoviev, *Lenin* (Petrograd, 1922), p. 51; *Leninskii Sbornik* 45:180.
17. Temkin, *Lenin,* p. 209.

material sabotage," he stated, but the only way to struggle against the war was by "moral sabotage." In particular, the voting of war credits could be a vital issue; the denial of credits would show the "simple soldier" that "the war is contrary to the interests of the people." The goal of the socialists should be "that the soldiers no longer fight with enthusiasm."

In turn, Lenin's supporters seemed relatively milder in their comments about other Russians. Zinoviev, noting that almost all speakers had expressed a substantial agreement with the resolution of the left, declared that Trotsky's draft manifesto was "a step forward" in comparison with the German draft. The draft's major flaw lay in its failure to enter the struggle "against Kautskyism."

In the evening session of September 7, Grimm finally called a halt to the discussions. The conference had in hand one draft resolution and three draft manifestos. Grimm proposed turning the draft manifestos over to an editorial commission but leaving "the question of a resolution open until a permanent organ is established." By a vote of nineteen to twelve, the conference concurred in tabling Radek's draft resolution; the leadership then proposed that the editorial commission include Lenin, Ledebour, Trotsky, Meyer, Martov, Modigliani, Merrheim, and Grimm; that is, three of its eight members would be Russians. Eventually the gathering chose a seven-member commission, including only two Russians: Grimm, Ledebour, Lenin, Merrheim, Trotsky, Rakovsky, and Modigliani.

The vote refusing to refer Radek's draft resolution to the editorial commission constituted the major test of strength in the conference. The lines, however, were far from clear. The Leninists in this case enjoyed the support of Chernov, Natanson, and Trotsky. Balabanova and Lemansky abstained, while Axelrod, Martov, Warski, and Łapiński voted against the resolution. The Russian and Polish participants in the conference had therefore supported the resolution by a vote of seven to four, with two abstentions.[18]

Trotsky later explained his support of the resolution by noting that the text had considerably modified the old Leninist program. It lacked the declaration that the "defeat of Russia is the lesser evil"; it did not demand the splitting of workers' organizations as a matter of principle; it recognized the "revolutionary significance of the struggle for peace,"

18. See, *ibid.,* pp. 234–35.

although it still misinterpreted the slogan "struggle for peace." In Trotsky's view, "everything was gone which had differentiated the position of *Sotsial'demokrat* from that of *Nashe Slovo*. . . . The representative of *Nashe Slovo* could only declare his solidarity with the basic theses of the resolution."[19] Such praise from *Nashe Slovo* undoubtedly contributed to the anger which Lenin later felt toward the Poles because of the concessions which he had made in accepting Radek's text.

Lenin's faction numbered some eight firm members: himself, Zinoviev, Platten, Berzin, Höglund, Radek, Nerman, and Julius Borchhardt. With the exception of Borchhardt, Lenin was at least ten years older than any other member of the group. Radek was barely thirty, and Berzin was the youngest, at twenty-eight. Lenin, at forty-five, actually stood among the older half of the participants in the conference. Again with the exception of Borchardt and perhaps Radek, Lenin's following consisted of either Russian emigrés or socialists from neutral countries.

The rest of the delegates lacked clear factional organization. Trotsky later claimed to distinguish three groups in all: Lenin's, the moderate element led by Ledebour, which only wanted to speak of peace, and a "center" group, which shared many of Lenin's views but considered organizational splitting still inopportune. He clearly considered himself the catalyst in the formation of this group. Martov objected, arguing that the differentiation of views in the conference had emerged entirely as a result of reactions to Lenin's initiative; he ridiculed Trotsky's pretentions to having led a "third force."[20]

To the Leninists, the divisions seemed clear. Zinoviev later declared that only the left had presented a "defined and whole program." The deliberations, he insisted, had consisted in a "duel" between Ledebour and the left. Of Trotsky he made no mention, saying only that the basic left group of seven or eight members occasionally swelled in size to ten or eleven.[21]

Trotsky's claim of having led a third faction at the conference rested on his work in the editorial commission, where he and Grimm undertook the writing of the conference's formal manifesto. Over the objection of Lenin, the commission decided not to select one of the three submitted texts but rather to produce its own. In Trotsky's words, how-

19. Trotskii, *Voina i revoliutsiia,* 2:56.
20. See, *ibid.,* 2:46, 55; *Nashe Slovo,* Jan. 6, 7, 1916.
21. G. Zinoviev and N. Lenin, *Protiv techeniia* (Petrograd, 1918), pp. 298–99.

ever, the fact that the commission selected him to work with Grimm on a final text "was no coincidence, but rather it corresponded to the groupings of the conference."

Trotsky claimed to see his contribution in putting the slogan of the struggle for peace on the "track of revolutionary-class tactics." He claimed to express the views of the conference's center, consisting of Roland-Holst, Kolarov of Bulgaria, Rakovsky, Platten, Grimm, Charles Naine of Switzerland, Balabanova, Modigliani, and two German delegates. (He insisted that it was a mistake to consider Platten a member of the Leninist camp.) In answer to challenges that this group had in fact split on the one major vote over referring the leftist resolution to the editorial commission, Trotsky scorned the idea of measuring the group and insisted that it had in fact existed.[22]

The editorial commission's manifesto began by asserting that the war had exposed the "naked form of modern capitalism." At fault for the war were capitalist society, monarchic and republican governments, secret diplomacy, bourgeois parties, the capitalist press, and the church. The socialist leadership in various countries had wrongly shelved the class struggle, voted war credits, and offered socialist ministers as "hostages."

In response to these conditions, "we Germans, French, Italians, Russians, Poles, Latvians, Rumanians, Bulgarians, Swedes, Norwegians, Dutch, and Swiss" had gathered to reaffirm the "international solidarity of the proletariat" and to renew the class struggle. Calling for a peace without annexations and without indemnities, the manifesto insisted the right of national self-determination had to lie at the basis of any settlement. The task of all socialists should be the "implacable proletarian class struggle" for "the holy aims of socialism, for the liberation of oppressed peoples and of the enslaved classes."[23]

Lenin, as the only member of the left on the editorial commission, had pressed for a sharper denunciation of defensist socialists, while Ledebour, supported by several others, had opposed all moves to demand that socialist deputies actively oppose all war credits. At one time or another, both men threatened not to sign the manifesto. The commission nevertheless reported its text to the conference in the evening of September 8.

22. See *Nashe Slovo*, Nov. 24, 1915.
23. Text in *Zimm. Bew.*, 1:166–69.

When Grimm opened the session, he turned to Lenin and specifically asked the Russian not to emphasize tactical differences at the cost of unity. Lenin's objections, he insisted, lay entirely in the realm of "elucidating the means of struggle" and not in principle. Roland-Holst nevertheless opened the discussion by presenting a declaration in the name of the left, calling for the refusal to vote war credits.

Martov then came forth in the name of "some Russian and Polish delegates," namely Axelrod, Warski, and Łapiński, arguing that the manifesto should be more specific about the "perspectives which await the proletariat after the war." Chernov followed him with two complaints: the manifesto should have denounced the role of Russian dynastic interests in the unfolding of the war, and the manifesto's conception that the proletariat alone had to bear the costs of the war was too narrow. In Russia, he argued, the peasants had to bear the brunt of the costs of war.

After desultory debate, all three efforts at amendment failed. Chernov announced that he could not support the manifesto as it stood. Lenin's group, on the other hand, contented itself with a new declaration that the manifesto did not satisfy it; the text offered no denunciation of opportunism. Nevertheless the group would support the manifesto as a "call to struggle."

Even at this point, the conference threatened to dissolve in disagreement. Morgari and Chernov criticized the manifesto. Others urged them to consider the impact of any refusal to support the declaration. Grimm insisted that the text had to be couched in the broadest possible terms, without specific references to individual countries and their problems. Balabanova added her argument: "You are here not just as a delegate; in your person the efforts for unity of the international proletariat find expression."

No less serious was the antagonism which the German delegates expressed toward Radek, who had been expelled from the German Social Democratic Party before the war. Ledebour threatened not to sign the manifesto if Radek's name should also be there.[24]

---

24. German Social Democrats scornfully attacked the Zimmerwald movement as the "Sobelsohnsche dritte Internationale" and the "edle Kämpfergruppe Grimm-Sobelsohn-Radek-Kradek-Parabellum." See *Internationale Korrespondenz,* Oct. 12, 1915, Mar. 7, 1916.

Grimm finally shut off debate and called for delegates supporting the manifesto to rise. Morgari joined the majority, but Chernov and Natanson, the two Russian Socialist Revolutionaries, remained seated. Other delegates turned on them, and finally, under pressure, they too arose. Grimm declared the vote to be unanimous, and the delegates joined together in singing the "Internationale."[25]

There remained yet a number of details. In contrast to Lenin's earlier willingness to publish the manifesto anonymously, the French and the German delegates insisted that the manifesto be published with signatures. Of the Russians, Lenin, Axelrod, and Natanson signed. Each of the three Polish representatives also signed, although Radek used Jakob Fürstenburg-Hanecki's name instead of his own.

In addition, the conference established a continuing executive body which, after some discussion, was named the International Socialist Commission in Bern. After Grimm had urged the delegates to contribute to the costs of the conference and of maintaining the ISC, the meeting ended at 2:30 in the morning of September 9.

News of the conference reached the general public only gradually. In the Swiss socialist press of September 18, 1915, Grimm and his colleagues in the ISC published an official summary of conference deliberations, mentioning parties and groups represented but without naming the delegates.[26] Publication in the warring countries met with a variety of difficulties.

In Paris, censors prohibited Trotsky from mentioning the conference in *Nashe Slovo,* but beginning on October 6 he proceeded to discuss the meeting without identifying it. Using as a form a fictitious diary, he delineated in great detail the organization and progress of the conference without specifying the time and the place. Only on October 19, after the French press had reported the conference, could Trotsky finally proclaim, "It did take place, this conference in Zimmerwald."[27]

The Zimmerwald meeting, to be sure, had included mainly individuals, opposition elements within regular socialist parties, and not official party

25. *Zimm. Bew.,* 1:157.
26. *Berner Tagwacht* and *Volksrecht,* Sept. 18, 1915. The Italian newspaper *Avanti* reported the conference on September 14. For the text of the communiqué, see *Zimm. Bew.,* 1:170–80.
27. Cf. *Ar. Monatte,* pp. 201–2.

representatives. Most of the participants had balked at the thought of splitting with the Second International. Nevertheless their action, and especially their decision to establish a continuing, executive agency, had in fact created a competitor to the International Socialist Bureau of the Second International. Lenin had wanted a firmer, more assertive action in this direction; the majority moved only hesitantly, uncertainly.

8

The Defensists

At the same time that the internationalists travelled to Zimmerwald, defensist Russian socialists gathered in Geneva. Both Social Democrats and Socialist Revolutionaries participated in the conference, and many observers found it ironic that G. V. Plekhanov, who had once played a great role in fostering the separate development of these two revolutionary lines, should now preside over an effort to coordinate them.

The defensists had already shown a considerable activity, centered in Paris. In the summer of 1915, a group of Social Democrats published a collection of articles entitled *The War*, including contributions by Ida Axelrod and Plekhanov.[1] Defensist Socialist Revolutionaries in Paris, led by A. A. Avksientiev, Fondaminsky-Bunakov, and A. A. Amfiteatrov, had also been publishing their own newspapers, *Novosti* (*News*) and *Za Rubezhom* (*Abroad*).

Contributors to *The War* took specific issue with the activities of the internationalists in Switzerland. In an account of the work of the socialist women's conference in Bern, one author complained that its resolution had given "a too general, abstract presentation of the question of the causes of the present war." Since Marxists had an obligation to distinguish who was the aggressor in any given conflict, the writer contrasted the Bern meeting with the work of the London conference of Entente socialists, which had "examined the concrete situation of the current war" and had

---

1. *Voina: Sbornik statei* (Paris, 1915). The collection was first planned in December 1914. Mark to Alexinsky, Dec. 17, 1914, Aleks. Ar. Voina, f. XII, 261.

drawn conclusions "which gave it the indisputable right to say of itself that it 'had remained true to the principles of the International.' "[2]

As their common ground, the contributors to *The War* declared, "We are all agreed with each other that the direct responsibility for the war falls on the German and Austrian governments, who attacked Serbia and violated the neutrality of Belgium." Lev Deich argued that a victory of the Entente powers presented no danger to democratic principles. Even though one could not believe the various promises of the Russian government, there was "nevertheless no basis to fear its emerging as the victor from the present war."[3]

Plekhanov took issue with those "obscurantists" who "warm up the thought of the anarchists (of a certain shade) that the defeat of any capitalist country will be harmful only to the interests of its bourgeoisie." Russia, he wrote, "belongs not to its Tsar but to its working population. Whoever holds dear the interests of this population cannot remain indifferent to the fate of Russia."[4]

G. A. Alexinsky attacked individuals by name. Unable to unite, he asserted, the internationalists even contradicted themselves. At one point, Alexinsky argued, Martov had seemed more enraptured with the idea of Russia's defeat than even Lenin had. Lunacharsky and Trotsky both found it possible to contribute essays against social patriotism to *Nashe Slovo* and at the same time to send "praises of Joan of Arc" to the Russian liberal publication *Kievskaia Mysl'*. Quoting *Nashe Slovo*, he criticized the internationalists for being united not on principle but only "on a position directly opposed to Plekhanov's point of view." The defeatists were not revolutionaries, he proclaimed: "They are simply liberal reformists, with the distinction that liberals usually await a constitution and freedom 'from above' from domestic authority while the Social Democratic liberal-defeatists await it also 'from above' but from foreign authority." The internationalists were only playing into the hands of the reaction, allowing it to categorize all Social Democrats as enemies of the people.[5]

The appearance of *The War* escalated the antagonisms between defensists and internationalists. Lenin called the publication "a collection of

2. V. Ol'gin, "Zhenskaia sotsialisticheskaia konferentisiia v Berne," *Voina*, pp. 84–90.

3. L. Deich, "Sovremennaia voina i sotsialisty," *Voina*, pp. 5–10.

4. G. V. Plekhanov, "Eshche o voine," *Voina*, pp. 11–48.

5. G. A. Aleksinskii, "S kem bol'shinstvo?" *Voina*, pp. 97–106. Cf. Isaac Deutscher's comments on Trotsky's journalistic work in his *The Prophet Armed* (New York, 1965), pp. 221–28.

sophisms and lies of the social chauvinists." He recommended it to all who wanted to study "the reasons for the collapse of the Second International." Anatole Lunacharsky criticized Deich's arguments as "naive" and Plekhanov's as "childish." Plekhanov, by equating revolution with military defeat, had actually come around to Lenin's position that defeatism facilitated revolution. Lunacharsky henceforth labelled Alexinsky a "Social Black Hundredite."[6]

Alexinsky remained the most active and prolific of the defensists. Publishing in various Russian, French, and English journals, the erstwhile Bolshevik travelled continually, lecturing throughout France and Switzerland.[7] In addition, he advised the French government about political currents among the Russian emigrés. Before the war, he had argued that the Russian government feared war. Now he argued that Russia was not responsible for the conflict.[8] In July 1915 he summarized his views of the war in a book, *Russia and the Great War*, which he published in both French and English. In August 1915 he founded his own newspaper, *Rossiia i Svoboda* (*Russia and Freedom*), which included among its contributors Benito Mussolini.

Alexinsky conceived of his work as having both positive and negative aspects. On the positive side, he supported Russia's war effort. His negative task consisted in offsetting the impact of *Zhizn'*, *Sotsial'demokrat*, and *Nashe Slovo*.[9] Toward this latter end, he became the first as well as the major exponent of the view that the Germans were subsidizing all the defeatist elements in the Russian emigration.

Writing for the Petrograd journal *Sovremmenyi mir* (*Contemporary World*) in the spring of 1915, Alexinsky attempted to link Lenin, Parvus-Helphand, and the Alliance for the Liberation of the Ukraine. The Leninists, he argued, had found it remarkably easy to leave Austria after the beginning of the war. Both Lenin and Parvus-Helphand had advocated the defeat of the Tsarist government. As for the Alliance, the new Ukrainian publication *Borotba* (*Struggle*), appearing in Geneva, had exposed its ties to the Austrian government.[10]

6. *Vperëd*, Aug. 25, 1915.

7. His subjects, in French or Russian, included "A moderate point of view," Geneva, December 1914, "Did Russia desire war?", Geneva and Zurich, February 1915, and "Should one fear victory by Russia?", Montreux, November 1915.

8. See his "Kann Russland einen Krieg wagen?", *Neue Zeit* 31 (1913):679, and "La Russie democratique et la guerre," *La Revue politique internationale*, no. 14 (1915), pp. 168–86.

9. *Rossiia i svoboda*, Aug. 29, 1915.

10. "O provokatsii," *Sovremennyi mir*, 1915, no. 3, pp. 50–63. See also the

In his book *Russia and the Great War*, Alexinsky repeated many of these charges while at the same time seeking to make clear his own attitude toward the Tsarist government. Of the action of the Duma deputies in refusing to vote for war credits he declared, "All we can say of them is that they acted like honest men—perhaps even too honest if we compare their attitude with the miserable conduct of their German 'comrades,' who have followed the battle car of their Kaiser like docile slaves." He also criticized the arrest of the Bolshevik deputies, since the basic incriminating document in their possession—Lenin's theses on the war—was "inoffensive in its complete stupidity."[11]

In his speeches, Alexinsky tended to argue that the defeatists came from the minority nationalities of Russia. In Zurich, he had once challenged an unsympathetic audience: "You Poles, Jews, and other nationalities, you keep your national identity. But let us Russians defend ourselves." In his book, however, he insisted that by and large the minorities had rallied to the Russian cause. As evidence, he cited the speeches delivered in the Duma's special session of August 8, 1914. By "one of the ironies of history," socialist thought had blunted the desire for national independence: "The very socialist labour movement which was always so persecuted by Tsarism is at present, objectively speaking, playing a part which is extremely useful in preserving the integrity and unity of the Russian state."[12]

The Tsarist government, to be sure, had done little to merit the loyalty of the population. Alexinsky considered it unfortunate that France and England had not exerted more influence on Russia's domestic policies. The arrest of Vladimir Burtsev, he declared, "shows us how destitute is the Russian government of elementary tact." The "stupid policy of the government," furthermore, "is damping the enthusiasm" of Jews for the Russian cause. Nevertheless, he considered that it was wrong to desire the defeat of Russia: "I believe that the people would suffer much more than Tsarism."[13]

The Germans and the Austrians, he charged, had engaged in "ignoble machinations" by attempting to corrupt the Russian revolutionary emigrés living in Switzerland. The Alliance for the Liberation of the

sequel, "Avstriiskie provokatory i rossiiskie putanniki," *Sovremennyi mir*, 1915, no. 6, pp. 145–69.

11. Gregor Alexinsky, *Russia and the Great War* (London, 1915), pp. 154, 176.

12. Okhrana report, Mar. 19/Apr. 1, 1915, OAr, XVId, f. 2; Alexinsky, *Russia and the Great War*, pp. 179ff.

13. *Russia and the Great War*, pp. 174, 199, 239.

Ukraine, under Parvus's direction, served only as an "ignoble agency of the Habsburg monarchy." Lenin's defeatist propaganda, which Alexinsky called "quasi-revolutionary hysteria," at best played into the hands of the Germans. Privately, Alexinsky did not hesitate to denounce individual Russians to the authorities as German or Austrian agents.[14]

Alexinsky's attacks had little effect on the internationalists in Switzerland. Much of his material had come in fact from internationalist publications, and they often complained of the way that he exploited their revelations. Those of his targets who answered him denied everything. The Ukrainian Alliance protested that it knew nothing of Alexinsky's charges; the Alliance was in essence a "nonparty, all-national organization."[15] Alexinsky even found himself attacked for having divulged the pseudonyms of revolutionaries in the public press and for having openly cited private conversations. He had thereby laid himself open to the charge of aiding and abetting the reactionary press.

In the pages of *Nashe Slovo*, Trotsky repeatedly attacked Alexinsky for his charges and insinuations that Christian Rakovsky was dealing with the Germans.[16] Other authors sought to ridicule his statements. In discussing the work of Zalizniak, Chernov questioned whether the self-styled Ukrainian Socialist Revolutionary held an Austrian or a Russian passport. If a Russian, Zalizniak would be a defeatist; but if an Austrian, Alexinsky would have to praise him as a defensist. Lunacharsky publicly announced that Alexinsky no longer had any right to call himself a member of the *Vperëd* group.[17]

Alexinsky and Plekhanov, despite their common views, did not work very closely together. On July 10, 1915, Plekhanov wrote a polite, formal note thanking Alexinsky for a copy of *Russia and the Great War*. In August the two men met in Geneva for what was apparently their only private conversation during the war. According to Alexinsky's notes, Plekhanov praised him for his work in exposing the work of the Germans among the emigrés, especially the Bolsheviks. Plekhanov reportedly asserted that Lenin had seized upon the opportunities offered by the war as the only

14. Cf. his denunciation of Trotsky, reported by the Parisian police, in A. Kriegel, "Le Dossier de Trotski à la préfecture de police de Paris," *Cahiers du monde russe et soviétique* 4:282.

15. *Po povodu stat'i G. Aleksinskogo v "Sov. mire."*, manifesto dated May 1915. See also *Nashe Slovo*, Nov. 5, 1915; *Borotba*, no. 4, 1915.

16. See *Nashe Slovo*, Apr. 25, May 30, 1915.

17. *Zhizn'*, June 27, 1915; *Vperëd*, Oct. 20, 1915.

means of recovering his position in the Social Democratic movement. But for the war, he would have been excluded from the Russian Social Democratic Party for his splitting tactics.[18]

The occasion for Alexinsky's meeting with Plekhanov arose with the preparation of a meeting to coordinate all the defensist elements of the various socialist factions. Four members of Plekhanov's *partiitsy* group gathered in Lausanne during August to define their own position on the war. Included in that meeting was I. A. Kisilev, a resident of Zurich, who provided Alexinsky with much of his information about currents among the emigration in Switzerland. (Kisilev also worked as an interpreter for Swiss authorities in dealing with Russian prisoners of war who had escaped from Germany or Austria.)[19]

The *partiitsy* meeting produced a series of resolutions on problems of organization, the war, neutrality, and the Duma faction. As before the war, they still called for the unity of the party and declared their opposition to "all new attempts to split or to disintegrate it." The war had arisen from the "appetites of the Austrian and German imperialists," and the Russian proletariat, "while participating in the defense of its own country, must not curtail its struggle with the reactionary government." The proletariat of the allied countries must take care that the war should not become an aggressive action. In conclusion, the meeting criticized the socialist faction in the Duma for excluding from its ranks a deputy who had taken a position supporting the war effort.[20] (During the summer of 1915, Plekhanov had begun to urge support for new war credits.)

From September 5 to 10, 1915, Social Democratic and Socialist Revolutionary defensists met in Geneva. The participants included Plekhanov, A. Liubimov, Alexinsky, Ida Axelrod, Avksientiev, Bunakov-Fondaminsky, A. Argunov, and V. I. Lebedev. After six sessions under Avksientiev's chairmanship, the group, who claimed to represent all the prewar factions of their respective parties, issued a manifesto and a proclamation.

Asserting the right of every nation to self-defense, the conference declared that the war, which had been forced on Russia, was taking a terrible toll, the burden of which fell on the toiling masses. Russia's defeat could only intensify the harmful consequences for the workers, thereby "retard-

---

18. Alexinsky's undated memorandum, Aleks. Ar., Voina, f. V, 110.
19. Kisilev's correspondence in Aleks. Ar., Voina, f. III, 77–108.
20. *Rezoliutsii priniatye na soveshchanii predstavitelei zagranichnykh sotsial-demokraticheskikh grupp partiitsev v avguste 1915* (Geneva, 1915); *Obzor,* pp. 38–40.

ing, if not completely curtailing, the cultural and social development" of Russia. This would in turn strengthen Tsarism. Therefore, in the interest of Russia's economic and political future, it was necessary to rally to the defense of the country. The road to victory led also to freedom; slogans opposing the war effort were "insipid and harmful."

The manifesto of the meeting, entitled "To the Class-conscious Working Population of Russia," declared that never before had Russia faced such a well-armed enemy. The workers must choose between the consequences of a German victory or participation in the self-defense of their country. Citing the consequences of the Franco-Prussian war of 1870–71 and the Russo-Japanese war of 1904–5, the manifesto warned that the Germans sought to colonize territory: "Never before have plunderers, dreaming about the exploitation of conquered peoples, displayed such cynical heartlessness." Indifference to the outcome of the war would be tantamount to "political suicide."[21]

The new "bloc of Socialist Revolutionaries and Social Democrats" also announced its intention of publishing its own newspaper, to be called *Prizyv* (*The Call*). Both Alexinsky and the Socialist Revolutionaries agreed to merge their publications in the new journal. By the end of September, groups supporting *Prizyv* had come into existence in Zurich (eighteen persons), Geneva (twelve), and Lausanne (fifteen).

From the beginning, the group was obviously an uneasy alliance. The balance between supporting the war effort and working for domestic change proved difficult to maintain, and not the least of the group's problems was the fact that it was rife with police agents, including the secretary of its Geneva group. On September 23 the Lausanne group, after listening to Avksientiev, endorsed the decisions of the Geneva meeting unanimously, but in a meeting two months later on November 21, the group was split. Two-thirds of the membership were unhappy with the editorial policies of *Prizyv*. Half of these felt that the journal had not espoused a clear line of revolution, and the other half felt that its position on national defense was not well enough developed.[22]

The supporters of *Prizyv* freely admitted that they comprised only a minority within the Russian emigration. In Lausanne, the Socialist Revolutionary group excluded the defensists from its ranks, as did the Men-

21. *Obzor*, pp. 58–67. Cf. the favorable comment in *Journal de Genève*, Nov. 2, 1915.

22. See *Prizyv*, Oct. 1, 1915; Okhrana report no. 1438, Dec. 10/23, 1915, OAr, XXIV(1).

shevik group. At the founding meeting of the *Prizyv* group in Lausanne, however, Alexinsky forced four men to leave when they refused to support the defensist resolution. In Zurich, the local Socialist group excluded the two leading defensists, Kisilev and R. Stepanov, declaring that it had tolerated them only so long as they did not represent a distinct faction or organization.

On September 20 a defensist emigré, Anton Savin, was bold enough to address a gathering of Russian Social Democrats in Zurich. After the speaker had called for the defense of Russia, Alexander Martynov, a member of the Menshevik Foreign Secretariat, led the attack by objecting that he had chosen as his examples Plekhanov and Lenin. Lenin was not typical of the internationalists, and Plekhanov employed "Hottentot logic." Martov, who spent the month of September in Zurich, objected that the speaker had sounded like Alexinsky and had ignored the problems of the class struggle. Astrov, another Menshevik, declared that Russia was an aggressor in the war. Both Riazanov and Rakovsky called for a program of "no victory, no defeat." In the words of one Okhrana agent, the Russian colony in Zurich was experiencing "an ever-sharpened relationship between the 'anti-defeatists' and the 'defeatists' or 'internationalists.' "[23]

The case of Stepanov and Kisilev represented, to a great degree, a last echo of Parvus's whirlwind visit to Switzerland in the spring of 1915. Writing in *Rossiia i Svoboda* in September, Alexinsky had renewed his attacks on the internationalists by charging that Parvus had distributed great sums of money among the emigrés. He specifically named various members of the *Nashe Slovo* group in Zurich as recipients of this largesse, and he cited Kisilev and Stepanov as his sources of information. He also made a point of identifying the nationality of Parvus's contacts—Georgians, Ukrainians, Jews, Armenians, and a woman who had connections with the Estonians.[24]

Kisilev had already raised a public scandal about Parvus's activities, charging that Martynov had requested that the Swiss Socialist Hermann Greulich intervene with the German authorities to aid Parvus in obtaining visas for the persons whom he had recruited to work in Copenhagen. In July, Greulich had issued a personal disclaimer of responsibility in the matter.

23. Okhrana reports no. 1202, Oct. 7/20, 1915, and no. 1230, Oct. 28/Nov. 10, 1915, OAr, XIIIb(1), 1915.

24. "Mezhdunarodnaia ober-provokatsiia," *Rossiia i svoboda,* Sept. 26, 1915.

After the publication of Alexinsky's new attack, Martynov replied that as in all cases of such literature, the "grains of truth are hidden in a heap of malicious lies, insinuations, misrepresentations, and so on." Asserting that he had visited Greulich only to testify to the character of one man, he denied having given Parvus any direct help. He admitted having heard various bad things about Parvus, but he could not refuse his help when it was requested. Furthermore, he felt that Greulich's involvement would keep the matter "absolutely clean." Why, Martynov asked, had Alexinsky so pointedly emphasized that each of the persons who had joined Parvus was a supporter of *Nashe Slovo?* The campaign against Parvus, he declared, was only a cover for a campaign against the Russian internationalists.[25]

The resolution of the Socialists in Zurich in excluding Kisilev had specified that he had "sought to cast shadows on the good name of several comrades" whose political views he did not share. Alexinsky responded with the charge that the internationalists were ready to defend Parvus but not Belgium. Kisilev argued that Martynov should in any case have warned Greulich that Parvus was behind his request.[26]

Martynov finally responded in an article attacking the organization of *Prizyv*. Noting that Plekhanov had now come out in favor of voting war credits and that Alexinsky had accused the internationalists of treason, he declared, "A greater humiliation of the banner of socialism we have never yet seen." *Prizyv* had passed beyond the tolerable boundaries for discussions between socialists. Although the Mensheviks generally opposed splitting, Martynov asserted, this represented an extreme case. The members of *Prizyv* could no longer be considered members of the August Bloc; they would no longer be "covered by our organizations as an umbrella."[27]

The socialists who had joined Parvus soon raised their own voices as a group in his defense. They took at face value, they declared, Parvus's statement that he was serving no power in the war. Alexinsky's

---

25. *Nashe Slovo*, Oct. 22, 1915. Even Trotsky, who condemned Parvus as a "social patriot," refused still to label him a German agent. See *Nashe Slovo*, Oct. 5, 1915.

26. I. A. Kisilev, *K razoblacheniiam o Parvuse: Otvet Martynovu* (n.p., n.d.), pp. 4–5, 9. See also *Prizyv*, Dec. 4, 1915; Okhrana report, Nov. 5/18, 1915, OAr, XVIb(6)(b), f. 1.

27. A. M., "Patrioticheskaia organizatsiia *Prizyv*," *Internatsional i voina* 1:146–48.

allegations constituted slander. Alleging that Parvus was a German citizen—which he in fact was not—they asserted that it was natural that he should support the German cause. The Russians then challenged Alexinsky to publish his charges in Switzerland or any other neutral country where they could sue him for libel.[28]

Alexinsky in turn lost no opportunity in pointing out that the group of Parvus's associates now formed the core of a *Nashe Slovo* group in Copenhagen. In particular he attacked Moisei Uritsky, an associate of Trotsky and later a Cheka official, G. Chudnovsky, who soon split with Parvus but nevertheless defended him, and A. G. Zurabov, at whom Alexinsky directed special barbs, since they had both been Social Democratic deputies in the Second Duma. Alexinsky and Zurabov had already clashed publicly in Zurich in November 1914, when Zurabov had challenged Alexinsky's view of "democracy in danger."[29]

Nashe Slovo eventually posed limits to "those whom Alexinsky has slandered or is slandering." The volume of protests sent to the newspaper had reached such proportions that the editorial board ruled it could handle only the most substantial cases: the comrades should simply remember, "Alexinsky's slander stains no one." For his own part, Alexinsky seemed to revel in the controversy. Attacking the members of the Zimmerwald conference, he insisted that the Social Democratic Party and the Socialist Revolutionary Party had empowered no one to attend in their names: "If a Martov, a Trotsky, or a Chernov gathered there, then they did this *only* on their own initiative." They represented not the Russian workers, but the "population of the Boulevard St. Michel."[30]

The Socialist Revolutionaries experienced difficulties similar to those of the Social Democrats. At the beginning of the war, the Delegation Abroad of the Central Committee of the Socialist Revolutionary Party had split four to four on the question of the proper position toward the war. By the fall of 1915 the ratio of internationalists to defensists had become four to two, but no move had yet been made to remove I. A. Rubanovich, a defensist, from his post as representative to the Inter-

28. *Kleveta g-na Aleksinskogo* (Copenhagen, 1915); *Nashe Slovo*, Oct. 14, 1915; *Nash Golos* (Samara), Jan. 17, 1916.
29. See Okhrana report, Nov. 12/25, 1914, OAr, XVIb(7), f. 8; *Informatsionnyi listok Bunda*, no. 9–10 (1915), pp. 25–26; A. Zurabov, *Itogi* (Copenhagen, 1915).
30. *Rossiia i svoboda*, Sept. 26, 1915; *Nashe Slovo*, Nov. 5, 1915.

national Socialist Bureau. The appearance of Chernov and Natanson at Zimmerwald and the appearance of four Socialist Revolutionaries at the Geneva meeting of defensists brought matters to a head.

In *Zhizn'* of October 3, Chernov attacked the defensist manifesto, which he attributed to Plekhanov, and then he turned on the Socialist Revolutionary participants in the conference. A new party, he declared, had been born, but a party which could not long survive. The group would have problems in maintaining discipline within its membership. The defensists had taken a "serious and weighty step" which would have to lead to yet more serious steps. The Socialist Revolutionary Party had been unable to agree upon a single position toward the war, but the defensists, Chernov argued, had in effect turned away from the mainstream of the party.

In a manifesto written in November, the members of the Delegation Abroad announced that they were hopelessly divided into two factions. Neither faction could take the responsibility for the other. Therefore the delegation henceforth could offer only technical assistance to party organizations. An Okhrana report interpreted this as meaning that the delegation was thereby liquidating itself and the Socialist Revolutionaries were breaking up into essentially two parties, one supporting and one opposing the Russian war effort.[31]

Plekhanov's own *partiitsy* also split; the Geneva group, labelling itself *"partiitsy-*internationalists,*"* declared that it had nothing to do with the defensists who had taken part in the September meeting. The "social patriots" represented no formal part of the *partiitsy* organization, and they had no right to use the name.[32]

Still other defensists joined no faction. A. A. Troianovsky, in Baugy, for instance, always represented a certain embarrassment for Lenin in that he, a member of the Bolshevik party, insisted that international socialism had always recognized the right of armed self-defense of a country. The proper course for socialists, he argued, was to "wish defeat for the victors and victory for the defeated." In the context of the situation in 1915, he was a defensist.[33]

31. Report of Feb. 6, 1916, OAr, IIe, f. 3, 102–5; *Zhizn'*, Dec. 5, 1915.
32. *Zhizn'*, Dec. 12, 1915.
33. See his articles in *Golos*, Dec. 1, 2, 1914. Also his *Voina i zadachi rabochego klassa v Rossii* (Geneva, 1915) and *Brauchen wir eine Internationale?* (Zurich, 1916); comments on his stand in *Internationale Korrespondenz*, Jan. 4, 1916, and by Manuilsky in *Nashe Slovo*, Nov. 3, 1915.

Prizyv began publication on October 1, 1915, in Paris. The Socialist Revolutionaries contributed the most to the newspaper's tone; Avksientiev alone wrote some forty articles for the sixty issues of the journal which appeared. Plekhanov and Alexinsky both maintained a certain reserve toward the newspaper. Differences in emphasis on the part of the contributors cropped up regularly; in the most notable example, Plekhanov argued in favor of supporting war credits and Avksentiev insisted that the socialist Duma deputies should abstain. Alexinsky favored direct personal attacks on the internationalists; Avksentiev opposed open polemics. Fondaminsky argued that Russian democracy could tolerate no interruption of Russia's defense; defeatism was "insane." Yet he also predicted a revolution which would lead to an intensification of Russia's war effort.[34]

Like Lenin, the *Prizyv* group concentrated its fire on the Mensheviks, arguing that their position was in essence defeatist. That of the Bolsheviks was at least "without masquerade" in favoring the defeat of Russia. The Mensheviks were no less defeatist, although they could not admit it.[35]

In contrast to the concentration of internationalists in Switzerland, the defensists, even though they had first organized in Geneva, chose to publish *Prizyv* in Paris. Whatever reservations individual contributors may have had about the war, the group found the French capital more congenial to their efforts. Their work in Switzerland was only sporadic.

34. See *Prizyv*, Oct. 1, Dec. 25, 1915, Jan. 22, 1916. The Okhrana Archive, XVId, f. 1, contains the minutes of the meetings of the Paris *Prizyv* group. See also Oliver Radkey, *The Agrarian Foes of Bolshevism* (New York, 1957), pp. 94–103.
35. *Prizyv*, Oct. 9, 17, 1915.

9

The Development of
the Zimmerwald Left

The Zimmerwald conference of internationalists, the Geneva conference of defensists, and the German military offensive into Russia combined to form a watershed in the course of Russian emigré politics in the fall of 1915. Although Lenin claimed that the new divisions among socialists were based on tendencies visible even before the war, the formal structure of those politics now changed radically.

The defensists considered it necessary to choose between the warring powers, favoring the defeat or the victory of one or the other camp. Most internationalists did not want to support the Tsar, but they feared the consequences of military defeat. Therefore they wanted to end the conflict as quickly as possible. Lenin's program, labelled "pan-defeatism" by his critics, demanded that Marxists work for the defeat of their own countries without favoring the victory of other powers. Under the circumstances, coalitions and alliances sprang up between former antagonists; former comrades fell out in bitter arguments. Out of the confusion, Lenin's program emerged as the most firmly articulated.

The Zimmerwald movement provided Lenin with an international public. To be sure, Robert Grimm dominated the work of the International Socialist Commission, just as he had the preparations for the Zimmerwald conference, but Lenin remained within the movement. Although frustrated, Lenin could still claim a series of mounting victories beginning with the women's conference in Bern. Some commentators have claimed that Lenin suffered a defeat at Zimmerwald in the rejection of Radek's draft resolution, but Lenin had not expected to carry a majority of the delegates. Only after the conference did he begin seriously to challenge Grimm, when he saw that Grimm intended to prevent the ISC from becoming a real rival to the International Socialist Bureau of the Second International.

Grimm viewed the activities of the Leninists as another eruption of the internal politics of the Russian emigration. Axelrod had long warned him against Lenin, but Grimm wanted only to keep free of the Russians' polemics. What happened in fact was that what had once been just a Russian dispute now quickly spread across the entire international socialist movement; Bolshevism assumed international significance.

Grimm attempted to be conciliatory toward all Russian factions. In a letter to the Socialist Revolutionary Delegation Abroad, he assured them that the Zimmerwald conference had had only the greatest sympathy for the points which Chernov had attempted to make. Unfortunately, the manifesto simply could not include specific details about the situation in each country: "Had one allowed more questions, then a full reworking of the text would have been necessary. Because of the short time, that was impossible."[1] The Mensheviks at first even praised Grimm. Martov considered the published account of the conference "really objective . . . Lenin and Co. will not like it."[2] Grimm soon found, however, that there was no satisfying all the Russians.

The first blow came with the publication in the October 15 *Berner Tagwacht* of an article by Radek describing a growth of revolutionary feeling in Russia. Radek, who used the pseudonym "Parabellum," gave all credit for the new wave to the Bolsheviks, and he equated the position of the Menshevik *Nasha Zaria* group to that of Plekhanov. Praising the heroism of the arrested Bolshevik Duma deputies, he quoted approvingly a sarcastic comment that the Tsar had permitted other Social Democrats to remain in the Duma as "decoration." The Organizational Committee, he declared, was working with the defensists in Russia even as the Foreign Secretariat sat with the internationalists at Zimmerwald.

Axelrod immediately protested to Grimm against opening the pages of the *Berner Tagwacht* to such an "unheard of, scandalous article." Such writing contributed only to splitting, not uniting, the ranks of the internationalists. The only explanation could be that Grimm "had read the article in question—from the standpoint of international Social De-

---

1. *Zimm. Bew.,* 2:108.
2. *Pis'ma P. B. Aksel'roda i Iu. O. Martova* (Berlin, 1924), pp. 351–52.

mocracy a criminal article—either not at all or else only cursorily." A person like Radek, influenced by Lenin, could compromise the work of the Zimmerwald conference. The article constituted "an especially illegal illustration of the true tendencies and goals of the Lenin-Radek clique in international party politics."[3]

The Mensheviks had received space in the *Berner Tagwacht* of October 16 for their own views of the Zimmerwald conference, but they also published a formal protest on October 19. Radek, they charged, had misrepresented both the Organizational Committee's position and that of *Nasha Zaria*. Radek's attack on N. S. Chkheidze and the other Menshevik Duma deputies constituted nothing less than infamy. Such attacks, the Mensheviks declared, were not uncommon in the Russian or the Polish press, but the Western European socialist press had never before entered into such factional struggle.

In an editorial addendum to the Mensheviks' complaint, Grimm explained that the Russian situation was so confused that an outsider could follow it only with difficulty. Therefore one had to take communications on the responsibility of the author. He then urged that the disputants settle the matter within the pages of the newspaper.

Radek's reply appeared on October 22. He retracted nothing, instead only reaffirming his basic points: "The charge of infamy . . . leaves me totally cool," for the Germans "pay me such compliments daily." Grimm asked Axelrod for a quick response so as to end this "unpleasant discussion," and the Mensheviks responded in the *Berner Tagwacht* of October 26. Radek had declared that he had seen no revolutionary proclamations issued by the Organizational Committee. The Mensheviks retorted that only in the last few weeks had the Bolsheviks themselves received any news from their colleagues in Russia. Radek must have read of the Organizational Committee's declarations in either *Nashe Slovo* or the publications of the Bund. "Up to now, none of these proclamations have been called not internationalist, even in the organ of Parabellum's mentor—Lenin."

In answer to Radek's call for supporting spontaneous revolutionary action, the Foreign Secretariat warned that the government had exploited such actions in organizing an anti-German pogrom in Moscow. Since Radek had singled out one proclamation in particular as patriotic, the Mensheviks sent Grimm a German translation of it, but he in turn

3. *Zimm. Bew.*, 2:175–76.

only declared that its wording could raise "misunderstanding." In any case, the *Tagwacht* now declared the polemic at an end.

Contrary to Grimm's hopes, however, the polemic was only beginning. Axelrod complained privately to Grimm that while his editorial comment might objectively and in itself be considered "very harmless," in context it made a very different impression. By not reacting to the attacks on the Menshevik Duma deputies, the *Berner Tagwacht* had only contributed to confusing party circles in Russia. The Mensheviks had never used the newspaper for attacks on the Bolsheviks, but Radek was obviously working for Lenin. Grimm only replied that he had no intention of attacking the Organizational Committee. News from Russia was scarce, and Radek was submitting informative articles. The answer for the Mensheviks lay in better communications.[4]

The same problem arose in connection with the publication of the *Bulletin* of the International Socialist Commission. In fulfilling the commission's mandate, Grimm requested that socialist parties adhering to the ISC designate correspondents and submit activity reports for publication and distribution. On October 20, Zinoviev sent in the Bolsheviks' report, asking that it be printed in full: "If because of a shortage of space an abridgement is absolutely necessary, then please send it back to us as quickly as possible and let us know how much it should be shortened." Grimm answered that it was indeed too long, but since he had no idea yet of the available space, the Bolsheviks should leave the job of abridging the text to him.[5]

Grimm's answer angered Lenin. Although Zinoviev assured the Swiss leader that the Bolsheviks only wanted to be sure that the basic character and tone of the report remained intact, Lenin complained angrily to his lieutenant, "What is the use of negotiations with Grimm?" Zinoviev should visit Grimm's office and request to see the passages to be excised. There remained then the alternatives of refusing to publish at all in the *Bulletin*, or of acceding to Grimm's demands and publishing the full text elsewhere with a notation, "This text uncensored."[6]

On October 22, Grimm had sought to protect his own position by notifying the Mensheviks of the lengthy report which he had received from the Bolsheviks. To avoid the impression of presenting only one

4. *Ibid.*, 2:218–19, 236–37. Cf. *PSS*, 27:242.
5. *Zimm. Bew.*, 2:180, 192–93.
6. *Ibid.*, 2:212–13; *PSS*, 49:167–68.

side, the *Bulletin* needed a report from the Mensheviks as soon as possible. Since the Central Committee had made extensive use of proclamations and manifestos published in Russia, the Mensheviks should probably do the same. In response to the Bolsheviks' attacks on the Duma deputies, Grimm proposed to publish the full text of a recent speech by the Georgian Menshevik Chkheidze.[7]

As a reward for these efforts, Grimm received another anguished letter from Axelrod. The Mensheviks had cut their report drastically to meet the demands of the *Bulletin,* and now Grimm spoke of a lengthy report from the Bolsheviks. Axelrod again insisted that Radek, "out of servility toward Lenin," had forced the Mensheviks to retaliate in self-defense. Western socialists, he warned, must understand those elements "which for five years I have publicly designated as our internal Black Hundreds and which I have charged with being criminal offenders against our movement." Grimm hastened to assure Axelrod that both Social Democratic factions would receive equal space in the *Bulletin.*[8]

Grimm also ran afoul of emigré politics in the problem of financing the ISC. After the Zimmerwald conference, Axelrod proposed to Lenin that the two Social Democratic factions agree to give the International Socialist Commission some three to four thousand francs from the so-called Schmidt inheritance, money then held in trust by a triumvirate of German socialists.[9] Lenin responded that he would have to discuss the matter with his colleagues. Axelrod also sought vainly to resolve the matter in direct negotiation with Klara Zetkin, one of the trustees. According to the Mensheviks, the Central Committee had to share equal rights to the fund with the Mensheviks, the Bund, the Social Democracy of Latvia, and the SDKPiL.

In the absence of an answer, Axelrod turned the matter over to Grimm, asking the ISC to pose the question directly to the Bolsheviks. When Radek relayed Grimm's inquiry, Lenin insisted that he had to consult with Zinoviev. At the same time, he complained that the Central Committee itself desperately lacked funds. Privately he called Axelrod an "idiot"; publicly he challenged the right of the Organizational Committee to make any claims on the money.[10]

7. *Zimm. Bew.,* 2:189, 233–37.
8. *Ibid.,* 2:250–51, 282.
9. On the prewar maneuvering over the Schmidt inheritance, see Leonhard Haas, *Lenin: Unbekannte Briefe 1912–1914* (Zurich, 1967).
10. *Zimm. Bew.,* 2:111–12, 125, 146–49, 166–67; *PSS,* 49:152–53.

In the end, Grimm had to settle for smaller contributions; by April 1916 he had received 222 francs from the Mensheviks, 200 from the Bolsheviks, 675 from the Socialist Revolutionaries, 49.40 from the Latvians, and 50 from the National Committee of the SDKPiL. The Bund, the Central Committee of the SDKPiL, and the PPS-Lewica made no contributions. The total of 1,196.40 francs, however, represented over one-third of the money received by the ISC in contributions from its member parties.[11]

Grimm also had his problems with the minority nationalities of the Tsarist Empire. In response to a request from the Bund that "Jews" be added to the listing of national representatives in the text of the Zimmerwald manifesto, Grimm declared that the ISC had no authority to do so. The Bund's representative at the conference should have made such a request at the proper time. When the Bolsheviks asked that the Ukrainians be added to the conference's declaration of sympathy with oppressed small nations, Grimm again refused to make any changes in the official documents, pointing to his answer to the Bund as a precedent.[12]

Not even the Swiss Socialist Party could now escape the influence of the Russian emigrés. When the party gathered in Aarau on November 20, 1915, for its annual congress, several Russian visitors attended the sessions—Riazanov, Isaac Bisk (an official of the League of Swiss Relief Societies), Martynov, and Balabanova. Among the 430 delegates there was also a Bolshevik, M. M. Kharitonov, representing Zurich.

The major item on the agenda was the question of the party's attitude toward the Zimmerwald conference, in which it had not officially participated. Eight of the ten members of the Central Committee of the party had opposed endorsing the conference, but the other two members, Hans Vogel and Fritz Platten, forced a public debate. Grimm then prepared a resolution for the party congress, supporting the official manifesto of the Zimmerwald conference. He expected to win approval without serious discussion, but unexpectedly, Kharitonov decided to amend the text.

Such diverse advisors as Axelrod and Radek had urged Kharitonov not to speak. Radek insisted that the position of the left should be repre-

---

11. Grimm Archive, IISH, 2. Teil. Grimm's expenses for the Zimmerwald conference totalled 299.95 francs. The second conference, held in April 1916, cost 501.20 francs.

12. *Zimm. Bew.*, 2:155–57, 158–59, 180, 192–93.

sented by Platten; it would be impolitic for a Russian to speak. Kharitonov nevertheless insisted on his right to the floor, and for this he won praise from Lenin: "I am very happy about your speech in Aarau, and I wholeheartedly congratulate you on your success. In my opinion it came out marvelously."[13]

Kharitonov's move consisted in an amendment offered to Grimm's resolution. Arguing that the Zimmerwald declaration was not clear enough, he proposed the addition of a sentence saying that "peace can be achieved only through revolutionary actions by the working class." When Herman Greulich and Otto Lang rose to attack the amendment, both Grimm and Platten rallied to its defense. Platten warned, "We must not let ourselves be led astray by the opportunistic objections of timid people." The assembly approved the amendment by a vote of 258 to 141 and then approved Grimm's resolution by 330 to 51.[14]

Kharitonov's effort at Aarau epitomized Lenin's approach to the Zimmerwald movement. For the Bolsheviks and their sympathizers, the Zimmerwald conference represented only a landmark along the way. According to Radek, the Zimmerwald majority had been too timid to take decisive action; the left had nevertheless signed the manifesto because not to do so, at the beginning of battle, would have been "doctrinarism and sectarianism." Zinoviev insisted that the meeting had constituted "the first stone of a new Third International." For Lenin, signing the conference's manifesto represented a compromise, but he repeatedly expressed the determination to force the Zimmerwald movement to the left, to a more radical, revolutionary program.[15]

Lenin supported the Zimmerwald movement while opposing Grimm's leadership. Immediately after the conference, Lenin had returned to Sörenberg, where he remained until the beginning of October. Since Zinoviev too had retreated to Hertenstein, Radek continued to serve as Lenin's link with Grimm and the ISC throughout September. Lenin's dissatisfaction mounted rapidly, as first Grimm refused to give Radek

13. *PSS*, 49:165. An Okhrana report of September 6, 1915, had spoken of Kharitonov as an "outstanding orator." No. 1046, OAr, XIIIb(1), 1915.

14. Yves Collart, *Le Parti Socialiste Suisse et l'Internationale 1914–1915* (Geneva, 1969), pp. 274ff.; M. M. Kharitonov, "Iz vospominanii," *Zapiski instituta Lenina* 2:129–35; Ia. G. Temkin, *Lenin i mezhdunarodnaia sotsial-demokratiia* (Moscow, 1968), pp. 308–10.

15. See *Zimm. Bew.*, 1:177n; G. Zinoviev and N. Lenin, *Protiv techeniia* (Moscow, 1918), p. 299.

copies of conference documents until they had appeared in the *Berner Tagwacht* and then, according to Lenin, the ISC introduced discrepancies in the published texts. Lenin considered Grimm's account of the conference one-sided and tendentious. He called Grimm a "scoundrel," and complained that Radek was "naive to the point of sanctity" in dealing with the ISC. When the ISC announced that it had no intention of replacing the International Socialist Bureau and would dissolve itself as soon as the ISB again assumed the leadership of the International, Lenin reacted violently, insisting that the conference had said nothing about the dissolution of the ISC.[16]

Balabanova, Grimm's chief collaborator in the ISC, offered nothing better in the eyes of the Bolsheviks. Krupskaya complained, "What strikes me is her insincerity. To you she says that she agrees completely, but behind your back she agitates against you; she does not fulfill her formal promises, and so on. It is difficult to work with such a person."[17]

On September 27, Grimm announced his intention of broadening the makeup of the ISC. The existing membership was simply not large enough to cope with the possible questions of the day. Since a new conference could not convene just "from one hour to the next," he intended to take the initiative in adding one to three members from each country. Above all, the Russian parties had to agree to this arrangement. "The representatives of the Central Committee, the Organizational Committee, and the Socialist Revolutionaries would each designate one representative who at the same time could represent the organizations standing near to his party (the Latvians, the Bundists, etc.)." Grimm further expressed the hope that the Poles could agree on a single delegate: "Through such an understanding one could avoid the impression that the expanded commission had a predominantly Russo-Polish character."[18]

The Bolshevik response, dated October 23, constituted a summa of their complaints about Grimm and the ISC. Agreeing in principle to Grimm's concern about giving the ISC a "Russo-Polish character," Lenin suggested that only "organizations or groups" who could prove

16. *PSS*, 49:139, 145–46, 153. Indicative of Grimm's conception of the ISC was the fact that at Zimmerwald he had proposed the name "International Exchange" for the office.

17. Temkin, *Lenin*, p. 243.

18. *Zimm. Bew.*, 1:183–89; Temkin, *Lenin*, pp. 345–47.

that they had been active in Russia for at least three years should be represented. This would effectively eliminate the *Nashe Slovo* group, whose presence at Zimmerwald Lenin had opposed.

The Bolsheviks named Zinoviev as their representative, with Lenin as his alternate. Lenin had intended to propose that Grimm further differentiate between the representation of large and small states by splitting even one vote into fractions so as not "to deprive of representation, groups which have their own nuances." He dropped this idea, however, at Zinoviev's suggestion.[19]

The chief task of the ISC should be the "exact delineation of the chief tendencies and orientations in international socialism at the present," the Bolsheviks declared. In order to avoid a purely pacifist position, the ISC must emphasize the class struggle and revolution: "The masses must not be lulled by the hope of peace without the destruction of imperialism." In this vein, the agenda of the ISC should specifically include the following questions: "The connections between the struggle for peace and revolutionary mass action or revolutionary class struggle on the part of the proletariat; the right of nations to self-determination; the connection between patriotism and opportunism."

In regard to the work of the ISC up to that time, Lenin lodged complaints about the changing of wording in the official documents of the Zimmerwald conference, the omission of Platten and Borchardt in the list of signers of the left's resolution, the failure even to publish the left's resolution, and the wastefulness of publishing the ISC's *Bulletin* in three languages. Since both the *Berner Tagwacht* and *La Sentinelle,* in La Chaux-de-Fonds, published much of the same material, the ISC should make use of their services. For English-language publications, Lenin offered to help Grimm find American connections.[20]

Lenin found himself faced with the task of further defining his own position on the war and at the same time publicizing the declarations of the left group at Zimmerwald. To some extent, the double number 45–46 of *Sotsial'demokrat* filled this gap, but only for Russian readers.[21]

19. Olga Hess Gankin and H. H. Fisher, *The Bolsheviks and the World War* (Stanford, 1940), p. 368.

20. Text in *Zimm. Bew.,* 2:196–201. Cf. Gankin and Fisher, *The Bolsheviks,* pp. 364–69, and *PSS,* 27:31–36.

21. Lenin managed to put out two issues of *Sotsial'demokrat* in quick succession—no. 45-46 of October 11 and no. 47 of October 13—by changing from Kuzma to another printer, Bentelli, in Bumplitz bei Bern.

Concerned now with developing an international following, Lenin put Inessa Armand to the task of preparing a French translation of *Socialism and the War,* and he corresponded with Alexandra Kollontai about arranging an English translation.

In an effort to broaden his organizational base, he co-opted Shliapnikov into the Bolshevik Central Committee: "Now there will be three members of the Central Committee abroad." Shliapnikov was also to recruit two or three workers in Russia for the Central Committee.[22] One factor behind this move may have been a certain concern about the image of the committee. Since the beginning of the war, Lenin and Zinoviev had spoken for the Central Committee. Lenin's only formal consultation of the Bolshevik membership had occurred at Bern in February 1915, and according to the Okhrana Lenin faced dissatisfaction within the ranks of the party. He had consulted with the Poles before Zimmerwald, but not with any formal gathering of Bolsheviks.

The most controversial point in Lenin's program remained his call for the military defeat of Russia. In an unpublished manuscript written in September 1915, he divided Russian revolutionaries into "chauvinist revolutionaries, who desire revolution so as to defeat Germany, and proletarian internationalist revolutionaries, who desire a revolution in Russia for the sake of the proletarian revolution in the West." The defeat of Russia, he insisted, "has proven to be the lesser evil, for it has tremendously enhanced the revolutionary crisis." Even his opponents, Lenin argued, had recognized the validity of his slogan.[23]

In answer to questions about what should be done in the event revolution occurred, Lenin published "Several Theses" in *Sotsial'demokrat.* Opposing the Mensheviks' call for a constituent assembly as the slogan of the liberals in 1905, he declared: "The most correct slogans would be the 'three pillars' (a democratic republic, confiscation of landed estates, and the eight-hour working day), with the addition of a call for international solidarity of workers in the struggle for socialism, for the revolutionary overthrow of warring governments, and against the war." The proletariat of Russia had the task of kindling the socialist revolution in Europe.

In the event of revolution in Russia, Social Democrats could join in a government of the "democratic petty bourgeoisie" but not in a govern-

---

22. *PSS,* 49:141. In a letter of September 19, Lenin complained that he was receiving "unbelievably little news from Russia." *PSS,* 49:149.
23. *PSS,* 27:26–30.

ment formed by the "revolutionary chauvinists." Once in power, the "party of the proletariat" would propose a general peace on the basis of the "liberation of the colonies and of all the dependent, oppressed, and deprived peoples." Since none of the warring governments could accept such terms, the revolutionary party should prepare and conduct a revolutionary war. Revolution in Russia would "create exceptionally favorable conditions for the development of revolution in Europe and Asia."[24]

Even as he reached out for new support, Lenin had to deal with divisions and conflicts within his own ranks. Conflicts arose with the *Kommunist* group of Piatakov, Bosh, and Bukharin, now located in Stockholm. In the fall, the three editors issued a set of theses on the national question which directly contradicted Lenin's position. Calling national self-determination a harmful dream in the era of capitalism, they insisted that to recognize that principle was equivalent to accepting the "right of the oppressed 'fatherland' to defend itself."[25]

Lenin eventually exercised the Central Committee's power to suppress the journal, and it began and ended its public life with a single issue, but he moved cautiously in the controversy. He had to isolate the three editors first so as to avoid a damaging split within the party. As a result, the dispute was to drag out over many months.

Closely associated with the *Kommunist* controversy were the issues in Lenin's relationship with the Polish dissidents. (An article by Radek had in fact served as a major factor in Lenin's dissatisfaction with the journal.) To gain the support of the Poles at Zimmerwald, Lenin had compromised on his basic slogans, agreeing even to leave the issue of defeatism out of the draft resolution of the left. After the conference, the Polish dissident organ in Zurich, *Gazeta Robotnicza,* argued that Lenin no longer attached significance to the slogan of defeat. For Lenin, such an interpretation of his efforts to unite the left constituted betrayal.[26]

---

24. *PSS,* 27:48–51. Many historians have cited these theses as background for the Bolshevik decree on peace in November 1917, but few have noted that they also constitute the basis for Kesküla's celebrated report to Romberg on the Bolsheviks' "conditions of peace." Cf. Z. A. B. Zeman, *Germany and the Revolution in Russia* (London, 1958), pp. 6–8.

25. See Gankin and Fisher, *The Bolsheviks,* pp. 219–21, 223–39; Demetrio Boersner, *The Bolsheviks and the National and Colonial Question 1917–1928* (Geneva, 1957), pp. 41–56.

26. See Temkin, *Lenin,* pp. 271–72. On the organization of the SDKPiL, see Bronislaw Radlak, *SDKPiL w latach 1914–1917* (Warsaw, 1967), pp. 97ff., 282ff.

Lenin summarized his problems in dealing with the Poles in a letter to Shliapnikov, written in March 1916: "Radek is the best of them; it has been useful to work with him (especially for the Zimmerwald Left), and so we worked. But Radek, too, vacillates. Our tactic here is two-fold . . . : on the one hand to help Radek move to the left, to unite all possible for the Zimmerwald Left. On the other hand *not by one iota* to allow vacillating on the basic position." He justified his cooperation in *Kommunist* as well as his work with the dissidents as necessary temporary alliances.[27]

Lenin's complaints about Radek were many. In a long article entitled "Annexations and Social Democracy," Radek argued that the slogan of national self-determination was illusory. Imperialism had made the national state obsolete; it was not in the interest of the working classes to support the establishment of new national states. That would constitute "turning back the wheel of history." Social Democrats should oppose all changes of boundaries "not out of love for the old map of Europe, but because socialism needs free, unbounded space for its development."[28]

Lenin's unpublished critique, entitled "The Revolutionary Proletariat and the Right of Nations to Self-Determination," charged that Radek himself was looking backward in not recognizing the strength and justice of the movement for national liberation in the colonial regions. The national question comprised an important part of the problem of democracy, and therefore one could not contrapose it to the problem of socialist revolution. Social Democrats must divide nations "into oppressing and oppressed." Social Democrats of oppressing nations "must demand the right of separation of oppressed nations." On the other hand, the Social Democrats of oppressed nations must uphold the "unity and merging of the workers of oppressed nations with the workers of the oppressing nations." Radek was "tilting with windmills" and "playing into the hands of the social imperialists."

Radek's program, Lenin continued, was vague enough to win the support of the German Social Democrats, Kautsky, Plekhanov, and even the pacifists. Since most socialists belonged to oppressing nations, the "struggle against annexations" had meaning only if the socialists "both

27. *PSS*, 49:193.

28. Parabellum, "Annexionen und Sozialdemokratie," *Berner Tagwacht*, Oct. 28, 29, 1915.

in peacetime and in wartime conduct propaganda for the freedom of secession of oppressed nations." Radek was "an excellent fighter against the German social patriots," but he was very poorly acquainted with Great Russian chauvinism.[29]

In the course of the fall of 1915, Lenin organized the Zimmerwald Left in a formal fashion. Writing to Kollontai on November 9, he spoke of a coming publication "in the name of the *Zimmerwald Left.* Under this name we would want to bring our left group at Zimmerwald . . . with its draft resolution and manifesto into the broadest possible circulation." With the appearance later in the month of the first issue of *Internationale Flugblätter,* subtitled *The Zimmerwald Left on the Tasks of the Working Class,* the Zimmerwald Left began its public life.[30]

The *Flugblätter* were to serve as popular publications for disseminating slogans, and Lenin also felt the need of a more theoretical organ. Therefore he agreed to join in a venture with Radek, together with the Dutch socialists Roland-Holst and Anton Pannekoek, to publish a journal entitled *Vorbote.* Pannekoek proposed an editorial board including himself, Roland-Holst, Willem van Ravesteyn, Lenin, Radek, and Trotsky. In explanation of the presence of "three Russian or Russo-Polish emigrés and three Dutch" on the board, he argued that these people "are the most concerned with problems of general international tactics." Socialists in the larger parties "have too many practical problems to solve."[31]

The execution of Pannekoek's plan proved difficult. Lenin seized on the idea enthusiastically, but he posed strict conditions for his participation, considering the editorial board a coalition of two groups: the Roland-Holst-Trotsky faction and the Zimmerwald Left. When Trotsky discovered that the journal would be published in Switzerland, under the eyes of the Leninists, he refused to participate.[32]

---

29. *PSS,* 27:61–68. Radek later explained his differences with Lenin as arising from his own inability to keep up with Lenin's thought. See his *Lenin: Sein Leben und Werk* (Berlin, 1924), pp. 22–24.

30. See Temkin, *Lenin,* pp. 257–60; *PSS,* 49:163. Ture Nerman later declared that Lenin had first organized the Zimmerwald Left immediately after the Zimmerwald conference. See his "20 Jahre Zimmerwald," *Berner Tagwacht,* Sept. 5, 1935.

31. *Zimm. Bew.,* 2:165, 188, 206–8, 214–15, 226–29.

32. See his letter to Roland-Holst, published in L. J. van Rossum, "Ein unveröffentlichter Brief Trockijs von Anfang 1916," *International Review of Social History* 14:251–66.

On January 15, 1915, the Bureau of the Zimmerwald Left, consisting of Zinoviev, Lenin, and Radek, insisted on controlling the editorial policies of the journal, over Radek's objections. Radek, for one, opposed the publication of Lenin's theses on national self-determination; Lenin warned, "This reeks of *war* with him." Although the matter seemed settled a few days later, on January 25, when the bureau met for the last time, Radek still opposed Lenin's demands for guarantees that any articles by him would automatically be accepted for publication.[33]

Roland-Holst assured Lenin, "You can be sure that in any case you can openly express yourself on all questions, even on ones with which we do not agree," but tensions within the editorial board persisted. In February 1916 Lenin left Bern, and Zinoviev later complained that there was "no collegial work" to be accomplished with Radek.[34] The Bureau of the Zimmerwald Left ceased to meet, and *Vorbote* ceased to publish in the spring of 1916 after just two issues.

Despite these personal conflicts, however, Lenin succeeded in spreading the name and the platform of the Zimmerwald Left throughout Europe, and even to the United States and into Siberia. To a degree, the conflicts represented a natural clash of independent personalities working toward the same ends. On the other hand, Lenin had frictions of some sort with almost all the leading personalities with whom he had to deal. Only a few collaborators escaped his wrath. Yet through all, he expanded his activities, reaching into the internal discussions of almost every major socialist party.

Pressed by the formation of the Zimmerwald Left, the ISC hung suspended uncertainly between Grimm's and Lenin's respective conceptions of its raison d'être. The very act of meeting at Zimmerwald had in itself meant a split with the ISB, and of course with the defensists. Yet Grimm and the majority of the delegates had refused to go so far as to proclaim a new International. The partisans of a new International, to be sure, offered little conception of its form and structure. Chernov and others could call for an "International of action," but beyond the contention that a new spirit was necessary, the advocates of reorganization had few positive proposals. Lenin limited himself for the moment to a demand for a statement of intention. Grimm would not provide even that.

33. *PSS,* 49:173–78; Temkin, *Lenin,* 260–61.
34. Temkin, *Lenin,* p. 263; *PSS,* 49:331.

10

The Emigré Colonies in Transition

As the split between defensists and internationalists meant in many cases a rupture between old friends, the political life of the Russian colonies in Switzerland changed drastically in the fall of 1915. Personal and factional feuds continued as of old, but the emigrés also manifested such new concerns as aid to Russian prisoners of war in Germany and in Austria-Hungary. Some new alliances arose, but for the most part the emigrés could not easily set aside old antagonisms.

Anatole Lunacharsky took the lead in September by calling for the unification of all Russian internationalists behind the Zimmerwald program. Although Lunacharsky later claimed that he had joined the Leninist camp immediately upon coming to Switzerland, in the fall of 1915 he was almost as critical of Lenin as he was of other internationalists. He praised Lenin for having signed the Zimmerwald manifesto: "We are glad that comrade Lenin is gradually studying reasonable 'opportunism.'" The Leninists, he explained, "are not distinguished for their clarity of thought."[1]

A gathering of Russians in Zurich on September 17 and 18, 1915, offered a typical example of the fate of Lunacharsky's call for unity. Present were Martov and Martynov of the Menshevik Organizational Committee, Natanson of the Socialist Revolutionaries, and D. M. Riazanov. Since Riazanov had only recently attacked the Organizational

---

1. *Vperëd*, Oct. 20, 1915; A. V. Lunacharskii, *Velikii perevorot* (Petrograd, 1919), p. 55; *Ar. Monatte*, p. 199.

Committee for having allegedly pirated an article of his in its *Izvestiia*, the meeting took place in a strained atmosphere. After agreeing to entrust Christian Rakovsky with the task of arranging the printing in Bulgaria of a Russian text of the Zimmerwald manifesto, the participants considered the problem of unity. The Mensheviks expressed reservations about working with Lenin, while Riazanov insisted that he was present only to exchange opinions. The group finally found common ground in discussing ways of raising more money to support *Nashe Slovo*.[2]

With Martov remaining in Switzerland for the time being, the Mensheviks embarked on a period of renewed activity, their major project being the publication of a collection of articles, *The International and the War*. Like many others before him, Martov now came to know the frustrations of dealing with Kuzma's printing establishment in Geneva. At one point he complained that it would have been faster to send the material to Paris, to be printed by *Nashe Slovo*.[3]

The International and the War contained articles by Martynov, Astrov, Larin, Ber, Ionov, and Martov, as well as the official documents of the Zimmerwald conference. F. M. Ionov, a member of the Foreign Committee of the Bund, contributed a particularly sharp attack on the position of *Nashe Slovo*. The Socialist Revolutionaries and Lenin's *Sotsial'demokrat* could be expected to take "semianarchist" positions, he argued, but *Nashe Slovo*'s destructive criticism of the old International offered nothing constructive and only played the anarchists' game. Martov felt constrained to add an editorial note to the effect that while *Nashe Slovo* at times indulged in "revolutionary oversimplification," Ionov had carried his criticisms too far.[4]

In November, the five members of the Foreign Secretariat of the Organizational Committee issued a new set of theses on the war, calling it an imperialist conflict and not a war of liberation, labelling the Russian government an aggressor, declaring that neither side in the war represented historical progress, rejecting both defeatist and defensist

2. Okhrana report no. 1214, Oct. 12/25, 1915, OAr, XIIIb(1), 1915. On the feud between Riazanov and the Organizational Committee, see *Nashe Slovo*, Aug. 31, Sept. 1, Nov. 20, 1915; *Pis'ma P. B. Aksel'roda i Iu. O. Martova* (Berlin, 1924), pp. 348–50.
3. *Pis'ma Aksel'roda i Martova*, p. 348.
4. F. M. Ionov (Koigen), "O takticheskoi i organizatsionnoi preemstvennosti (k pozitsii "Nashego Slova")," *Internatsional i voina* (Geneva, 1915), 62–76. Cf. *Pis'ma Aksel'roda i Martova*, p. 351.

arguments, and urging the proletariat to regenerate itself and to struggle for a quick end to the conflict.[5]

Despite Martov's effort at achieving an objective balance in his comment on Ionov's article, his feud with Trotsky grew in the fall of 1915. When Trotsky published his own views of the Zimmerwald conference Martov accused him of subjectivism. Trotsky responded with the charge that Martov had not even been present for most of the conference. Martov again insisted that Trotsky's alleged "third position" at Zimmerwald had existed only in his head. He ridiculed Trotsky's claim that Platten was not firmly in the Leninist camp, and in answer to Trotsky's assertion that he had not noticed Martov's activity at the conference, the Menshevik snorted, "If you look too long in the mirror, you won't see much." Trotsky replied that Martov's "persecuted appearance" had become a "point of view."[6]

Although Trotsky was distancing himself further and further from the Mensheviks, he, like Lunacharsky, still maintained that the Leninist position was wrong. Lenin's views, he insisted, suffered from "a failure to understand the slogan of peace, the subordination of questions of political action to questions of organizational division, and a uniform, inimical attitude toward all who did not share the basic principles" of his program. He referred to the Leninists as the "extremists."[7]

Much as he scorned both the Mensheviks and the Bolsheviks, Trotsky attacked the Bund still more sharply. When he heard of the Bund's request that the Jews be added to the list of nations supporting the Zimmerwald manifesto, Trotsky noted that at the conference, Lemansky had declared that the Foreign Committee had no power to make basic policy decisions. Had the group now changed its mind? Or, he questioned sarcastically, did the Bund want to rewrite the manifesto by adding "and Jews for informational purposes only" to the listing of nationalities. On this point, he fully agreed with Lenin, who accused the Bund of seeking the best of both sides of the fence, both joining and rejecting the new movement.[8]

In November 1915, the Foreign Committee of the Bund met in

5. OAr, XVIb(6), f. 1e; *Zimm. Bew.*, 2:269:80. See also A. Martynov, "Velikaia istoricheskaia proverka," *Krasnaia nov'*, 1923, no. 4, pp. 201–3.
6. *Nashe Slovo*, Jan. 6, 7, 13, 1916.
7. *Ibid.*, Nov. 24, 1915.
8. *Ibid.*, Nov. 5, 1915; *Sotsial'demokrat*, Oct. 11, 1915.

Lausanne to consider the new course of socialist politics. Although the group agreed to accede to the Zimmerwald manifesto, the gathering, according to Okhrana reports, evidenced more antagonism toward Lenin than toward the defensists. The committee refused to join in the work of the International Socialist Commission out of fear that even that group represented an untoward step in the direction of creating a new International. As for Lunacharsky's call for unity, the Bund leaders declared that they would join no new tightly organized structure, but that they would participate in any interparty discussions.[9]

In his published comments on the Zimmerwald conference, Lemansky claimed to see two basic tendencies in its discussions, the one "the primordial Russian custom of deciding everything for the people but without the people," and the other more democratic. In the end, the conference had taken a middle position, closest to that of Trotsky. Kosovsky agreed with Lemansky's account, adding that the Russian emigrés at the conference had been in a poor position "to organize a campaign of peace among Russian workers." Both men opposed any idea of creating a Third International, and called for a "careful watch on the activities of the ISC."[10]

The internationalist Socialist Revolutionaries were more enthusiastic about the Zimmerwald movement, although Chernov repeatedly expressed reservations. On September 28, he told an audience in Geneva that Zimmerwald had launched no new International. It had lacked representation from many important and indispensable socialist parties, and therefore it could make no pretensions yet of being a broadly based international movement.[11]

In *Zhizn'* of September 26, Chernov explained his views of a new International further: "There will be a new International, but it will not be created by the flourish of a pen at a gathering of a few dozen persons." No one political party, furthermore, would dominate the new International. The Third International, however, was "not yet ready internally." The basic tone of the Zimmerwald conference Chernov described as having been one of "general solidarity, enthusiasm, and efforts for mutual understanding and mutual loyalty."

Chernov listed himself as having abstained on the vote for the con-

---

9. OAr, IIe, f. 3, 93–99; XVIIIa, f. 2.
10. Both accounts in *Informatsionnyi listok Bunda,* no. 9–10, 1915.
11. Okhrana report, Oct. 10/23, 1915, OAr, XVIIg, f. 2.

ference's manifesto, declaring that he had objected not to what the manifesto said but to what it did not say. The manifesto had ignored the peasantry; its generalizations on imperialism had failed to consider the peculiar conditions of Tsarist Russia; in all, the manifesto was irrelevant to conditions in Russia. Nevertheless, Chernov assured his readers, his abstention did not mean that he supported the International Socialist Commission any the less.[12]

Like the various Social Democratic factions, the Socialist Revolutionaries indicated little willingness to smooth over ideological differences with other groups. They attacked the Bolsheviks in particular. Responding to criticisms by Zinoviev, one writer noted, "The Leninist *Kommunist,* for example, calls the Organizational Committee nothing but a 'venerable fiction,' and in response to this, the Leninist Central Committee receives the name 'a group of usurpers.' " The "secret of Zinoviev's unique logic" lay in the Leninist practice of taking two or three loyal followers and declaring, "This is the real 'core of the party' . . . *Rome n'est plus dans Rome; Rome est la ou je suis.*" Another writer attacked Zinoviev more directly, declaring that Lenin's lieutenant had but one task: "to take any 'thought' from Lenin and to pass it on to the reader in caricature—or if it is itself a caricature, then in a 'super'-caricature."[13]

The Socialist Revolutionaries did not spare the Bund either, accusing Kosovsky of idolizing the German Social Democrats. At one time, one writer declared, Plekhanov and the Bund had both served as symbols of orthodox Marxist beliefs; now they both represented only a "blind, traditional belief in 'live bodies' and 'dead souls.' "[14]

The example of the defensist *Prizyv* groups inspired the internationalists to make some attempts at interparty cooperation, but while individuals might cross party lines, factional divisions usually posed insuperable obstacles. Even such a mild endeavor as a picnic could prove difficult, as the *Zhizn'* and *Nashe Slovo* groups in Geneva discovered in September. The Social Democrats complained that the Socialist Revolutionaries had not worked hard enough on the preparations, and as if that were not enough, they had then "sparkled by their ab-

12. Cf. the hostile characterization of Chernov at Zimmerwald in Ture Nerman, "20 Jahre Zimmerwald," *Berner Tagwacht,* Sept. 5, 1935.
13. See B. O-n, "Plennoe narodnichestvo," and B. Kamkov, "Zashchita beznadezhnykh pozitsii," *Zhizn',* Oct. 10, 1915.
14. A. F-r, "Svoeobraznaia ortodoksiia," *Zhizn',* Oct. 17, 1915.

sence." Chernov attempted to put the blame on bad weather, but he nevertheless issued a public apology.[15]

In November, socialists in Geneva planned a celebration in honor of the tenth anniversary of the Russian revolution of 1905. The Leninists declared that they would participate only if the attendance were limited to supporters of the Zimmerwald manifesto. When the *Zhizn'* group rejected these conditions, the Bolsheviks boycotted the gathering, which included representatives of *Zhizn', Nashe Slovo,* the Bund, *Vperëd,* and other groups. Manuilsky, Lunacharsky, and G. Ia. Sokolnikov-Briliant spoke. Although formerly a supporter of Plekhanov, Sokolnikov, the secretary of the *Nashe Slovo* group at Geneva, took a Leninist line at this occasion, insisting that "only through defeat will we achieve freedom." Lunacharsky, criticizing Axelrod as well as Plekhanov, proclaimed, "The dawn of the second revolution is already breaking."[16]

Still another example of interparty tensions occurred in December, again in Geneva, when Georgian Mensheviks cancelled a planned meeting because of a furor over whether to invite the Tolstoyans. The Leninists, now joined by the *Vperëd* group, objected strenuously, insisting on the presence only of Marxist internationalists.[17]

On December 26, 1915, Social Democrats and Socialist Revolutionaries gathered in Bern to discuss the possibilities of organizing a joint publication along the lines of *Prizyv.* Reportedly present were Martov, Martynov, Axelrod, Zinoviev, and Chernov. Although generally agreeing on publishing a newspaper in Geneva and on the need of seeking funds from emigré groups, the meeting broke up without concrete results. A similar meeting in Zurich on January 4, 1916, included only Social Democrats, who expressed themselves in favor of a new publication without the Socialist Revolutionaries. The presence of the SR's, they declared, would give the enterprise a "direction undefined and even contradictory to Marxism."[18]

In Geneva, possibilities of uniting socialists behind the Zimmerwald program had to take second place to problems of simply attempting to achieve economic cooperation. In contrast to the situation in most other Russian colonies in Switzerland, the Russians in Geneva had been un-

15. Okhrana report no. 1276, Oct. 27/Nov. 9, 1915, OAr, XIIIb(1), 1915.
16. Okhrana report no. 1412, Dec. 3/16, 1915, OAr, XIIIb(1), 1915. See also *Zhizn',* Nov. 28, 1915; OAr, XVIb(3), f. 5(c).
17. Okhrana report no. 67, Jan. 21/Feb. 3, 1916, OAr, XIIIb(1), 1916.
18. Okhrana report, Feb. 3/16, 1916, OAr, XVIc, f. 4.

able to unite in a single emigré fund for the help of impoverished comrades. In 1914, torn by complaints about the behavior of anarchist members and by charges that the Social Democrats and Bundists had been drawing the benefits of contributions made by Socialist Revolutionaries, the old fund had split, the Socialist Revolutionaries forming their own. Despite a strong tradition of party cooperation—and even the existence of a small group of women specializing as members of interparty organizations—the two groups had rejected all efforts to bring them back together.

In the name of the League of Swiss Relief Societies, Feliks Kon came to Geneva several times during December 1915 and January 1916 in an effort to reunite the rival emigré funds. The task was difficult; a discussion about organizing a dining room for emigrés broke down among reminiscences of previous failures and stories of "disorder, poor food, and embezzlement." Working with B. Ia. Nalivaisky, an SR, and Elizabeth Dicker, a Bolshevik, Kon organized a Geneva Union for Aid to Political Exiles and Prisoners, but in fact, the rival funds continued on as before.[19]

A number of emigré aid groups now turned their attention to Russian prisoners of war in Germany and in Austria-Hungary. The numbers of prisoners had of course swelled as a result of the German military offensive of 1915, but the Russian government had long feared that the emigrés might attempt to do something in this direction. In December 1914 the Okhrana had nervously quoted Chernov as saying, "The prisoners are our army,"[20] while from the very beginning of the war the Germans had permitted *Golos* and *Mysl'* and their successors to reach the prisoners relatively unhindered. The Germans also distributed their own newspapers, *Russkii Vestnik, Russkie Izvestiia,* and *Rodnaia Rech',* in the camps. The Alliance for the Liberation of the Ukraine provided political instructors to work with Ukrainian prisoners.

On September 30 and October 1, 1915, the Central Committee of the Committee for Aid to Russian Citizens in Switzerland, in its fourth plenary meeting, offered aid to all socialist organizations in Switzerland helping the prisoners. The committee, still chaired by Naum Reichesberg, also expressed interest in organizing a newspaper and in establish-

19. Okhrana reports nos. 64, 130, 171, Jan. 21/Feb. 3, Feb. 8/21, Feb. 18/Mar. 2, 1916, OAr, XIIIb(1), 1916, and Jan. 8/21, 1916, XVId, f. 1.
20. Report no. 1697, Dec. 13/26, 1914, OAr, XIIIb(1), 1914.

ing libraries in the prison camps. Now somewhat embarrassed about its period of cooperation with the Russian mission in Bern, the committee made clear its desire to work only with the political emigrés, specifying N. A. Rubakin and K. M. Oberuchev as consultants in the new endeavor.[21]

Konstantin Mikhailovich Oberuchev, a "retired colonel" of artillery, represented, in the eyes of the Okhrana, the moving spirit in the work among Russian prisoners of war. Arrested in Moscow in 1913 for political activities, he had been exiled from Russia for a period of three years. Like a number of other emigrés, he offered his military services to his homeland in the first days of the war, but he was refused. He then turned to relief work and slowly made the transition to an internationalist position. As a leading member of the Russian club in Montreux, he participated actively in the debates of the emigrés. In the fall of 1915 he attended the organizational meeting of the *Prizyv* group in Lausanne, but Alexinsky forced him to leave the hall when he refused to sign a defensist resolution. On the other hand, he criticized Lenin's position as simplistic.[22]

Oberuchev argued that because the Tsarist government considered them to be traitors, special efforts were necessary on behalf of the prisoners of war. Relief from Russia was severely limited. In turn, the emigrés' financial resources were so meagre that after lecturing in Paris at the end of 1915, Oberuchev eventually left for the United States in his search for more funds.[23]

The Socialist Revolutionaries took the lead in organizing a publication, *Na Chuzhbine (In Foreign Land)*, assigning to the task all their resources previously used for *Zhizn'*. The new parent organization took the name Committee for Intellectual Aid to Russian Prisoners of War in Germany and in Austria. Its leadership included Chernov, Natanson, and Boris Kats-Kamkov. The editorial board of *Na Chuzhbine* was headed by Jacques Dicker, and it included Alexander Tsivin, B. I.

21. Protocol of the meeting in the papers of Isaac Bisk, Nicolaevsky collection, Hoover Institution, Stanford, California. The committee eventually published a summary of the activities of groups aiding prisoners of war, *Rapports et comptes rendus des comités de secours aux prisonniers de guerre russes, 1914–1916* (Bumpliz, 1916).

22. See K. M. Oberuchev, *V dni revoliutsii* (New York, 1919), pp. 8–15. A police summary of his activities is in Okhrana report no. 153, Feb. 13/26, 1916, OAr, XIIIb(1), 1916.

23. Oberuchev, *V dni revoliutsii*, p. 18.

Nalivaisky, Vladimir Vnorovsky, A. Cherniavsky, and Boris Klushin.[24]

Jacques Dicker, or Iakob Dikker, represented the most striking exception to the general practice of the Russians—up to this time—of ignoring Swiss politics and institutions. Born in Russia in 1879, he had joined the Socialist Revolutionary Party in 1897. As a student at the University of Kiev he had experienced his first political arrest, and after being arrested again in Petrograd during the 1905 revolution he eventually made his way to Geneva where, in the fall of 1906, he enrolled in the school of law. In 1915, now a practicing lawyer, he received his citizenship in Geneva. As a member of the Socialist Party of Geneva, he served briefly in the city's Grand Conseil in 1917, and in 1922 he became *Nationalrat* from Geneva. His political opponents in Switzerland often attacked him for his Russian-Jewish background and also for the fact that his wife was a well-known member of the Bolshevik Party.[25]

The editorial policy of *Na Chuzhbine* consisted in bringing news of Russia and questioning the idea of fighting on behalf of the Tsar: " 'I am not your enemy,' each should say to his opponent; 'Our masters are the enemy.' These masters are not only enemies of each other; they are enemies to their own people."[26] In its first issue, *Na Chuzhbine* demanded a constituent assembly independent of the old government. Devoting a great deal of space to the conditions of the peasantry, the journal argued for a greater class consciousness, and it warned the soldiers against the inquisitiveness of both officers and Red Cross nurses.

The Russian mission in Bern demanded several times that the Swiss government suppress *Na Chuzhbine* as a violation of Swiss neutrality, and it singled out Dicker as particularly culpable. The Swiss government, however, rejected each demand; the police in Geneva reported, "The contents can perhaps be designated as 'revolutionary' by Russian conceptions, but not by ours."[27]

The Bolsheviks had called for the development of a program for

24. Okhrana report no. 1166, Nov. 12/25, 1916, OAr, XIIIb(1), 1916. See also Oliver Radkey, *The Agrarian Foes of Bolshevism* (New York, 1957), pp. 120–22.

25. See Leon Nicole, *Notre Comarade, Jacques Dicker: Dernier adieu* (Geneva, 1942), and the file of newspaper clippings on Dicker in the Archive d'Etat, Geneva. For examples of the personal attacks on Dicker, see *Le Pilori*, 1923–24, and René-Louis Piachaud, *Contre Me Jacques Dicker, Conseillor Anti-National* (Geneva, 1924).

26. *Na Chuzhbine*, 1916, no. 2, p. 21.

27. BBAr, Pd, Russen in der Schweiz, Bd. 17.

prisoners of war at their conference in Bern in March 1915. Under the aegis of the Committee for Foreign Organizations, G. L. Shklovsky undertook the chairmanship of a Commission for Intellectual Aid to Prisoners. By the fall of 1915, the group had established contacts in Germany, and in the course of 1916, the Bolsheviks sent over 5,000 pounds of books, brochures, journals, and other publications, including 500 copies of each issue of *Sotsial'demokrat* and 600 copies of *Kommunist*. Krupskaya supplemented the work of the group by conducting an extensive correspondence of her own with individual prisoners.[28]

The Geneva-based Society for Aid to Russian Prisoners of War in Germany and Austria-Hungary had a more indefinite party physiognomy, as it was directed by Pavel Biriukov. Nevertheless, its announced aim was the dissemination of "revolutionary propaganda by all possible means." In Zurich the Committee for Aid to Prisoners of War included representatives from a number of party groups, but it was also distinguished by the fact that it cooperated with the Russian mission in Bern. Organized in October 1915, its leadership was dominated by defensists, but its membership also included internationalists. It sent goods and money through the mission, but it also claimed to have sent fifteen packages of revolutionary literature in 1916.[29]

The minority nationalities also organized their own relief groups. The Lithuanians at the University of Fribourg formed a relief group, Lituania, which soon obtained funds from Lithuanians living in the United States. It sent food and publications into Germany. A Polish student society in Geneva, Ognisko, attempted to help both refugees and prisoners of war, without consideration of party affiliations.[30]

Inevitably, those interested in working with the prisoners of war had to enter into contact with the diplomats of the Central Powers, either at a consulate or at the mission in Bern. The prison camp commandants repeatedly wrote to Romberg requesting information on the various groups in Switzerland, and for the German minister this provided his only serious discussions with Russian socialist emigrés. Nevertheless, it did not significantly widen his circle of agents.

28. *V plenu,* 1917, no. 1.
29. Okhrana report no. 1253, Dec. 16/29, 1916, OAr, XIIIb(1), 1916.
30. Report dated Dec. 15, 1915, HHSAr, PA, 904/8e/85; J. Puryckis, "Lietuviu veikimas Šveicarijoje didžiojo karo metu," *Pirmasis nepriklausumos Lietuvos dešimtmetis* (London, 1954), pp. 63–64; Romberg to Berlin, Mar. 17, 1916, AAM, T136/21.

Nikolai Rubakin, the noted Russian bibliographer, was probably the most important emigré to negotiate with Romberg. In June 1915 Stepankowski, who apparently knew Rubakin through the Ukrainian Socialist Revolutionary Party, had mentioned to Romberg the possibility of working with him. On July 15, Stepankowski described Rubakin's plans for a newspaper for the prison camps and for a "bill of indictment" (*Anklageschrift*) against the Russian government, to be made up of secret diplomatic documents.[31]

The Auswärtiges Amt immediately expressed a strong interest in pursuing the matter; Zimmermann spoke of Rubakin as "a force suitable for anti-Russian propaganda." Romberg, however, did not meet Rubakin until the fall. On September 17, Keskküla presented Rubakin's terms: aid in publishing his indictment, and a request for a guaranteed annual income of 12,500 Swiss francs. Keskküla's own evaluation of Rubakin was that he had "an important name but no organization behind him." On another occasion, Keskküla indicated a strong dislike of the man: "I would really prefer to have nothing to do with the fellow—I hope soon to be in such a position."[32]

On September 22 Romberg, Keskküla, Rubakin, and Schubert met at the German mission. Rubakin called German propaganda among the prisoners of war ineffective, too blatant. Instead, he recommended the establishment of small libraries of perhaps 600 books at each camp, heavily stocked with reprints of various of his own works. He was willing to give the Germans the reprint rights to his works for 2,000 francs apiece.

Romberg characterized Rubakin as on the one hand "an idealist" and on the other "a shopkeeper." He would be difficult to deal with, but his cooperation could be invaluable. On October 5, attempting to demonstrate his interest in Rubakin's work, Romberg offered him a typewriter, to which Rubakin answered on the seventh, declaring that he had an opportunity to buy a good used one for 275 francs; Romberg could just send him the money. In delivering his proposed list of books for the prisoner of war camps, Rubakin declared that through his contacts he could buy the works for a discount under the list price.

The Auswärtiges Amt, for all its interest, warned that it would not give Rubakin limitless funds. The War Ministry eventually agreed to

---

31. AAM, T120/5224/K489037.
32. AAM, T120/5224/K489189-90, K489233.

establish three trial libraries for the prisoners, but at the cost of only 100 rubles each. By the time Rubakin had finished negotiating with Romberg, the Auswärtiges Amt had agreed to pay the difference between the 300 rubles offered by the War Ministry and the 2,250 rubles which, according to Rubakin, the books actually cost.

Although Rubakin also received at least 10,000 francs for the publication rights to five of his books, he complained bitterly when German authorities refused to publish several others. The Germans, he argued, should have agreed to publish his works as a whole body of literature.

The fate of Rubakin's "bill of indictment" typified the whole course of his relationship with Romberg. In September 1915, through Kesküla, Rubakin had declared that he needed 16,000 francs to complete the work. By May 1916, his needs had risen to 50,000 francs. The work was to appear simultaneously in English, French, German, and Russian. Eventually a Polish publication came into the question as he opened negotiations with Szymon Askenazy of the group La Pologne et la Guerre. The Auswärtiges Amt had declared from the beginning that it had no interest in the publication, but it permitted Romberg to offer Rubakin money under the pretext of supporting the book. (When Rubakin demanded aid in conducting his research, the Auswärtiges Amt only referred him to the Zentralbibliothek in Zurich.)

By February 1917 Romberg had paid Rubakin 20,000 francs in support of this project. When, in the summer of 1918, Rubakin again came to the Germans with a request for 40,000 francs for the completion of his manuscript and for another 200,000 francs with which to establish a pacifist institute, the Auswärtiges Amt flatly refused. (Nor would it have anything to do with Rubakin's offer to act as a mediator between the German government and President Woodrow Wilson of the United States.)[33]

Rubakin's program for the prisoners of war represented, it must be noted, an integral part of his lifelong concern for encouraging literacy and for sharpening the social consciousness of individuals. Throughout his life, he regularly drew up reading programs for his correspondents, carefully matching the books with the readers. In October 1916 he participated in founding a section for bibliopsychology in the Rousseau

33. See AAM, T120/4818 and 5224; AAB, Gesandtschaft Bern, Russland II, Sonderhefte über Personen, Bd. 1–2.

Institute in Geneva. In his overflowing library, Rubakin reserved a special section for books written by persons whom he had helped.

Rubakin, furthermore, was ready to seek financial assistance from any source, while at the same time he felt that he could maintain his own independence. When Louis Lochner, of the Ford Peace Mission, came to Switzerland in February, Rubakin, through Henri Guilbeaux, asked for financial support. The Russian freely admitted his contacts with the Germans, telling Lochner, "I had figured correctly that the German authorities would be caught by my denunciation of the Tsar, and that on this score they would be glad to have the literature admitted, hoping that from their hatred of the Tsar, they would turn to a love of the Kaiser. That I was merely using the Tsar as a type, but that in reality my propaganda was directed against all exploitation of the many by the few—this the German military censors were too stupid to understand. My readers, however, understood. And when Russia's great moment comes, this propaganda work will bear fruit a hundredfold."[34]

The German military censors, however, proved more observant than Rubakin thought. Complaining that Rubakin's model libraries had too much socialist literature and not enough belles-lettres—the book which the prisoners most requested was Tolstoy's *War and Peace*—the Germans eventually broke up the collections, refusing to distribute many of the books.

For all his investment, Romberg apparently never penetrated Rubakin's circle of acquaintances. The relationship between the two remained strictly a business venture. Rubakin does not seem to have offered any information on the activities of other Russian emigrés, and Romberg does not even seem to have requested any.

The emigrés' concerns for prisoners of war testified to the care with which they watched international events, but with perhaps the exception of Lenin and a few others, they paid little attention to events in Switzerland. As of January 1, 1916, the Western powers imposed an economic arrangement on Switzerland aimed at limiting the possibilities for contraband materials to make their way into Germany. In the course of the month, the Swiss government was shaken by the "affair of the colonels,"

---

34. Louis P. Lochner, "Henry Ford and His Peace Venture," Louis Lochner Papers, Wisconsin State Historical Society, Box 53. Cited with the permission of Mr. Lochner.

when three officials of the General Staff were arrested on the charge of having passed secret reports to the Germans. At the same time, a crowd attacked the German consulate in Lausanne. These events, however, passed virtually without notice in the world of the emigrés, wrapped up as they were in their concerns with their homeland and in their own polemics.

11

The Campaign Against the Mensheviks

In the fall of 1915, Lenin had launched a new offensive on the international level, challenging Grimm's direction of the ISC. Even earlier, the Bolshevik leader had deplored the influence which the Mensheviks had on the Swiss, and it was only a matter of time before he would publicly link the two. In the first months of 1916, he brought his attacks on the Mensheviks to an international audience.

At the beginning of the year, however, life among the emigrés went ahead in routine fashion, as gatherings throughout Switzerland commemorated Bloody Sunday in 1905. The oratory reflected the current divisions among the socialists. In Geneva, on January 22, Martov supervised a meeting which excluded all defensists; only internationalists could speak. In Zurich, some 300 persons gathered on January 30 to hear Martynov and Kon.[1]

The *Prizyv* groups, too, made their voices heard. Excluded from the Geneva meeting, they issued their own manifesto, calling for the defense of Russia while recognizing the irony of fighting on the side of the "enemy of yesterday and tomorrow." In Zurich, a defensist speaker attacked the "political illusions of the present time," labelling the Bolsheviks "political fantasts."[2]

1. Okhrana reports nos. 127, 205, Feb. 6/19, Feb. 26/Mar. 10, 1916, OAr, XIIIb(1), 1916.
2. Okhrana report no. 196, Feb. 26/Mar. 10, 1916, OAr, XIIIb(1), 1916; also OAr, XVIIr(1), f. 5.

The emigrés all felt to some degree isolated. News from Russia came only intermittently, and wartime censorship played havoc with their mail. Martov complained to Axelrod that the French Post Office had confiscated an article of his intended for publication in the United States: "This means a loss of 150–200 francs; I made no copy of the article and in any case it is probably too late."[3]

Lenin had to share the frustrations of the other emigrés, but at the same time, he exploited his time by engaging in research. In January 1916 he agreed to a proposal made by M. N. Pokrovsky and Maxim Gorky that he undertake a study of contemporary imperialism. He had already begun collecting materials for such a work several months earlier, but now he applied himself to the task with new enthusiasm.[4] His first step was to plan a trip to Zurich in order to visit the Zurich Zentralbibliothek, but he had to put off his departure for a few days when Grimm announced that the expanded International Socialist Commission would meet on February 5.

Grimm had not been able to realize all his hopes for the ISC, but renewed activity by the International Socialist Bureau, together with a series of attacks on the Zimmerwald movement made by Camille Huysmans and Emile Vandervelde, forced him to accelerate his own work. His announcement caught many interested parties short. Neither the French nor the British could send delegates on such short notice, and Trotsky complained bitterly, "Why didn't you write to us two or three weeks earlier?"[5] The *Nashe Slovo* group had to content itself with sending a draft manifesto for the consideration of the ISC.

When the commission gathered in Bern on Saturday evening, February 5, Russians and Poles were present in roughly the same proportion which they had enjoyed at Zimmerwald. Although Zinoviev was the official representative of the Bolshevik Central Committee, Lenin too attended the meeting; others included Natanson, Martov, Radek, Warski, Łapiński and Balabanova. The official protocol listed twenty-one delegates, including the members of the ISC, but omitting Lenin's name.[6]

Of the twenty-one parties and groups which Grimm announced as having acceded to the Zimmerwald program, Russian groups accounted for six. Grimm had listed the three Polish parties as just one entry, but

3. *Pis'ma P. B. Aksel'roda i Iu. O. Martova* (Berlin, 1924), p. 355.
4. See M. N. Pokrovskii, "Kak rozhdalsia 'Imperializm,'" in *Vospominaniia o V. I. Lenine*, 5 vols. (Moscow, 1961), 2:364–68.
5. *Zimm. Bew.*, 2:439.
6. *Ibid.*, 1:197–98.

he had still to give separate places to the Bolsheviks, the Mensheviks, the Socialist Revolutionaries, the Bund, and the Social Democratic Party of Latvia. No other country had more than three entries.[7]

In his opening speech, Grimm noted that since French and English delegates had been unable to attend the meeting, "the gathering naturally cannot serve as a gathering of the enlarged commission." It could have only an "advisory" character and could make no binding decisions.

When the report of the ISC had concluded and the delegates turned to their work, new procedural issues immediately arose concerning the claims of the Zimmerwald Left. Radek claimed to have the mandate of Roland-Holst, and Lenin insisted on representing Julian Borchardt's International Socialists of Germany. When Modigliani questioned the idea of a country's being represented by a national of another country, Radek pointed out that Rosa Luxemburg had once given a mandate to Kautsky to represent the SDKPiL in the International Socialist Bureau. Grimm appealed directly to Lenin, saying that it would make a bad impression in Germany to have a Russian represent a German group.[8] Lenin insisted that mandates were permissible; Borchardt's group existed and deserved to be heard. The subsequent debate revolved about the question whether the International Socialists of Germany constituted a significant group in Germany. In the end, the group decided that since it had only consultative powers, it should make no decision.[9]

The Russian representatives, most of whom had not left Switzerland since the time of the Zimmerwald conference, gave no reports on developments within Russia, but they commented freely on the activities of socialists in other countries, and they participated energetically in the general discussions. In the rambling discussion over whether the meeting should issue a manifesto, Martov took the lead—in opposition to Grimm and Lenin—in proposing that a circular letter be sent to organizations adhering to the Zimmerwald program. When the meeting accepted a resolution to this effect put forth by Łapiński and Rakovsky, it named a seven-member editorial commission which included Martov, Balabanova, and Zinoviev.[10]

---

7. *Ibid.,* 1:201.

8. See *Internationale Korrespondenz,* Mar. 7, 1916: "Was könnte nun den ausländischen Genossen der russische Emigrant Lenin über Deutschland erzählen? Er ist einer der engköpfigsten Vertreter der russischen Fluchtlingsphäre."

9. *Zimm. Bew.,* 2:206–10.

10. Lenin had been proposed at first, but he withdrew in favor of Zinoviev. *Ibid.,* 1:242.

Early in their deliberations, the delegates agreed to the calling of a second internationalist conference, to open on Easter Sunday, April 23. The details of the conference's organization proved to be another problem. After some discussion, the assembly agreed to Grimm's proposal that participation be limited to "representatives of such political or labor organizations, or individuals, who accept the platform of the Zimmerwald conference." It also accepted Rakovsky's amendment that all delegates to the Zimmerwald conference had the right to attend the next conference. It rejected Martov's proposal that all "newspapers and periodicals which struggle in the spirit of the Zimmerwald decisions have the right to send representatives with advisory votes to the conference."[11] From the Russian standpoint, these decisions meant that *Nashe Slovo* could send no representative, but that Trotsky could attend the meeting in a personal capacity.

Next came the question of the agenda for the upcoming conference. Lenin opened the discussion by offering four points: the struggle against the war, tactics of the international proletariat against imperialism, methods and means of the international association of the proletariat, and the right of national self-determination. Some delegates questioned his third point as introducing the idea of a Third International; others opposed discussion of national self-determination. Radek proposed as an agenda: reports, the struggle against the war, peace proposals and the action of the proletariat, and the relationship to the ISB. Martov immediately arose to offer the wording "struggle for peace" instead of "struggle against the war." The final agenda drawn up by the ISC contained elements of all these suggestions.[12]

On the evening of February 9, Grimm presented the meeting with the draft letter to be circulated by the ISC. The discussions in the editorial commission had culminated in a stormy debate between Martov and Zinoviev. According to one Russian account, the other members of the commission stood aside, declaring that "if the 'Russians' came to an agreement with each other, then they had nothing more to do."[13] Using as a base a text prepared by Grimm, the two Russians eventually found common ground. The plenary session adopted the text unanimously

11. *Ibid.*, 1:244–45.

12. *Ibid.*, 1:245–46.

13. G. L. Shklovskii, "Tsimmerval'd," *Proletarskaia Revoliutsiia*, 1925, no. 9, p. 99.

and without discussion, although Lenin, Zinoviev, and Radek declared that they were voting for it "without fully agreeing with individual sentences."[14]

The text of the circular was much more forceful than that of the Zimmerwald manifesto five months earlier. It came out explicitly against any support of war credits; it criticized the ISB for deceiving the masses; it dismissed the thought of a "reciprocal amnesty of the compromised opportunist leaders" as a "pact against socialism"; and it called for "uniting the proletariat of all countries into a vital revolutionary power."[15]

The antagonism between Bolsheviks and Mensheviks flared several times in the course of the meeting. At one point, according to Martov, Grimm criticized the Bolsheviks for their public characterization of the socialist Duma deputies as "decoration."[16] At the final session, Zinoviev began to read a declaration asserting that the representatives of the Organizational Committee should be regarded as only a minority faction, since the majority of the committee had taken defensist positions. Grimm interrupted him to ask the gathering whether Zinoviev should be allowed to continue. Supported by Rakovsky, Modigliani, and Serrati, Martov argued that the very fact that the Organizational Committee had empowered him to represent it should put the lie to Zinoviev's accusations. The majority of the participants then voted against allowing Zinoviev to finish his statement.[17]

For purposes of secrecy, Grimm informed the members of the ISC that he would announce the site of the second internationalist conference as being The Hague. He urged his listeners not to talk publicly about their discussions, and at the end of February, the *Bulletin* of the ISC reported the ISC session only briefly and announced the general plans for the conference.[18]

As late as mid-April, Lunacharsky's *Vperëd* attempted to maintain the fiction that the internationalist conference would take place in Holland. In a report dated March 21, 1916, the Okhrana accepted this assertion; its summary of the ISC meeting, moreover, added a number

14. *Zimm. Bew.*, 1:251.
15. English text in Olga Hess Gankin and H. H. Fisher, *The Bolsheviks and the World War* (Stanford, 1960), pp. 385–89.
16. *Izvestiia ZSOK*, Apr. 10, 1916.
17. *Ibid.; Zimm. Bew.*, 1:251; *Sotsial'demokrat*, Mar. 25, 1916.
18. *Zimm. Bew.*, 1:259–62.

of frills, reporting that Axelrod, Martynov, Łapiński, Riazanov, and Kon had participated in the discussions. Furthermore, Willi Münzenberg had allegedly been dispatched to Russia to invite socialists to attend the conference. Any persons attempting to leave Russia for this purpose, provided they were not Duma deputies, were to be arrested.[19]

On the other hand, Stepankowski informed Romberg on February 10 of the general course of the ISC's discussions, and on February 16 he told the German minister that the upcoming conference would take place in Switzerland, not in the Netherlands. Stepankowski's source was Edmondo Peluso, a member of the ISC. Romberg's interest in the socialists, however, was so limited that he passed the information on to Berlin only on March 23, 1916. His report at that time discussed, in the main, the activities and declarations of the German socialists. He gave almost no note to the activities of the Russians.[20]

The members of the ISC, to be sure, had made no secret of their presence in Bern. On the evening of February 8, Modigliani, Rakovsky, Grimm, and Lenin had addressed a public gathering which had packed the hall of the Bern Volkshaus. On this occasion, Lenin made clear that his opposition to the war had nothing in common with pacifism: "Not in vain will millions fall in the war and as a result of the war. The millions who starve, the millions who offer their lives in the trenches, they do not just suffer; they gather strength, they think about the true causes of the war, they strengthen their wills, and they come to a clearer and clearer revolutionary understanding."[21]

Within the ISC, Lenin had challenged the mandate of the Organizational Committee's representatives, and he opposed the idea of inviting the German centrists to the internationalist conference. Despite Grimm's pleas that the internationalists should not engage in internecine polemics, Lenin emphasized still more strongly, during the first months of 1916, his demand for the sharpest possible definition of internationalism and for the clearest possible differentiation of those who could claim to be internationalists. To this end he did not even spare his own followers and supporters; he mercilessly pointed out the errors of all.

Writing directly to Radek, for example, Lenin insisted that a common

19. OAr, IIe, f. 3, 117–19. See also Alfred Rosmer, *Le mouvement ouvrier pendant la guerre*, 2 vols. (Paris, 1936–1953), 2:78–79.
20. AAM, T120/5224/K489607, K489707; *Zimm. Bew.*, 1:491–92.
21. *PSS*, 27:234; *Berner Tagwacht*, Feb. 9, 1916.

struggle by the Bolsheviks and the SDKPiL was impossible so long as the Poles did not support the need for ideological splitting. The Poles had criticized his position of defeatism, and he considered this an act in the spirit of the ill-fated Brussels conference of July 1914. Writing to Zinoviev, Lenin put his anger in more personal terms, labelling Radek a *Dreckseele* and complaining because he was "conducting himself so foully."[22]

In regard to the continuing controversy with the *Kommunist* group, Lenin wrote to Shliapnikov, "The question of splitting is basic." To compromise would be a crime. The Poles, Trotsky, the Organizational Committee, and the *Kommunist* group all wavered to some degree on splitting. Since Shliapnikov himself showed signs of supporting Bosh, Bukharin, and Piatakov, Lenin couched his views in more moderate language than he used in writing to Zinoviev. Nevertheless, to keep *Kommunist* alive, he argued, would "open the door to squabbling and wavering."[23]

Even Zinoviev aroused Lenin's anger because he had invited Shliapnikov to come to Switzerland for the internationalist conference. Lenin objected to this on two grounds: Shliapnikov, who served as a vital communications link with Russia, had already travelled out of Scandinavia more than he should, and, moreover, he had displayed too much sympathy for the *Kommunist* group. Shliapnikov did not come.[24]

Despite these disputes, however, Lenin showed concern for the lot of his errant followers, and he sought to maintain useful contacts with even those whom he most violently opposed. When Bukharin was arrested in Stockholm, Lenin asked Riazanov to seek Herman Greulich's and even Kautsky's intervention with the Swedish Social Democrats. Through Zinoviev, he remained in touch with Radek and continued to consult with him on certain matters.[25]

After the question of splitting, the major ideological sore point between Lenin and his supporters was the problem of national self-determination. Lenin had begun to expound on this subject in the fall of 1915, but it became a matter of more intensive discussion in the late winter and spring of 1916. Radek, Bukharin, and the Dutch all expressed

22. *PSS*, 49:181–82, 188.
23. *PSS*, 49:192–96.
24. Ia. G. Temkin, *Lenin i mezhdunarodnaia sotsial-demokratiia, 1914–1917* (Moscow, 1967), p. 373.
25. *PSS*, 49:212–13.

reservations or opposition to the principle of national determination, and Lenin came to fear a possible alliance of these diverse elements against himself.

When Lenin scheduled a public lecture in Zurich entitled "Conditions of Peace in Connection with the National Question," the Mensheviks in that city turned out in force, hoping to embarrass him about his relations with the Poles, but Lenin proved too resourceful for them. Beginning his speech at nine in the evening, he continued on until midnight, the curfew hour. Martov and Semkovsky protested heatedly that they must yet have an opportunity for discussion. The proprietor of the restaurant where the group was meeting ordered them to leave. The Mensheviks finally decided to meet the next night for a discussion, but Lenin refused to attend.[26] On March 1, Lenin gave the same talk in Geneva to an enthusiastic crowd of several hundred persons.[27]

After lecturing in western Switzerland, Lenin returned not to Bern but to Zurich. He had originally intended to stay in Zurich for only a few weeks, to use the library; now he chose to settle there. The reasons for this decision remain somewhat unclear, but the vitality of the city apparently played a major role. Krupskaya later complained of having been "cooped up in a petty-bourgeois democratic cage in Bern."[28]

The intellectual life in Zurich corresponded to the general hopes and despair of wartime more than did the atmosphere in Bern. Although Switzerland remained neutral throughout the war, the Swiss, too, suffered from wartime shortages. During the winter of 1915–16 the cost of living took a sharp turn upward, and, reflecting the tensions of the time, the Zurich city council in January 1916 forbade the wearing of masks in public places during Carnival. The influx of foreigners into Switzerland during 1915 had also raised new fears of *Überfremdung*. On January 1, 1916, a writer for the *Neue Zürcher Zeitung* openly declared, "The canton of Zurich already has enough foreigners on *Toleranz*"; on January 24, another writer warned that the *Überfremdung* of Zurich had "made disturbing progress" in recent years. Meetings discussing prospects of peace and meetings discussing problems of resident foreigners drew equally large audiences in the city.

26. M. M. Kharitonov, "Iz vospominanii," *Zapiski Instituta Lenina* 2:122; Okhrana report, Mar. 17/30, 1916, OAr, XVIIa, f. 1B.

27. In one of his few comments on Lenin, Stepankowski told Romberg that Lenin's appearance in Geneva had to be considered a success for the Bolshevik leader. AAM, T120/5224/K489651.

28. N. K. Krupskaya, *Reminiscences of Lenin* (Moscow, 1959), pp. 311–12.

Lenin settled in the Niederdorf region of the city, just a few minutes from the home of the Eintracht Society. To be sure, Eintracht, reflecting the wartime changes in Zurich, had fallen on bad times. In the summer of 1915, its chairman had reported that membership had dropped to 421 from the 844 of the last months before the war. The losses were due partially to the departure of German and Austrian workers for their homelands, but the group also found itself torn by internal differences. Several factions broke away to found their own organizations. A summary of the group's activities published in March 1916 noted sadly that while once the attendance at meetings had been greater than the membership, and attendants had been necessary at the doors, now the small hall in the building sufficed for all those interested. The members who had left, moreover, had constituted the elite of the group.[29]

The reduced membership still struggled to keep Eintracht alive. In the winter of 1915–16 Charles Rappoport, Radek, and Grimm gave lectures; Mieczyslaw Bronski and Riazanov offered courses. In March 1916, led by Bronski and Radek, the society came out in favor of splitting within the German Social Democratic Party: "It is a harmful illusion to believe that a battle-worthy party can be created without splitting." The decline of the organization, however, could not be stayed. Meeting on August 23, 1916, the membership, by a vote of forty-four to eleven, decided to dissolve as of January 1, 1917.[30]

As Eintracht declined, other organizations sprang up. Although a variety of writers have maintained that the Russian emigrés in Zurich had kept to themselves in isolation and that the Swiss public knew nothing of them, in fact, Russians participated in almost all the new intellectual currents. When a group of artists, calling themselves the Cabaret Voltaire, met at the Cafe Meier on February 5, 1916, "there were many Russians there. They organized a balalaika orchestra of at least twenty persons and wanted to remain permanent guests." Out of that gathering grew Dadaism. On February 26, a Russian chorus sang in the cabaret, and a Russian soiree took place on March 3.[31]

---

29. See *Volksrecht*, July 30, 1915, Mar. 2, 1916.

30. *Ibid.*, Aug. 24, Dec. 30, 1916. See also "Bericht an die ordentliche Generalversammlung der 'Eintracht' am 26.7.1916," Eintracht file, ZSSAr.

31. See Miklavz Prosenic, *Die Dadaisten in Zürich* (Bonn, 1967), pp. 38–45; Richard Hulsenbeck, "Zürich 1916, wie es wirklich war," *Die Neue Bücherschau* 6 (1928): 615; Hugo Ball, *Die Flucht aus der Zeit* (Lucerne, 1946), p. 72. The *Neue Zürcher Zeitung*, February 9, 1916, spoke of six Russians comprising a balalaika orchestra with guitar accompaniment.

The group which most interested Lenin was a radical political group calling itself the Kegelklub (Bowling Club). Like the Cabaret Voltaire, the Kegelklub had descended from soirees organized by Fritz Brupbacher even before the war. Although the group had no regular membership, it admitted newcomers only by invitation, carefully recruiting discreet persons holding responsible positions in the youth organizations, trade unions, or Socialist Party.[32] When Lenin joined the group, he attempted to convert it from a discussion group to a more active political organization.[33]

Throughout March, Lenin worked on his theses for the internationalist conference. Arguing that an imperialist war could end only in an imperialist peace unless a social revolution intervened, he warned that socialists could not be satisfied with simply mouthing pious slogans such as "no annexations" and "self-determination of nations." They must give the slogans a concrete program: "As annexation, one can consider only the adding of a territory *against the will* of its population; in other words, the understanding of annexation is indivisibly connected with the understanding of self-determination of nations." The task of a socialist must therefore be to "demand the immediate and unconditional *freedom of separation* for all colonies and nations oppressed by *his own* 'fatherland.' " In so doing, the socialist must also realize and accept the fact that "revolutionary actions in time of war are impossible without the threat of defeat for 'one's own' government and that any defeat of the government in a reactionary war facilitates revolution, which alone can bring a lasting and democratic peace." In conclusion, Lenin again insisted that a complete split with the policies and institutions of the Second International was absolutely necessary.[34]

After having sent the theses off to Zinoviev with instructions that the latter's wife type four or five copies of them for distribution, Lenin urgently instructed him to add another point: "The only unconditional demand which Social Democrats can raise as a program of peace, without playing into the hands of the opportunists, is *the refusal to pay war*

---

32. Dr. Ferdinand Böhny, interview, Feb. 13, 1970.

33. See Markus Mattmüller, *Leonhard Ragaz,* 2 vols. (Zurich, 1957–68), 2:127; Kharitonov, "Iz vospominanii," pp. 135–38; Fritz Brupbacher, *Zürich während Krieg und Landesstreik* (Zurich, 1928), pp. 65–66; Babette Gross, *Willi Münzenberg* (Stuttgart, 1967), pp. 69–70. The name of the group has been variously explained as a joke and as a disguise.

34. *PSS,* 27:282–93; *Zimm. Bew.,* 2:512–18.

debts." The call for the annulment of war debts had originated with
Dutch socialists, and the Eintracht Society had endorsed it during the
month of March.[35]

A second phase of Lenin's preparations for the upcoming conference
involved an all-out attack on the credentials of the Foreign Secretariat
of the Organizational Committee. Although Grimm refused to publish
one attack on the Mensheviks in the ISC *Bulletin*, the Bolsheviks went
on to deliver a formal challenge to Martov's mandate to participate in
the conference. Martov and Axelrod, Lenin insisted, could only claim
to represent the Foreign Secretariat and a few like-minded comrades.
The Organizational Committee as a whole could not be represented,
since Mensheviks in Russia were supporting the War Industries Committees which had been set up by the Tsarist government in order to
increase industrial production.[36]

The Mensheviks produced their own manifesto for the internationalist
conference, charging that the capitalists were attempting to resolve the
"irreconcilable contradictions of the capitalist order" through war, and
predicting that the capitalists would be unable to achieve a stable settlement to the conflict. The Mensheviks supported the idea of "national
self-determination" but insisted that only social revolution could bring
it about; in the capitalist system, "small, nominally independent states"
tended to become "vassals" of the great capitalist powers. The task of
socialists lay in working for the "full economic and political unification
of all civilized nations."[37]

Lenin's attacks on the Organizational Committee found an approving
audience among other emigré groups. Through the late winter of 1916,
the antagonism between Martov and Trotsky continued to intensify, and
attacks in *Nashe Slovo* on the Mensheviks grew apace. Manuilsky and
Zalewski both contributed articles critical of the Organizational Committee in Russia, and the editorial board defended them against rejoin-
ders by the Mensheviks. The editorial board also enraged the Mensheviks, not to speak of some of its own members, by printing an appeal
for financial support of *Sotsial'demokrat*.[38]

---

35. *PSS*, 49:203–4, 27:274, 290; *Volksrecht*, Apr. 7, 1916; *Zimm. Bew.*, 2:
528–29.
36. *Zimm. Bew.*, 2:521–24; *PSS*, 27:240–45.
37. *Kriegs- und Friedensprobleme der Arbeiterklasse: Entwurf eines Manifestes
vorgelegt der zweiten Zimmerwalder Konferenz* (Zurich, 1916).
38. See *Nashe Slovo*, Feb. 2, 11, Mar. 7, Apr. 8, 9, 1916. The Okhrana issued

The Mensheviks neither knew nor cared that the board of *Nashe Slovo* had its own deep division in its attitude toward the Bolsheviks. In a telegram to Lenin congratulating *Sotsial'demokrat* on the occasion of its fiftieth issue, the Bolshevik section in Paris summarized the situation in the following way: "A-v [Antonov-Ovseenko] deeply regrets that he can greet the celebrant only in his own name, and not in the name of his family. His spouse Natal'ia Savel'evna [*Nashe Slovo*] disagrees with him and is unsympathetic toward the celebrant. He also regrets that his old friend Golosov [*Golos*] is no longer among the living, for he was favorably inclined toward the celebrant and would certainly have celebrated this occasion. His words touched us all; this was a sheer hymn to the whole activity of Solomon Davidovich [*Sotsial'demokrat*]."[39]

On March 18, Martov sent *Nashe Slovo* his resignation, but because of postal delays the board learned the news only in April, and then from reading the *Izvestiia* of the Foreign Secretariat. In explanation of his action, Martov declared that he had remained on the staff so long as he saw any hope for proper direction and for the protection of the minority from "the worst excesses of partisan arbitrariness."

In characteristically sarcastic fashion, the board asserted that Martov had opposed all attacks on the defensists and had interfered with efforts to distinguish "passive internationalism and proletarian pacifism on the one hand, and, on the other, social-revolutionary internationalism, which alone fits the tasks of the working class in the new era." Martov's resignation, the board insisted, gave no cause for any reevaluation of its editorial policy.[40]

Nashe Slovo now turned on the Mensheviks even more sharply, but Trotsky and his comrades were still not ready to join the Bolshevik camp. Trotsky welcomed what he saw as a rewording of Lenin's slogan of defeat—from the defeat of Russia as the lesser evil to a call for "revolution without fear of defeat"—but he still questioned the long-range significance of the change. *Sotsial'demokrat*, he declared, still took inconsistent and contradictory positions.[41]

Despite *Nashe Slovo*'s declarations, Lenin still considered Trotsky "a

orders for its agents to work against fund-raising efforts on behalf of *Sotsial'demokrat*. OAr, IIe, f. 3, 106.

39. Anton Rakitin, *Imenem revoliutsii* (Moscow, 1965), p. 60.

40. *Nashe Slovo*, Apr. 19, 1916. See the analysis of Martov's internationalism in Israel Getzler, *Martov* (Oxford, 1967).

41. *Nashe Slovo*, Mar. 21, Apr. 11–12, 1916.

Kautskyite, i.e., he wants unity with the Kautskyites in the International, with the Chkheidze faction in Russia." Even though Trotsky "had been forced to recognize now the inevitability of splitting with the patriots, i.e., with the party of the Organizational Committee," he nevertheless took faulty positions in such a vital question as national self-determination.[42]

The Mensheviks saw little difference between Lenin and Trotsky. Axelrod admitted that Russian military reverses had strengthened defensist tendencies in Russia, but he argued that defensists of the *Prizyv* variety were still rare. The members of the Organizational Committee had chosen to participate in the War Industries Committees because they viewed this as a unique opportunity to reach the workers. The Foreign Secretariat refused to consider this a defensist action, however much it disagreed with the decision.[43]

Although the various socialist emigré factions might not have considered that they were responding directly to Lenin's call for splitting, the August Bloc of 1912, which had seemingly triumphed at the Brussels conference of 1914, now lay in shambles. The Zimmerwald Left, to be sure, was suffering its own internal fissures, but Lenin faced no serious rival among the Russians.

42. *PSS*, 27:236, 273, 49:191–92.
43. *Izvestiia ZSOK*, Feb. 5, 1916.

12

Kiental and After

The Second International Socialist Zimmerwald Conference opened in the Volkshaus in Bern on the evening of April 24, 1916, Easter Monday. Among the forty-one delegates were again a considerable number of Polish and Russian emigrés. From the Socialist Revolutionary Party came Natanson and two others using the pseudonyms of Vlasiev and Savelev; representing the Mensheviks were Martov and Axelrod; Bolshevik delegates were Lenin, Zinoviev, and Inessa Armand; Poles included Warski, Łapiński, Radek, Stein-Dąbrowski, and Bronski. Zinoviev also held a mandate from the Latvian Social Democrats. On the other hand Austria, England, Bulgaria, Sweden, Rumania, and Holland all lacked official representation.

Notable by his absence was Trotsky. The decision of the ISC to invite all participants of the Zimmerwald Conference had remained secret, and Grimm found it necessary several times to explain the invitations for the second conference. The exclusion of any official representation of *Nashe Slovo* angered many Russians, and the fact that Trotsky could not come to Switzerland for the meeting only added to the dispute.[1]

In the summer of 1916, Manuilsky publicly charged that the Bolsheviks and the Mensheviks had conspired to exclude Trotsky and *Nashe*

---

1. See Riazanov's exchange with Grimm in *Zimm. Bew.*, 2:444, 450, 456, 464, 467. When Solomon Grumbach commented on Trotsky's absence from the conference, *Nashe Slovo* of May 13, 1916, explained, "The masters of his [Grumbach's] masters do not give out passports to Russian emigrés in general and to Zimmerwalders in particular."

Slovo from the conference.[2] Lunacharsky used a different tactic, notifying Grimm that the Social Democratic "unified group of Petrograd" had recognized *Nashe Slovo* as its official organ: "In the name of all comrades who struggle sincerely for agreement between Russian internationalists, I ask you, Comrade, to insist on our right to be represented at the conference."[3] In Trotsky's absence, *Nashe Slovo* would probably have been represented by Lunacharsky, Manuilsky, or Riazanov.

Also absent was the Bund. In the name of the Foreign Committee, S. Kursky notified Grimm that "against our will," the Bund had to limit itself to a greeting. According to Okhrana reports, the Bundists found themselves sharply divided at this time. Since "comradely relations" had always substituted for discipline in the party ranks, the organization could take no single stand toward the Zimmerwald movement. In March 1916, two Bundists in Paris had joined *Prizyv,* and at the same time, the Bund group in Geneva complained with increasing bitterness that the Foreign Committee, under Kosovsky's domination, had systematically blocked efforts to take an unequivocally internationalist stand and had refused to call a conference of Bund groups in Switzerland. Under the circumstances, the Foreign Committee sent no delegate to the internationalist conference.[4]

Despite their numbers, the Russians did not play any major role in the formal organization of the conference, taking none of the elected posts of the meeting—with the exception that Balabanova, who represented the ISC and the Italian Socialist Party, served as secretary, together with Ernest Nobs of Zurich. Nevertheless Stepankowski, in his report to Romberg, erred in declaring that since "no one had come from Russia," the Russians and the Poles "therefore had no significance."[5]

At the end of the brief organizational meeting of April 24, Grimm announced that since Bern was "overrun with dubious elements," the conference would shift its site.[6] At seven-fifteen in the morning on

2. *Vpered,* June 8, 1916. See also Martov's answer in *Izvestiia ZSOK,* Sept. 12, 1916.

3. *Zimm. Bew.,* 2:600–602.

4. See *Zimm. Bew.,* 1:351, 2:536–40; Okhrana report, Aug. 6/19, 1916, OAr, XVIIIb, f. 4; circular letter of Geneva Bund group, Feb. 9, 1917, Vperiod Ar.

5. Romberg to Berlin, May 20, 1916, AAM, T120/5224/K489943. On this occasion, the Okhrana's information proved more reliable, as agents obtained a copy of Inessa Armand's summary of the discussions. Report of June 23/July 6, 1916, OAr, XVIc, f. 5.

6. The Austrian military attaché claimed that an Austrian agent, disguised

Tuesday the twenty-fifth, the delegates assembled at the train station, and the ISC provided them with tickets to Kiental, on the Lake of Thun, where the conference resumed on the same afternoon.

The Russians gave no reports on activities in the Tsarist Empire, but as soon as the German and the French delegates had finished their speeches, the Russians made their presence felt. A group of nineteen delegates, including Natanson, Lenin, Zinoviev, Radek, Bronski, Dąbrowski, Savelev, Vlasiev, and Armand, presented a formal declaration protesting the action of the French Socialist parliamentary deputies in voting for war credits. Martov spoke immediately in opposition to the declaration, and when the meeting threatened to dissolve in turmoil, Modigliani proposed that consideration of the declaration be postponed. The conference agreed and adjourned for the day.[7]

On the following day, Lenin received two setbacks at the very start. The mandates commission rejected Radek's claim to represent the Revolutionary Union of Holland, and it refused to consider Lenin's charge that Martov and Axelrod did not represent the majority of the Organizational Committee. In the discussions on "the struggle for ending the war," "the position of the proletariat on questions of peace," and "agitation and propaganda," the Leninist camp enjoyed more success.

The Bolsheviks and the Mensheviks offered the conference competing drafts on the problems of war and peace. In the name of the Polish dissidents, the Bolsheviks, and the Bremen opposition, Radek proposed a resolution calling the war "a struggle of capitalist world powers for a new division of the undeveloped lands." All talk of a democratic peace under capitalism constituted only a delusion; imperialism, however, "was digging its own grave." The proletariat's peace program demanded the annulment of war debts, unemployment compensation, a democratic republic, the rejection of all annexations, freedom for the colonies, the elimination of frontiers, and equality of nations.

On behalf of Axelrod, Łapiński, and himself, Martov presented a draft manifesto which agreed that the warring powers themselves could produce no stable peace. The manifesto also joined in attacking the practice and theory of "official socialism." The Mensheviks' slogans included: "Against all forcible annexations, open or masked," "Dis-

---

"mit angeklebtem Schnurrbart und roter Krawatte," attended the meeting. Clemens von Walzell, *Kundschaftsdienst oder Spionage?* (Leipzig, 1934), p. 102.

7. *Zimm. Bew.,* 1:307–9. Unless otherwise noted, all citations of the debates at Kiental are taken from *Zimm. Bew.,* 1.

armament of government by means of a radical democratization of the system of armed force," "Down with the war," "No indemnities," and "Down with secret diplomacy."

After prolonged discussion, the conference named two commissions to consider the major issues which the participants had defined. One, to write a resolution on the position of the proletariat toward problems of peace, included Martov, Radek, and Natanson among its nine members. The other, charged with drafting a resolution on relationships with the International Socialist Bureau, had seven members, including Lenin, Axelrod, and Warski.

The commission on the International Socialist Bureau reported back first, bringing in a resolution calling for the reorganization of the Executive Committee of the ISB—its membership to be made up of socialists from neutral countries—the exclusion of all socialists holding posts in warring governments, the refusal to vote war credits, and a demand for "a peace without annexations, without war indemnities, and which recognizes the right of self-determination of nations."

On behalf of the commission's minority, led by Lenin, Warski objected to any call for the ISB to meet for any reason. The German government, he charged, was seeking to exploit the ISB to promote an imperialist peace. Therefore, the minority resolution read, "The new International . . . can only be born from the revolutionary class struggle of the proletarian masses." Only a mass movement, and not an understanding between socialist leaders, could determine the fate of the International. "The Second International Conference therefore views the idea of convening the International Bureau as entirely misguided and harmful."

Lenin reiterated his view that nothing could be gained by discussions with the ISB: "The people with whom you want to reestablish the International have died; they live no more, not literally but politically." Grimm insisted that the conference should not demand the convening of the ISB, but that its representatives should attend if such a meeting took place. Axelrod, who had stood with the commission's majority, demanded the earliest possible meeting of the ISB; Martov suggested that the conference adopt no resolution at all concerning the convening of the ISB.

Łapiński offered a resolution calling for a careful watch of the ISB and declaring the intention of Zimmerwald supporters to attend any meeting in order to make their position clear. Zinoviev eventually offered a new resolution ordering that should the ISB meet, the ISC must convene at least its expanded membership "in order to discuss the question of a common stand of the Zimmerwaldists."

Grimm hoped to find a generally acceptable compromise formula from the discussion; some delegates wanted to avoid any vote at all; but Lenin pushed for a test of strength between the minority and the majority resolutions, demanding a vote on all proposals. The Italians threatened to leave the conference if the delegates voted to abandon the Second International. The Zimmerwald Left did in fact leave the meeting hall briefly when Grimm questioned whether the proponents of the various resolutions were truly concerned with the question on the agenda or whether they had other motives.[8]

At the suggestion of Martov, supported by Lenin, the conference finally agreed to a "completely platonic vote" to establish the attitudes toward the various resolutions, and a commission would then draw up the text which would unite the assembly. The minority resolution in fact drew twelve votes, to the ten of the majority resolution. The conference, however, rejected both by giving Łapiński's formula fifteen votes and Zinoviev's nineteen. Since Zinoviev's proposal was considered essentially a procedural declaration and complementary to Łapiński's proposal, Łapiński's text served as the basis for the discussions of the commission, which was enlarged by the addition of Zinoviev, Serrati, Łapiński, and Nobs.

The commission's final text criticized the inactivity of the ISB during the war and condemned the support given the Entente cause by its chairman, Vandervelde. The International could become a strong force again only when the proletariat ended the civil peace and resumed the class struggle. If the ISB convened, the ISC would consider the role to be taken by the Zimmerwald movement.[9]

Lenin, together with Zinoviev, Nobs, and Bertha Thalheimer, indicated that the resolution had failed to go as far as he wanted. Nevertheless, since the assembly had shown its preference for Łapiński's version, he would not oppose it. Some delegates opposed the resolution on the grounds that it leaned too far toward the left. In particular they attacked the call for a renewed class struggle and for mass action by the proletariat. As proposals for amendment mounted, Radek intervened to complain that the "resolution is becoming more and more colorless;

---

8. *Zimm. Bew.*, 1:372; Ernst Nobs, "Lenin und die Schweizer Sozialdemokraten," *Rote Revue* 33:59.

9. See Ia. G. Temkin, *Lenin i mezhdunarodnaia sotsial-demokratiia* (Moscow, 1968), pp. 412–13.

we protest this." In the end, the text was accepted essentially unchanged, by a vote of twenty-one to one, with several abstentions (including Axelrod's).[10]

Turning to the problem of the position of the proletariat on questions of peace, the conference adopted a text prepared on the basis of theses presented by Grimm. Consisting of fourteen points, the theses asserted that only forceful action by the proletariat, not pacifist ideas, could bring a lasting peace. Repeating the calls for a peace with no annexations and no indemnities, the theses concluded with a call for "a common international struggle for socialism."

In the discussion, both left and right again emphasized their reservations about the text but asserted their willingness, in the interest of unity, to support the document. Radek read a resolution, signed by eight delegates, including Lenin, Zinoviev, Armand, Dąbrowski, Platten, and Bronski, asserting that the theses represented a step forward in their "rejection of social pacifistic utopias," but that they still did not go far enough. Martov too objected to aspects of the document, but in the final vote only Warski, who declared "I have read the theses and I cannot digest them," voted against acceptance.

In the early morning of April 30, a five-man commission, which included Łapiński, Martov, and Radek, presented the conference with a draft manifesto. Two years of war, it declared, had brought no decisive result, "no victors, no losers, or rather everything lost, that is, all bleeding, all ruined, all exhausted, that will be the balance of this horrible war." The war could bring no good result; no war could put an end to war. "Lasting peace will be the fruit only of a victorious socialism." In conclusion, the manifesto called upon the proletariat to oppose all war credits: "Down with the war! Long live peace, immediate peace, without annexations! Long live international socialism!"[11]

The conference closed at four A.M. on Sunday, April 30. Some of the delegates had already departed. The publication and editing of the conference's documents was entrusted to the ISC. Most observers judged the tone of the conference to be considerably to the left of that of the first conference at Zimmerwald. Some attributed this to Lenin; Grimm claimed that the movement had matured and was gradually realizing its strength.[12]

---

10. *Zimm. Bew.,* 1:374–76; Temkin, *Lenin,* p. 413.
11. *Zimm. Bew.,* 1:403–6.
12. See Branko Lazitch, *Lénine et la IIIe Internationale* (Paris, 1951), pp. 64–67.

Lenin could find both victories and defeats in the deliberations of the conference. On some specific issues he had been highly successful. The final resolution of the conference, however, had ignored his call for civil war; the delegates still refused to break openly with the Second International. Nevertheless, the Bolsheviks could claim that the meeting "represented a new step forward. . . . Unwillingly and resisting," the Zimmerwald majority had "to go on the path which we propose."[13]

The twelve votes for the Leninist resolution on the ISB included four veterans of the original Zimmerwald Left—Lenin, Zinoviev, Radek, and Platten. The other four members of the original Zimmerwald Left had been unable to come to Kiental. Three of Lenin's new votes came from an increased representation for the Bolshevik Central Committee and the Polish dissidents, Armand, Dąbrowski, and Bronski. Serrati of Italy represented the only convert from the original Zimmerwald majority, and the other four votes came from persons who had not been at Zimmerwald—Robman, Nobs, Kanclerovic, and Fröhlich. Subsequently Lenin lost the support of Nobs, but he won others to his side, including Henri Guilbeaux.

In his memoirs, Guilbeaux claimed that Lenin, at Kiental, had converted him from following the lead of Martov. In fact, Guilbeaux seems to have accepted the Zimmerwald program only in the course of the month of April, suddenly, after having associated himself first with the pacifist approach of the Ford Mission and of the Committee for a Durable Peace. Guilbeaux soon became one of Lenin's most important supporters in French-speaking Switzerland.[14]

According to *Nashe Slovo* of June 3, "At the second conference, the 'Zimmerwald Left' was weaker as an organization than at the first, but the ideas of revolutionary internationalism were significantly more strongly represented." Lenin had drawn sharper attacks from his opponents than ever before. Axelrod had told the gathering, "I would and should say much more against the views of Comrade Lenin and his friends than is possible in this brief time."[15] Nevertheless, Lenin's prestige grew as a result of the conference.

On May 2, the expanded International Socialist Commission again met in Bern, this time with six of the fourteen delegates representing

13. Temkin, *Lenin*, p. 418.
14. See Henri Guilbeaux, *Vladimir Il'ich Lenin* (Leningrad, 1925), pp. 149–50; Guilbeaux's letters to Auguste Forel, March to May 1916, in Forel Ar. IV.A.67.
15. *Zimm. Bew.*, 1:365–66.

Polish and Russian groups: Natanson, Martov, Zinoviev, Radek, Warski, and Łapiński. Without Lenin, the left seemed to have less clear direction, but Zinoviev and Radek still made their presence felt by objecting to the idea of encouraging Zimmerwaldists to attend a meeting of socialists from neutral countries, called by the ISB for The Hague at the end of June 1916.[16]

Lenin now returned to Zurich, where he began an entirely new phase of his activity. Although the Bureau of the Zimmerwald Left had ceased to function as such, Lenin kept the name and the idea of the group alive, devoting a special issue of *Sotsial'demokrat* to the Kiental conference and reproducing a special report on the conference for distribution in Russia.[17] The second and last issue of *Vorbote,* dated April 1916, appeared with a lengthy article by Zinoviev summarizing the Kiental conference. Lenin also embarked on another series of lectures, speaking in Zurich on May 15, in Geneva on June 2, and in Lausanne on June 3.

At the same time, he worked industriously on his manuscript for *Imperialism: The Highest Stage of Capitalism.* Completed in June, the work first saw publication in the summer of 1917. Lenin offered it as documentation of the basic views on the war which he had been advancing since 1914, and the study quickly took its place as one of his major writings.

Offering a myriad of statistics as evidence, Lenin argued that monopolies and imperialist competition inevitably developed together with the capitalist system. Needing markets and raw materials, the capitalist states competed with foreign investments and armies: "So long as capitalism remains capitalism, surplus capital will not be used to raise the standard of living of the masses in a given country, for this would mean a decrease in profits for the capitalists. Rather, it will be used to raise profits by the export of capital abroad, to the backward countries." The system, moreover, inevitably led to war: "The capitalists divide up the world not because of some personal wickedness, but because the degree of concentration which has been achieved forces them to take this course in order to obtain profits." Only a socialist revolution could end this costly competition; the capitalist system could not be reformed.

Lenin angrily criticized the German socialist Karl Kautsky, whom he

16. *Ibid.,* 1:393–425. Temkin, *Lenin,* p. 422, noted that Lenin was at the same time encouraging Scandinavian radicals to attend the meeting.

17. *Sotsial'demokrat,* June 10, 1916; Temkin, *Lenin,* p. 432; *Volksrecht,* May 5, 1916.

accused of breaking with Marxism "by defending, in the period of finance capital, the 'reactionary ideal' of 'peaceful democracy.' " Kautsky's thought had "nothing but reactionariness and bourgeois reformism in it."

In conclusion, Lenin argued that imperialism represented "transitional or, better, dying capitalism." Profits might allow the capitalists to corrupt "various strata of workers, temporarily even a substantial minority of them," and therefore revolutionaries must understand that the "struggle with imperialism, if it is not indivisibly linked with a struggle against opportunism, is an empty and false phrase."[18]

While Lenin worked to discredit the leaders of the Second International and to split socialist parties of all countries, the continuing controversy with the *Kommunist* group plagued him with the spectre of the younger members of his own party, together with younger Swiss and Dutch socialists, splitting with him to follow new paths. Lenin's view of imperialism, for example, clashed sharply with the views advanced by the *Kommunist* group, who carried their critique to the point of opposing the principle of national self-determination as an illusion in the imperialist epoch and of claiming to see no useful distinctions between different forms of capitalist society.

Lenin explained his views again and again; the *Kommunist* group would not accept them, and even won support from others. When Radek began to intervene, Lenin finally proposed that the *Kommunist* group simply continue to publish its journal, but without any connection with the Central Committee. The Central Committee itself would now offer a new publication, *Sbornik Sotsial'demokrata. Kommunist* did not appear again.[19]

Lenin also found himself plagued by routine financial and organizational problems. Shliapnikov discovered that during his travels someone had stolen his official stationery as representative of the Central Committee. *Sotsial'demokrat* of June 10, 1916, carried an anguished appeal by Shklovsky to "comrades in New York," asking them to respond to letters and to send money. In April, moreover, *Sotsial'demokrat* had had to raise its price because of a raise in wages to typographical workers. With the appearance in June of the special issue on Kiental, *Sotsial'-*

18. *PSS*, 27:299–426.
19. See *PSS*, 30:69–70, 49:220ff; Olga Hess Gankin and H. H. Fisher, *The Bolsheviks and the World War* (Stanford, 1960), pp. 219–30; Temkin, *Lenin*, pp. 435–53.

demokrat ceased publication until November 1916. Since Lenin even lacked money for himself, Krupskaya accepted the post of secretary of the Central Secretariat of Russian Emigré Funds in Switzerland.[20]

In contrast to the Zimmerwald conference, the Kiental conference seemed to leave the Russian emigrés pensive. The exhilaration of Zimmerwald was gone; the emigrés looked more carefully and thoughtfully at what they were doing. Zinoviev questioned whether Zimmerwald would be "only a passing episode" or whether it would be "on the contrary, a stage on the road to the creation of a new international association of workers, without the social chauvinists and against them." K. Zalewski criticized the conference for having failed to press toward a new International, "centralized, with international, not state-national political orientation." On the other hand, Lunacharsky questioned whether the conference had not committed itself too strongly to a "purely revolutionary and antireformist position."[21]

Martov and Axelrod continued to support the work of Grimm and the ISC as it stood. The defensists had protested the Kiental meeting even before it had taken place, and in the summer of 1916 they gave their support to the attacks on the Zimmerwald movement made by Solomon Grumbach.[22] For the most part, however, the activities of the emigrés after the conference focussed more sharply on local issues and organizations than on such larger problems as the competition between the ISC and the ISB.

The financial problems which plagued Lenin were common throughout the emigration, and the emigré funds found demands on their resources growing. The Zurich fund, the strongest, took the initiative in calling for coordination of the work of all the funds, and on April 23 and 24 a general conference took place in Bern.

Delegates came to Bern from eight Swiss cities. In agreeing to the formation of a Central Secretariat, they drew up a constitution limiting membership to political emigrés. Although the representatives of Bern and Geneva had opposed this limitation—arguing that they needed the aid of politically neutral emigrés—the Zurich group forced its accep-

20. N. K. Krupskaya, *Reminiscences of Lenin* (Moscow, 1959), pp. 333–34.
21. See G. Zinoviev and N. Lenin, *Protiv techeniia* (Moscow, 1918), p. 355; *Nashe Slovo*, July 27, 1916; *Vperëd*, June 8, 1916.
22. See Grumbach's *Der Irrtum von Zimmerwald-Kiental* (Bern, 1916); reprinted in abridged form in Gankin and Fisher, *The Bolsheviks*, pp. 452–62, and reviewed in *Berner Tagwacht*, July 26, 1916, and *Nashe Slovo*, Aug. 22, 1916.

tance. Felix Kon took the post of chairman of the Central Secretariat and Krupskaya became its secretary.

In the subsequent months, Krupskaya helped in the formation of new funds in La Chaux-de-Fonds and in Clarens. Since the emigrés in La Chaux-de-Fonds almost all had well-paying work, many in the watch industry, they made significant contributions to the treasury of the Central Secretariat. Krupskaya also investigated the problem of employment of emigrés, finding that of the able-bodied persons, only the "emigrés of the intellectual professions" truly had trouble finding work.[23]

By the beginning of summer, 1916, the Russian socialist emigrés had become strangely quiet. The Kiental resolutions seemed to have reached the limits of possible political action for the time being. The emigrés turned to their personal troubles. Lenin and Krupskaya retired for a vacation in Tschudiwiese, where, according to Krupskaya, they received no visitors. Zinoviev again spent the summer in Hertenstein, Radek went to Davos. Inessa Armand vacationed in Hertenstein. For the time being, the stage belonged to other elements in the emigration.

23. See Okhrana report, OAr, XXVb, f. 3; S. M. Lebidova and S. A. Pavlotskaia, *Nadezhda Konstantinovna Krupskaia* (Leningrad, 1962), pp. 114–16; Alfred Erich Senn, "Russian Emigré Funds in Switzerland, 1916: An Okhrana Report," *International Review of Social History* 13:76–84.

13

The Russian
Parliamentary Delegation

In the course of May and June of 1916, the attention of the emigré colonies in Switzerland and throughout Western Europe focussed on the visit to Western capitals of a Russian parliamentary delegation which included Paul Miliukov, the leader of the parliamentary opposition in Russia. The mission originated in an invitation issued by the British government to Duma deputies to visit England. France added an invitation to visit the military front, and eventually the Italians joined the call. Miliukov had originally proposed that the delegation should include no more than three deputies, but in the end seventeen persons made the trip. (The British government reportedly had requested that the delegation include representatives of the right.)[1]

Miliukov, long a bitter opponent of the Tsarist government, had adopted the Russian cause in World War I as his own. He firmly believed in the alliance with England and France as a progressive factor in Russia's future, and repeatedly expressed his faith in the "liberating goals of this war."[2] He particularly supported Russia's desire to gain Constantinople.

The Tsarist government had at first attempted to maintain the war effort without the Duma. After its special session of August 8, 1914, when it approved war credits, the Duma did not meet again until January 1915, when it worked for only three days. In the shadow of

1. *Rech'*, Feb. 22, 1916.
2. See Thomas Riha, *A Russian European: Paul Miliukov in Russian Politics* (Notre Dame, 1969), pp. 216–18.

Russia's military defeats in the summer of 1915, Miliukov pieced together a coalition of Duma deputies called the Progressive Bloc. In contrast to his prewar tactics, he now sought his political allies from the political center and right rather than from the left.[3] When the Duma convened again in August 1915, Miliukov stood as the leader of a majority of the deputies. The Bloc could not unseat the cabinet of ministers, however, and the Tsar soon prorogued the session.

When Tsar Nicholas personally took over the command of the armed forces in the fall of 1915 and thereby left the reins of power more or less in the hands of the Empress, the conflict between the Duma and the throne intensified. In January 1916, Boris Stürmer replaced I. L. Goremykin as chairman of the Council of Ministers, but Miliukov saw this as no improvement. At the opening of the new session of the Duma in February 1916, the Tsar himself came to address the body for the first time, but, in Miliukov's words, "Nicholas's visit changed exactly nothing. Politics remained the same." The Duma remained in session only long enough to debate the budget; in the meantime, the throne continued its process of removing administrative officials sympathetic to the Progressive Bloc. The legislative session ended on April 18, eleven days before Miliukov's departure for Western Europe.[4]

For Miliukov, the trip had a number of useful aspects. Even though the Progressive Bloc was having internal problems, Miliukov did not doubt that the Western powers wanted to use the parliamentary delegation at the same time to strengthen the image of Russia in their own countries and to tie Russia more closely to the Entente's war effort: "The existence of the Progressive Bloc offered the possibility for the first time of showing off abroad the representatives of the Russian legislative institutions as a whole in the spirit of the 'sacred union.' " On the other hand, the Progressive Bloc could improve its own bargaining position vis-à-vis the throne by winning official European recognition.[5] Eventually the trip also served to color very strongly Miliukov's personal images of the war, of the Russian throne, and of the socialist emigrés.

3. *Ibid.,* pp. 223–24.

4. See Paul Miliukov, *Political Memoirs 1905–1917,* ed. Arthur P. Mendel (Ann Arbor, 1967), pp. 328–29; P. N. Miliukov, *Vospominaniia,* 2 vols. (New York, 1955), 2:218–31.

5. Miliukov, *Political Memoirs,* p. 340; *Vospominaniia,* 2:232. Riha, *A Russian European,* pp. 250–51, makes an interesting comparison between this trip and an earlier one which Miliukov made in 1909.

When the delegation departed Petrograd on April 29, 1916, it included six representatives of the State Council and eleven Duma deputies. The group suffered from serious internal tensions. Miliukov often seemed to be the leader of the delegation, but the official chairman was A. D. Protopopov, the deputy chairman of the Duma, whom the Russian ambassador in London called "an imbecile." Baron Roman Rosen, a member of the State Council and former Russian ambassador to Washington, tended to overshadow Protopopov in the formal diplomatic receptions, but the other delegates reportedly made "some very offensive remarks in reference to Baron Rosen's alien origin and German proclivities."[6] Miliukov, moreover, had clashed with Rosen over a decade earlier when he had foregone a reception with the President of the United States rather than submit to being introduced by Ambassador Rosen.[7]

To Miliukov's regret, no socialists participated in the delegation, although they had been invited. Three representatives of minority nationalities made the trip—Count Zygmunt Wielopolski and F. F. Raczkowski of Poland, and a Lithuanian, Martynas Yčas, a member of Miliukov's Kadet Party. Miliukov later complained that all three men seemed more interested in meeting their compatriots than in the work of the delegation, but in all, the delegation probably discussed the national question in Russia more than it did any other problem.[8]

In Sweden, where the delegation met a rather cold reception, Miliukov, on his own, immediately plunged into socialist and pacifist circles. He and Yčas together visited the offices of the Ford Mission in Stockholm, but he had little sympathy for the pacifist spirit of that organization.[9] Miliukov also spoke at some length with Carl Lindhagen, Burgomeister of Stockholm. He thought he saw German influences behind the questions of his hosts, and he dismissed their views by saying, "The opinions of the neutrals could not influence the aims of the belligerents."[10]

After a day or two in Norway, the delegation finally arrived in England

6. Constantin Nabokoff, *The Ordeal of a Diplomat* (London, 1921), p. 53.

7. Riha, *A Russian European*, p. 162.

8. On the delegation's journey, see, besides works already cited, Roman Rosen, *Forty Years of Diplomacy*, 2 vols. (New York, 1922), 2:213–21; Martynas Yčas, *Atsiminimai nepriklausomybes keliais*, 3 vols. (Kaunas, 1935), 2:184ff.; "Dnevnik P. N. Miliukova," *Krasnyi Arkhiv*, 54-55:3–48; "Russkaia 'parlamentskaia' delegatsiia za granitsei v 1916g.," Krasnyi Arkhiv, 58:3–23.

9. "Dnevnik," p. 26. Miliukov did not mention Yčas's having accompanied him, but the visit is described in Ada Morse Grose, "Candle in the Dark," Louis Lochner Papers, Wisconsin State Historical Society.

10. Miliukov, *Political Memoirs*, p. 343; *Vospominaniia*, 2:236; "Dnevnik," p. 27.

on May 5, landing, for reasons of security, in northern Scotland. Taken by special train to London, they settled into the Hotel Claridge on the morning of the sixth, much chagrined by the failure of the Russian ambassador to meet them at the train station. The warmth of their British hosts, however, soon overcame their pique.

On the seventh, Miliukov travelled to Brighton to see Peter Kropotkin. Visits with emigrés played a major role in Miliukov's program, and he had in fact met many of them before, including the internationalists. Alexinsky and he had argued in 1905; Chernov had been his student in Moscow; and he had once even visited Lenin in London. On this trip, however, Miliukov chose to deal mainly with defensists. Kropotkin, for example, expressed great concern about the successes of the Zimmerwald movement.[11]

On May 9, King George V received the delegation, paying special attention to Miliukov. The travellers all responded well to such formal receptions, and they were obviously impressed by their visits to British defense plants. In a festive gathering on May 10, the tenth anniversary of the Russian Duma, the British House of Commons formally honored the delegation. In all, the group remained in England until May 20.

In Paris, the delegation's reception proved even more impressive. Izvolsky, the Russian ambassador, acted as a gracious host, and Miliukov felt that his talks in Paris were more productive than those in London. Aristide Briand and Raymond Poincaré spoke with the group, and in a flurry of parties, the delegates met such figures as Thomas Masaryk, the Czech leader, and Sir Arthur Conan Doyle. The Sorbonne briefly flew the Russian flag together with the French flag.

Protopopov usually represented the delegation in statements to the foreign press, but other members of the group also spoke with newspapermen on occasion. Miliukov represented the left wing of the delegation and Count Wielopolski spoke on behalf of the minorities. For the most part, the speakers emphasized the unity of the peoples of Russia in pursuing the war effort, but the national question kept reemerging through their comments.

In England, Miliukov, commenting on the Polish question, insisted that Poland must remain a part of Russia, under an autonomous arrangement along the lines of Irish Home Rule.[12] Miliukov, a political liberal,

11. Miliukov, *Political Memoirs,* p. 345; *Vospominaniia,* 2:238; "Dnevnik," p. 33.
12. *Manchester Guardian,* May 20, 1916.

could not countenance the thought of breaking up the Russian Empire. Count Wielopolski, a National Democrat, publicly declared his solidarity with Miliukov: "Our future is possible only in union with Russia." The presence of two Poles in the delegation, Wielopolski declared, was "the greatest proof that we are and will remain faithful to the attitude which we took at the beginning of the war."[13]

Although the Russian government officially considered the Polish question a purely domestic issue, Miliukov found it necessary to discuss Tsarist policies toward the national minorities at almost every occasion. In speaking with British Foreign Minister Sir Edward Grey, Miliukov himself raised the issue of Poland, asking, "What do you think of the Polish question?" Grey responded, "This is Russia's affair. We naturally would like her to give the Poles autonomy, but we cannot interfere." Miliukov then declared, "For us, too, the Polish question is a domestic question. . . . We are against mentioning the internal constitution of Poland in any international act." In a conversation with the historian R. W. Seton-Watson, Miliukov found that the Polish question represented their major point of disagreement; Seton-Watson insisted that an international act on Poland was essential.[14]

Miliukov also spoke freely on the question of the Armenians in Russia, and he discussed the treatment of Russian Jews with the Rothschilds. (In Russia, conservatives later accused him of having sold promises on the future treatment of Jews in Russia.) He publicly advocated a more tolerant policy on the part of the Tsarist government toward all its national minorities, but he could not bring himself to support any extensive political concessions.

On the first leg of the trip through Scandinavia, Miliukov had already debated the Polish question at length with Wielopolski in private. Miliukov's conception of the maximum possible concessions to the Poles barely touched Wielopolski's conception of the absolutely minimal Polish demands. Wielopolski had written the official Polish translation of the Grand Duke's declaration on Poland in August 1914, and he openly declared that his major purpose in joining the parliamentary delegation had been to take the opportunity to discuss the national question with Miliukov.

Wielopolski argued strongly in favor of an international declaration on Poland's future; in this way, if Germany won the war, Berlin too

---

13. *Journal de Genève*, June 8, 1916.
14. "Dnevnik," pp. 42, 45.

would have to recognize Polish rights. Miliukov objected to any consideration of the possibility that the Allies might lose the war. He pointed out that a project for Polish autonomy lay before the Russian government, and he expressed his confidence that it would be promulgated. He insisted again and again that France and England must take no stand on Poland.[15]

On May 30, the delegation left Paris and broke up into several groups, all of which were to convene again in Italy in a few days. Miliukov and Yčas detoured into Switzerland, where, following separate paths, they sampled the climate of the Russian emigration. Miliukov characterized Switzerland as the "classic land of all kinds of emigrations and nationalist propagandas," and he explained his trip as being a search for information. Switzerland offered even better sources of information than did Sweden. Yčas frankly wanted to meet with Gabrys and other Lithuanians.[16]

According to Yčas, Miliukov met with Bolsheviks in Lausanne, but the liberal leader spoke only of having conferred with Polish leaders in western Switzerland. He called his conversation with Erasmus Piltz, "a comparatively moderate representative of the 'Russian orientation,' " particularly helpful. Miliukov also met with Stepankowski and Gabrys, who claimed to have told him that Russian "centralism was irretrievably doomed." Like any other Russian intellectual touring Switzerland, Miliukov found time to travel to Baugy to visit Rubakin.[17]

Miliukov left behind him in Lausanne a new information agency, Agence Russe d'Information, headed by Vladimir Viktorov-Toporov, a correspondent of Miliukov's newspaper *Rech'*. Stepankowski immediately made the acquaintance of Toporov, and thereafter ranked him with Sviatkovsky as one of his major sources for reports to the German mission.

Yčas dealt only with Lithuanians; indeed, German sources reported that he had brought some 100,000 Swiss francs for the purpose of winning the Lithuanian emigrés to the Russian cause.[18] He found that

---

15. "Dnevnik," pp. 16ff. See also Wielopolski's testimony in *Padenie Tsarskogo Rezhima,* 7 vols. (Moscow, 1927), 6:27–48.

16. Miliukov, *Political Memoirs,* pp. 355–56; *Vospominaniia,* 2:251; Yčas, *Atsiminimai,* 3:7–11.

17. See Juozas Gabrys, *Vers l'independance lituanienne* (Lausanne, 1920), pp. 108–9; Romberg to Berlin, July 22, 1916, AAM, T120/4820/L244712. For Miliukov's views of Gabrys, see his *Natsional'nyi vopros.* An Austrian report claimed that there was a woman involved in Miliukov's visit to Switzerland. HHSAr, PA, XXVII/56/Ber/31.

18. Steputat to Berlin, Nov. 11, 1916, AAM, T136/22.

Gabrys had made considerable progress in publicizing the Lithuanian national movement. In March, a Lithuanian conference in Bern had called for Lithuania's independence of both Poland and Russia; in April, another conference, allegedly in The Hague, reaffirmed this call. Both meetings had in fact taken place in Bern, and they had consisted basically of Gabrys, three priests from Fribourg, and a great deal of publicity.[19]

Gabrys was feeling a certain amount of pressure from all quarters at just this point. A secret French military report, full of errors, spoke of his having received money from the Entente and yet travelling freely between London, Paris, Berlin, and Vienna. At the very least, the document meant that Gabrys's French friends had doubts about him. A German report noted that Gabrys had suspiciously large amounts of money at his disposal. Gabrys's contacts among the American Lithuanians, who had given him a considerable amount of financial support in the past, were now complaining about his profligate ways.[20] Nevertheless Gabrys pushed ahead, organizing a conference with Yčas as chairman in Lausanne, May 31 to June 4, 1916.

Yčas later complained that although he had met only with Lithuanians in Switzerland, by the time he returned to Paris in the middle of June, Russian agents could present him with a complete account of his activities in Lausanne. If anything, however, he underestimated the leaky security in wartime Switzerland. He left the country on June 4, and the Austrians received a report of the Lausanne meeting on June 8. Romberg, on the other hand, had begun receiving reports on Yčas the day before his arrival in Switzerland.[21]

Both Yčas and Miliukov hurried from Switzerland to rejoin their delegation in Italy. In Rome, Miliukov met Plekhanov and apparently won the old socialist's approval of the war program of the Progressive Bloc. After another brief stop in Switzerland—Miliukov stayed in Geneva from June 15 to 17—the delegation eventually returned to Russia at the beginning of July.

Although Miliukov's determination to see the war through to a successful end had undoubtedly intensified as a result of his meetings

19. See Malbone W. Graham, *New Governments of Eastern Europe* (London, 1928), p. 360; Juozas Gabrys, "Tevynes sargyboje," MS, 2:137; A. Steponaitis, *Tevyneje ir pasauly* (New York, 1962), pp. 95–100; Okhrana report no. 231, Mar. 4/17, 1916, OAr, XXII, f. 1B.

20. French report in OAr, VIIIb, f. 1B; AAM, T120/5224/K489739; K. Rutkauskas to Gabrys, letter dated February 29, 1916, in the papers of Juozas Gabrys, held by Dr. Albertas Gerutis, Bern, Switzerland.

21. HHSAr, PA, 904/8e/231; AAM, T120/4820/L244712.

in western Europe, the delegation's work failed in a number of ways. According to Sviatkovsky, it had not made a really good impression in either London or Paris.[22] Miliukov and Yčas had both failed to change the currents of thought among the emigrés to any significant degree. Most critical, however, was the scandal raised over reports that the head of the delegation, Protopopov, had met in Stockholm with Max Warburg, an influential Hamburg banker. In Miliukov's view, this action contributed to rumors of treason in Petrograd.[23]

The initiative for the Stockholm meeting actually came from Count Dmitri Olsufiev, a member of the State Council. In the shadow of Yčas and Miliukov, Olsufiev too had travelled to Switzerland, but among his contacts was Romain Rolland. Rolland considered Olsufiev, who had known Tolstoy, a Christian conservative who seemed more congenial than most socialists. His political ignorance, however, distressed the French writer. Possibly influenced by his talks in Switzerland, Olsufiev let it be known in Stockholm that he would like to speak to a German; when the meeting was arranged, Protopopov came along. Warburg considered Protopopov to be definitely the greater man of the world.

The meeting amounted to no more than an exchange of opinions, but once back in Petrograd, Protopopov spoke of it openly and freely. He even claimed to have organized it. When challenged, he eventually insisted that his sole purpose had been curiosity: "There is nothing serious here and nothing important here. This was an interesting occasion." He protested against charges that he had compromised the work of the delegation, but apparently the controversy around the affair eventually contributed to the breakdown of his health.[24]

After his return, Miliukov remained in Petrograd only briefly before hurrying back to England, now in an unofficial capacity, to accept an invitation from Professor Bernard Pares to give lectures at Cambridge University. Roman Dmowski participated in the same program. Miliukov's real attraction in Western Europe, however, was again Switzerland, "where I wanted to gather data, from sources unavailable in Russia,

22. Romberg to Berlin, July 22, 1916, AAM, T120/4820/L244712.
23. P. N. Miliukov, *Istoriia vtoroi russkoi revoliutsii*, 2 vols. (Sofia, 1921), 1:31–32.
24. See *Padenie Tsarskogo Rezhima*, 1:113, 118, 138–39, 156–57; 6:338; 7:35–37; *L'All. et la paix*, pp. 392–94; report of Feb. 17, 1917, in AAB, PA, WK2 geh., Bd. 30; Romain Rolland, *Journal des années de guerre 1914–1919* (Paris, 1952), pp. 803–5.

on secret contacts between German and Russian circles." His work in Cambridge done, he hurried again to Lausanne, where emigrés gave him "a whole bouquet of facts—authentic, doubtful, and unlikely." Unlike Alexinsky, Miliukov directed his suspicions not against the socialists but against court circles. On November 14, back again in Petrograd, he cited events in Switzerland extensively in his challenge to the Russian government, charging secret contacts with the Germans and questioning, "Is this stupidity or treason?"[25]

Miliukov's voyages to Western Europe had brought the official opposition in Russia into contact with the political emigration. His disputes on the national question, as well as his scorn for both pacifism and the Zimmerwald movement, boded ill for the day when he might come to power in Russia.

25. Miliukov, *Political Memoirs,* pp. 359–60.

14

The League of
Alien Peoples of Russia

In the spring of 1916, the principle of national self-determination had established itself firmly as a major topic of debate for the socialist emigrés, and the parliamentary delegation had also spent a surprising amount of time discussing the national question in the Tsarist Empire. The discussions drew their significance from the German occupation of Russia's western borderlands and the growing problem of the future of these territories. In April, the German government announced that the Reich had no intention of allowing the regions occupied by its troops to return to Russian sovereignty. Baron Romberg, the German minister to Bern, saw in all this a justification of his own predilection for working among the emigrés from the national minorities of Tsarist Russia, and his agents did all that they could to encourage him.

Stepankowski and Gabrys lost no opportunity to persuade German authorities that Tsarist Russia feared nothing more than a revolution by the minority nationalities. When a leading Russian police official visited French Switzerland, Stepankowski reported that his purpose was to investigate the activities of the nationalities. He said the same of Miliukov's visit. Gabrys assured Romberg that Yčas had come to Switzerland at the direction of Foreign Minister Sazonov, with the aim of combatting anti-Russian feelings among the Lithuanian emigrés. Romberg, in turn, seemed more and more inclined to believe in the possibilities of arousing the nationalities.

On March 10, 1916, when Gabrys came to Romberg with the idea of founding a "League of the Small Nationalities of Russia," the German minister listened with interest. At about the same time, Berlin notified Romberg of its interest in a plan to exploit the "non-Russian peoples of Russia." A group in Germany headed by a Baltic nobleman, Baron Friedrich von der Ropp, had proposed a call to world opinion against the Tsarist government, a propaganda campaign against Russian "atrocities," and development of a mass movement "Away from Russia" (*Los von Russland*) among the minority nationalities.[1]

On April 15, Romberg transmitted to Berlin Gabrys's formal proposal for the organization of a League of Alien Nationalities of Russia (Ligue des nationalités allogènes de Russie). Proposing first the establishment of only a steering committee, Gabrys anticipated formally organizing the league only after the cessation of hostilities. Romberg emphasized that Gabrys had good organizational talents, and he expressed his own opinion that Germany should have a strong interest in the plan.[2]

Berlin seized upon Gabrys's plan with an enthusiasm which even he could not have anticipated. A week later, Baron Bernhard von Uexküll, traveling under the name Benno von Ullrich, was on his way to Bern, charged with the task of organizing the League of Alien Peoples of Russia (Ligue des peuples allogènes de Russie, or Fremdvölkerbund Russlands). Working with von der Ropp, Uexküll set up a front organization in Berlin under the name Neutrale Korrespondenz.

Uexküll met Gabrys in Bern on April 26. On the twenty-seventh he journeyed to Lausanne where he talked further with Gabrys, Stepankowski, and Tyszkiewicz. On the twenty-eighth he wrote to Ropp, describing "our Swiss organization" as "perfect." He also claimed to have won the cooperation, through cash payments, of several Western newspaper correspondents who promised to publicize the activities of the league.[3]

The first project of the league was the publication of an appeal to United States President Woodrow Wilson on behalf of the oppressed nationalities of Russia. Most of the signers lived in Germany or Scandinavia, but while in Switzerland Uexküll, through Gabrys and Stepan-

1. See AAM, T120/5224/K489668, K489754–57; AAB, Wk 11c geh., 11.
2. AAM, T120/5224/K489770–78. Here, as elsewhere, the views of Romberg and Schubert cannot be distinguished. The draft of the letter was in Schubert's handwriting although it bore Romberg's signature.
3. AAM, T120/5224/K489785–93. The correspondents allegedly included Jean Pelissier, a French friend of Gabrys's who worked for the Deuxième Bureau; Edmondo Peluso; and John White, an English friend of Stepankowski's, who had reportedly just become an official agent of the British government.

kowski, claimed to have won the support of the Groupe lettone en Suisse, which he claimed to have founded, the Edition juive en Suisse, and the Ukrainisches Sozialdemokratisches Comité.[4]

When the letter to Wilson appeared on May 7, published simultaneously in Stockholm and Lausanne, it bore the signatures of, among others, Ropp, Michael Lempicki, Dmytro Dontsov, the Groupe ukrainien en Suisse, and the Comité lituanien de Berne.[5] Praising Wilson as the "most ardent defender of humanity and justice," the appeal recounted the complaints of Finns, Balts, Lithuanians, Belorussians, Poles, Jews, Ukrainians, Moslems, and Georgians. "Such are the abuses of the Russian government toward its own subjects," the document concluded; "Come to our help! Save us from destruction!"

Although the German press faithfully reproduced and publicized the appeal, it had little effect. The American government took no note of it. Miliukov called the text surprisingly mild. The Entente powers, on the other hand, took careful note of the names, and an Okhrana circular called for the arrest at the Russian frontier of any of the signers, with the exception of Lempicki, who still enjoyed the immunity of a Duma deputy.[6]

Another project of the league involved the translation of a manuscript entitled "Do You Know Russia?", written apparently by von der Ropp. The text, which had an intentionally sensational tone, aimed at exposing the oppression of minority nationalities in Russia and at challenging the Russian Empire's right to exist: "Every friend of humanity and civilization must deny the right of existence to a state which for centuries has systematically persecuted and oppressed the beliefs, nationality, and freedom of its inhabitants."[7]

Gabrys agreed to undertake the translation into French, even though he knew but little German. The result of his endeavour was an essentially new book, entitled *La Russie et les peuples allogènes*. (Gabrys used the pseudonym Inorodetz, the Russian equivalent of *allogène*.) When the

4. See Uexküll to Ropp, Apr. 29, 1916, AAB, Wk 11c geh., Bd. 12.

5. AAM, T120/5224/K489911–13. When Gabrys published the text in his memoirs, *Vers l'independance lituanienne* (Lausanne, 1920), pp. 277–82, he altered the Lithuanian signature to "Groupe lituanien en Suisse."

6. Circular, Oct. 29, 1916, OAr, IIe, f. 3, 133–41; P. N. Miliukov, *Vospominaniia*, 2 vols. (New York, 1956), 2:253.

7. See *Kennen Sie Russland?* by "twelve Russian subjects" (Berlin, 1916); AAM, T120/5224/K489790.

work appeared in 1917, von der Ropp praised it as excellent, "better than the German original."[8]

From its inception, the league met with problems in dealing with its supporters as well as with other German agencies. Nominally independent, it worked with the Auswärtiges Amt through the person of Otto Gunther von Wesendonck. It had little influence, however, in the regions of Russia under German occupation where the army reigned supreme. When von der Ropp and Uexküll began to seek contacts among the intellectuals in the occupied areas, they found that for Erich Ludendorff, in Steputat's words, "all unofficial political activities are unclear and unpleasant." Only under pressure did Ludendorff permit three Lithuanians to sign the letter to Wilson.[9]

On the other hand, the various persons who adhered to the league had their own ambitions. Gabrys, for instance, apparently gave the Germans no information about the pronouncedly anti-German resolutions adopted by the Lithuanian meeting with Yčas in Lausanne at the beginning of May. Gabrys also made the Germans uncomfortable by his willingness to meet and work with French and Belgians. As the league developed its activities, it found Ludendorff and the German High Command in its way repeatedly, questioning the activities of such persons as Gabrys and von der Ropp.

The most significant and most successful effort of the League of Alien Peoples came in its campaign to dominate the Third Conference of Nationalities called for Lausanne at the end of June 1916. The Union of Nationalities had held its first meeting in 1912 and its second in June 1915, both times in Paris. Neither meeting had drawn much attention from either diplomats or political agents.[10]

The union's call for a new conference, inviting "all dissatisfied nationalities of Europe" to attend, offered a great opportunity to the Germans. In February 1915, Kesküla had raised the idea of organizing a

8. Von der Ropp to Stepankowski, Feb. 8, 1917, AAM, T136/22. See Gabrys, *Vers l'independance lituannienne,* p. 119, and Friedrich von der Ropp, *Zwischen gestern und morgen* (Stuttgart, 1961), p. 109.

9. See Fritz Fischer, "Deutsche Kriegsziele: Revolutionierung und Separatfrieden im Osten 1914–1918," *Historische Zeitschrift* 188:288; Fischer, *Griff nach der Weltmacht* (Düsseldorf, 1964), p. 145.

10. The Paris Okhrana had not seen enough political significance in the meeting of 1915 to report it to Petrograd. See OAr, IIe, f. 34, 727–29, and report no. 1278, Dec. 18/31, 1916, XIIIb(1), 1916.

"bloc of nationalities" of Imperial Russia and staging a congress. In the course of the year, others had taken up the same thought, but the problem of avoiding the charge of simply being a German machination seemed insurmountable. Now the League of Alien Peoples planned to take over the Conference of Nationalities.[11]

In external appearance, the Union of Nationalities still had a pronouncedly pro-Entente image. Belgian and Italian sections had just recently joined the organization. The membership lists still included leading French figures, such as the historian Charles Seignobos. The first announcement of the conference designated Edouard Milhaud, a professor at the University of Geneva and a close friend of Aristide Briand, as the president of the meeting.

As plans progressed, however, Milhaud withdrew, and Paul Otlet, a well-known Belgian bibliographer, assumed the presidency. A participant in the second conference in 1915, Otlet had come to Switzerland in September of that year, reportedly with the aim of conducting pro-Entente propaganda. In December he had attended the pacifist conference "Pour la paix durable" in Geneva. His circle of friends included Romain Rolland, Biriukov, and Rubakin.

The ultimate judge of the validity of the mandates of delegates attending the conference was, however, Gabrys, and the Germans anticipated no difficulty in winning admission for their friends. The Auswärtiges Amt provided funds for its chosen delegates, and the league found that its greatest problem came from Ludendorff, who objected to Uexküll's suggestion that Lithuanian and Belorussian assemblies be permitted to choose delegates. The army instead simply named delegates, sending three Lithuanians and two Belorussians.

In a letter of June 2 to Gabrys, von der Ropp summarized the arrangements: Gabrys received 10,000 francs to cover expenses such as bribing newspapermen; the delegates would arrive in Lausanne on the evening of June 24; Gabrys should find a suitable location for a private meeting of the league's delegates on the twenty-fifth; he should also find "not too expensive" lodgings for the group. The league should control at least nine votes at the conference. Gabrys in turn informed Romberg that the conference would have a basically anti-Russian tone,

11. The invitation in Office de l'Union des Nationalités, *Annales des Nationalités. IIIe Conférence des Nationalités. Documents préliminaires* (Lausanne, 1916), p. 3.

but that because of circumstances, it would also have to have a pro-French "gloss."[12]

Entente sources, without fully understanding the scope of the German activity, evidenced considerable unease about the meeting. Although the Okhrana, by the end of June, had identified von der Ropp as the author of the appeal to Wilson, it seems not to have drawn any connection between the League of Alien Peoples and the Conference of Nationalities. At the same time, the Entente watched the preparations for the conference carefully. At the last moment, Izvolsky reportedly succeeded in persuading Czech and Serbian delegates to withdraw. Lausanne, already a hotbed of wartime intrigue, became even more tense as the opening of the conference drew near. Many commentators later challenged the significance of the conference, but in the month of June, anticipation ran high.

Probably the sharpest critics of the work of the League of Alien Peoples were the Latvians in Switzerland, who had immediately identified the hand of the Baltic Germans in the enterprise. Although the Balts were themselves a minority in the Russian Empire, the Latvians, who saw them as the landowners and privileged class in the Baltic area, refused to recognize them as an "oppressed" people.

The Latvian socialists in Bern, headed by Felikss Cielens, had protested against the letter to Wilson as soon as they had learned of it. The Latvian Committee in Switzerland, organized in the fall of 1915 under the chairmanship of the writer Janis Rainis, published a denunciation of the League of Alien Peoples as the creation of the Baltic German barons von der Ropp and Sylvio Broedrich. The "groupe letton," the committee declared, was a "mystification." The Latvian people saw the solution of the national question not in "separation from Russia" but rather "in common with the true Russia—the Russian democracy." On June 21, Kesküla, who was just then leaving Stockholm to attend the conference, anxiously warned Berlin to postpone the gathering. The Latvians, he declared, were preparing "unpleasant surprises."[13]

On June 25, the League of Alien Peoples held a secret organizational meeting in Lausanne. Present were von der Ropp, three Lithuanians

---

12. AAM, T120/5224/K489986–87; T136/21.
13. See Edgars Andersons, *Latvijas vesture 1914–1920* (Stockholm, 1967), pp. 141–43; Felikss Cielens, *Laikmetu maina,* 2 vols. (Lidingo, 1961), 1:393ff.; Austra Osolin, *Selbstbefreiung oder Selbstvergewaltigung* (Olten, 1917).

(Steponas Kairys, Jurgis Šaulys, and Antanas Smetona), two Poles (Lempicki and W. Sieroszewski), three Finns (Konni Zilliacus, Samuli Sario, and Herman Gummerus), Michael Tseretelli of Georgia, and Stepankowski. All but Smetona, Gummerus, and Stepankowski had signed the appeal to Wilson; only Stepankowski had been a resident of Switzerland up to this time. The group immediately named Lempicki president of the league, and it voted to accept the Belorussian and Moslem delegates into the organization.

Besides agreeing on tactics for the conference—including a promise not to attack each other and to act as an informal bloc—the group adopted a program amounting to a constitution. The document provided for contributions by member groups, plans for activity among emigrés in the United States, a variety of publications, and the establishment of special agencies to collect and disseminate information on Tsarist nationality policies. As their executive committee, the delegates chose von der Ropp, Stepankowski, Gummerus, Lempicki, and Šaulys.[14]

The Lithuanian delegation to the conference represented a keystone in the plans of the league. In the previous months, Gabrys had prepared the way for a declaration of Lithuanian independence, but he did not have a free hand in delivering the Lithuanian delegation to the league. Besides the three delegates from occupied Lithuania, representatives of Lithuanians in Russia and in the United States had now arrived in Switzerland. In response, the Germans sent Steputat to Switzerland. Gabrys repeatedly told Romberg that only with difficulty could he restrain the Lithuanians in Switzerland from following a pro-Russian line. Steputat, in turn, informed his superiors that only with difficulty could he keep Gabrys on a pro-German line.

Complicating the situation was the presence of an American-Lithuanian priest, the Reverend Vincas Bartuška, who had visited occupied Lithuania in the spring of 1916 on a fact-finding mission for an American-Lithuanian group. German officials in Lithuania had arrested him and fined him 1,000 marks on charges of illegal correspondence, contact with persons disloyal to the German administration, and unauthorized travel.[15]

Gabrys had requested the intervention of the German mission in

14. Protocol of the meeting in AAM, T136/22.
15. V. Bartuška, *Lietuvos nepriklausomybes kryžiaus keliais* (Klaipeda, 1937), pp. 56–57; AAM, T120/4820/L245033.

Bern to obtain Bartuška's release, and he had pressed the Germans to allow the priest to come to Switzerland. Nevertheless, Bartuška immediately upbraided Gabrys for the latter's cooperation with Berlin; Gabrys in turn complained that the Germans should be more careful in using his name. In an effort to assuage the irascible priest's feelings, the Auswärtiges Amt announced that it was donating 1,000 marks to Lithuanian war relief in Bartuška's name. When this failed, Romberg gave him 1,000 marks from his own secret fund.[16]

The delegates from occupied Lithuania urged Bartuška to hold his tongue. Steputat warned all concerned that criticism of Germany could lead to reprisals in Lithuania. On the other hand, Bartuška criticized Yčas for his reluctance to support Lithuanian independence. In the end, Bartuška agreed to represent Lithuania at the conference. For Gabrys and the Germans, this constituted a major victory.

When the conference opened on June 27, the League of Alien Peoples was ready to take command. On the surface, the meeting still appeared to be neutral or even pro-Entente. Public displays depicted the work and the troubles of minority nationalities on both sides in the war. Otlet's credentials as a Belgian nationalist were impeccable. But at Otlet's side sat Gabrys, whose advice Otlet had agreed to ask on the various personalities who might request the floor. In his opening speech Otlet discoursed on the principle of nationality, defended the right of self-determination even for small nations, and concluded by characterizing Belgium as the "symbol of the right of sacrificed peoples to defend themselves."[17]

In the afternoon session, devoted to reading and discussing a proposed "Declaration of the Rights of Nationalities," the League of Alien Peoples opened its first attacks on the Russian Empire. Tseretelli insisted that one should react to the "assassination of a nation" in the same way as to the assassination of a man, and he offered Poland, Lithuania, and Georgia as examples.

The meeting took a sharper form on the second day, as Edmond Privat dismissed criticism of the conference, questioning whether it was "Germanophile to speak of the rights of Belgium or those of Serbia." Ironically, the German agents at the conference who knew nothing of

16. Romberg to Berlin, Aug. 4, 1916, AAB, Wk 11c, geh., Bd. 15.
17. Unless otherwise noted, all citations from the conference's debates have been taken from *Compte rendu sommaire de la IIIme Conférence des Nationalités reunié à Lausanne 27–29 juin 1916* (Lausanne, 1916).

the League of Alien Peoples thought that a pro-Entente spirit dominated well into the second day, and that the anti-Russian spirit came entirely from the delegates and not from the administration of the conference. One observer complained of Otlet's "arbitrariness bordering on perfidy" and criticized von der Ropp's "pro-Entente intrigues."[18]

From the beginning, von der Ropp assumed a confusing role. He had signed the appeal to Wilson as a Latvian, but when the Latvians in Switzerland began to attack him he dubbed himself, with Gabrys's blessings, a Lithuanian. In the second day's discussions, he exploited his position at the head table to speak first, bemoaning Lithuania's unhappy position between the danger "on the one hand of being Prussified and on the other of being Russified." When an Egyptian delegate criticized the English, von der Ropp protested that Egypt had progressed under British rule. The ensuing confusion threatened to disrupt the meeting, but finally Otlet was able to restore order. Von der Ropp reportedly apologized to the Egyptian in private, saying, "I am sorry, Monsieur, if I have hurt your feelings as a patriot."[19]

The two major challenges to the principle of self-determination for the peoples of Russia came in the cases of Latvia and Georgia. The Latvian representatives came out against separation from Russia and for the military victory of the Allied Powers, arguing that they hoped for a better future within a democratic Russia. Gabrys intervened to block an attack on von der Ropp, but for this he won the enmity of the Swiss scientist Auguste Forel, who had accompanied the Latvians. Forel later complained that Gabrys had been "actually rude to me." Gabrys suppressed the Latvian statement in the protocols of the conference.[20]

After Michael Tseretelli had given an impassioned speech for Georgian independence, another man arose to demand the floor. Otlet asked him whether he wanted to speak for or against Tseretelli's presentation, and he answered, against. When Otlet then yielded, German observers expected trouble.

The speaker, Viktor Tevzaia, held the post of *Privat Dozent* on the law faculty of the University of Geneva, and he belonged to the Georgian club in that city. A Menshevik, he argued that the 1905 revolution in Russia had forged a bond between the Russian and the Georgian

18. See AAM, T120/4820/L244667–71; T120/5224/K490075.
19. AAM, T120/5224/K490079.
20. Statement in AAM, T120/22. See also Forel's *Out of My Life and Work* (New York, 1937), p. 316.

peoples, with the result that the Georgians, rather than seeking independence, only wanted to fight in alliance with the Russians for the democratization of Russia. Tseretelli angrily insisted that the Georgians and the Russians had absolutely nothing in common.

One after another, the members of the League of Alien Peoples worked to develop an anti-Russian atmosphere. Poland served as the focus of their enthusiasm, and the league's greatest single triumph came in the reading of a declaration from several Polish groups in Switzerland endorsing the work of the conference. The Poles, led by Szymon Askenazy, had at first planned to attack it, but Lempicki persuaded them to change their stand. The signers included Kucharzewski's society, La Pologne et la Guerre, the pro-Austrian press bureau in Bern, the National Democrats' agency in Lausanne, and the Comité de publication encyclopedique sur la Pologne.[21]

When Lempicki took the podium on the last day, June 29, the delegates greeted him with calls of "Vive la Pologne! He responded in kind: "The true sense of Russian policy is the struggle against Poland, a regime of terror; and the promises of the Grand Duke to grant independence to Poland were made with the intention not to keep to them. The conduct of the Russians after the invasion of Galicia surpasses the horrors of Dante's inferno." Amid the loud cheers, von der Ropp arose to proclaim, "Let Poland, which is the key to the future, go ahead, and we will follow!"

In his report to the Auswärtiges Amt, von der Ropp asserted that at this point "stormy jubilation filled the hall, the delegates of the non-Russian peoples fell into each other's arms and kissed. All present stood under the charm of this singular fraternization and unity of the non-Russian peoples."[22]

In his final speech von der Ropp sought, in his own way, to drive a wedge between the Entente powers: "Citizen soldiers of France, defend all that is sacred to you and to civilization, defend France, which is the throne of beauty and of taste! Citizen soldiers of England, defend your Empire, which has assured prosperity to all nations! But Frenchmen and Englishmen, do not shed your blood in support of the enslavement of the numerous nations groaning under the Russian yoke! Help to reestablish just relations between the peoples of a new Europe!"

---

21. AAM, T120/4820/L244708; Gabrys, "Tautos sargyboje," MS, 2:160–61.
22. Report dated July 6, 1916, AAM, T136/22.

Otlet attempted to put the discussion back on a more general plane in his own final speech, but the League of Alien Peoples had succeeded in dominating and directing the tone of the conference. Whether it represented a personal triumph for von der Ropp, however, was another question.

Romberg received glowing reports about the meeting from all his informants. Even those complaining about both Otlet and von der Ropp considered that of the major powers, Germany and Turkey had emerged from the speeches with the best images. Germany had enjoyed a great success as a result of the "strong demonstration" against Russia in "fanatically French-oriented Lausanne." Gabrys had manipulated Otlet "extraordinarily skillfully." Romberg in turn reported to Berlin in the same vein.[23]

Von der Ropp found himself both praised and attacked. In self-justification, he insisted that he had learned of a plan by Izvolsky to disrupt the conference, making it appear to be a German puppet and then claiming a violation of Swiss neutrality. Von der Ropp had therefore taken it upon himself to attack Russia and to disarm Izvolsky at the same time. Romberg endorsed von der Ropp's actions, admitting that they may have been exaggerated but emphasizing that they had been successful. Other Germans were not so generous, as Steputat complained that von der Ropp had emerged as the warmest defender of England and France at the conference. The Auswärtiges Amt also found it necessary to defend von der Ropp against criticisms from the military.[24]

Other reactions to the conference varied widely. The *Journal de Genève* of July 2 reported that it had received at least a dozen protests about the gathering's anti-Entente character. The *Gazette de Lausanne* carried several criticisms of the meeting. *Le Temps* of July 7 spoke of "inopportune zeal" and charged that since many of the delegates had come through German territory, they were "at least suspect of partiality towards the Central Empires." The Okhrana blamed Otlet for the anti-Russian character of the speeches and criticized the conference as a "misuse of the hospitality of Switzerland." Later, the Russians speculated that Gabrys had received money from the Austrians.[25]

Socialist reactions to the conference also varied. Radek considered

23. AAM, T120/4820/L244632.
24. See reports in AAM, T136/22.
25. Okhrana reports no. 699, July 6/19, 1916, and no. 33, Jan. 9/22, 1917, OAr, XIIIb(1), 1916 and 1917.

that the delegates, who represented "all the nations in the dictionary and yet a few more," constituted a veritable "Noah's Ark," or rather a "Tower of Babel," in Lausanne. Radek scornfully declared that the delegates "also do not understand that their goal is impossible; it is historically settled." Another commentator noted that even these "oppressed 'nations' " had shown a "latent imperialism."[26]

Writing to Robert Grimm, Edmondo Peluso described the meeting as "an entirely platonic demonstration." D. Z. Manuilsky dismissed the work of the delegates as only demonstrating their knowledge of various languages and their "timidity and ideological impotence." More interesting to him was the question of who stood behind the conference. The delegates had obviously had an easier time reaching Switzerland than had the delegates to the Kiental conference.[27]

Trotsky, on the other hand, commented that the meeting had shown "that the majority of oppressed nationalities live within the boundaries of the Entente liberators." He could not understand how anyone could defend Russia's record in its treatment of national minorities. Tevzaia responded to this by attacking "Baltic barons and Polish anti-Semites" and criticizing Trotsky for not having noted his challenge to Tseretelli. Trotsky declared that he knew nothing of Tevzaia's speech, but he repeated his assertion that the conference had offered a "bright illustration of the Entente's international policies."[28]

Almost overlooked in the discussions was the conference's major resolution, reaffirming the principle of national self-determination and proclaiming that the rights of minority nationalities should be recognized by international law. The existence of nationalities, the resolution asserted, "forms a natural and rational basis for the division of the population of the globe into governmental units."[29]

The conference's effect lay in the image of Russia which it had produced. It aroused no mass movements or campaigns. Romberg insisted,

26. *Berner Tagwacht*, July 7, 1916; *Demain*, 1:45. The editor of *Demain*, Henri Guilbeaux, saw the English hand behind the conference. See his *Du Kremlin au Cherche-Midi* (Paris, 1933), p. 111.

27. *Zimm. Bew.*, 2:539; *Nashe Slovo*, July 29–30, 1916. In his financial reports, Stepankowski listed payments to Peluso of 320 francs in September and 400 francs in October. He also listed a payment of 200 francs to Manuilsky in September. AAM, T120/4820/L245099, L245306.

28. *Nashe Slovo*, July 13, Aug. 2, 1916; L. Trotskii, *Voina i revoliutsiia* (Moscow, 1918), 1:196–97.

29. Text in AAM, T136/22.

on the basis of information from Gabrys and Stepankowski, that the Russian government was greatly concerned over the success of the conference, but Steputat insisted that the significance of the conference had been overestimated. The League of Alien Peoples itself retired from public view, leaving only an office in Bern, to be manned by Stepankowski and Dontsov. The effectiveness of its propaganda cannot be measured.

To be sure, the conference did succeed in stimulating some of its opponents to act. The Latvians, who had met with such an unfriendly reception at Lausanne, organized a Comité d'etudes en faveur des Lettons, as well as two information agencies in Basel. Conflict immediately arose, however, as Rainis, declaring himself to be a socialist, refused to participate in the committee, which was directed by a nationalist who favored an Entente victory.[30]

Uexküll and von der Ropp now invested heavily in subsidizing Gabrys's activities as a publicist. They advanced him 20,000 francs for the preparation of the protocols of the conference and another 5,000 for the translation of *Do You Know Russia?* At the same time they worried about both his national prejudices and his cavalier attitudes toward their money. Von der Ropp, who insisted on the necessity of reviewing the text of his speeches for the protocol, instructed Schubert to watch that Gabrys did not minimize the role of the Poles: "Please tell Gabrys that my heart beats for Lithuania, but that it would be politically unwise to put Lithuania in the foreground." Uexküll complained that Gabrys not only claimed high expenses without providing receipts, but even went on to add up the figures wrong—in his own favor.[31]

Gabrys himself enjoyed a considerable success in the aftermath of the conference as the Lithuanians agreed to form a council in Switzerland, to include representatives from Russia, the United States, and the occupied territories. The council was to be a secret organization, concealed behind Gabrys's Lithuanian Information Bureau.[32]

At the same time, as the Auswärtiges Amt now initiated a policy more sympathetic to the minority nationalities of Russia, the significance of

30. See Rainis's letters to Forel, Forel Ar., IV.A.137.
31. AAM, T120/4820/L244636, L244766–77.
32. See Juozas Puryckis, "Lietuviu veikimas Šveicarijoj Didžiojo Karo metu," *Pirmasis nepriklausomos Lietuvos dešimtmetis* (London, 1955), pp. 68–70; Borje Colliander, *Die Beziehungen zwischen Litauen und Deutschland während der Okkupation 1915–1918* (Abo, 1935), pp. 42–47.

the activity in Switzerland had to wane. *Nolens volens,* the German High Command gradually had to allow a greater activity among the population of the occupied territories. In the case of the Lithuanians, Jurgis Šaulys now travelled frequently to Berlin, and in the fall of 1916, Yčas, returning from a trip to the United States, met with German agents in Stockholm. In this broader program, Gabrys's significance for the Auswärtiges Amt had to wane.

Gabrys, however, did not put all his hopes on Germany. One factor in his expense accounts to the Germans may well have been the work which he was simultaneously devoting to the preparation of a volume of documents concerning German occupation policies in Lithuania, which he eventually published under the name Marie Camille Rivas and which he called "our Big Bertha."[33] The League of Alien Peoples, by supporting the development of the national question in Eastern Europe, was contributing also to the embarrassment of German policies.

33. C. Rivas, *La Lituanie sous le joug allemand 1915–1918* (Lausanne, 1918); Gabrys, "Tautos sargyboje," 3:1ff.

15

National Self-Determination in Action

The Conference of Nationalities had pleased Romberg and other German officials, but no great power could claim to control either the principle of national self-determination or the direction of any given national movement. The powers could only contribute to the development of the national question and hope that their sympathizers would triumph and remain loyal. Romberg invested heavily in the cause of various minority nationalities; his goal was the disintegration of Tsarist Russia. A certain degree of personal ambition and pride may also have entered the picture, however; his success with the Conference of Nationalities had won him greater notice in Berlin. When the Auswärtiges Amt subsequently began to question the activities and accomplishments of his agents, he came energetically to their defense. With time, he also became more and more generous in supporting agents of dubious value.

Just as the internationalist socialists had moved toward more radical positions in the course of the war, the various national movements, with the Poles foremost, could claim progress in their development. On November 5, 1916, a joint proclamation of the German and the Austrian emperors announced the reestablishment of the Polish state. The Central Powers had agreed upon the action at a meeting of their respective chancellors on August 11–12. The new state would have no power to conduct its own foreign policy; its territory included only the Russian-held portion of Poland; and Germany would control its armed forces. Although the German Chancellor, Bethmann-Hollweg, thought that the proclamation should be issued as soon as possible, the governments chose to delay action so as not to compromise current hopes for a separate peace with Russia.[1]

Throughout September and October 1916, Switzerland reverberated with rumors of secret talks between the official and unofficial agents of the German and the Russian governments, aiming at bringing about a separate peace between the two states. Miliukov heard them and he was shocked. Lenin took note of them and hastened to tell his followers that such a peace represented only an imperialist tactic and that it could produce no lasting, positive results.[2]

On October 8, the Prussian cabinet met with General von Beseler, the German Governor General in Warsaw, and generally indicated its support for the establishment of an independent Poland. The consideration that perhaps three divisions, 36,000 men, might thereby become available to the armed forces of the Central Powers outweighed all other factors. Poland could serve as a buffer state, pushing the Russian frontier back to the east but at the same time not overburdening the German Empire with a Catholic, Slavic population.

Ten days later, German and Austrian officials again agreed to issue the proclamation as soon as possible. Austrians and Germans alike complained that Russia represented a "sphinx." The proclamation of Polish independence would undoubtedly compromise the efforts at a separate peace, but, as Bethmann-Hollweg argued, everything depended on "the determination and strength of the peace party" in Russia.[3]

The formal proclamation on November 5 came from von Beseler's office in Warsaw. The parts of Poland "snatched with heavy sacrifices from Russian power" would become "an independent state with a hereditary monarch and constitution." The question of the frontiers of the new Kingdom of Poland was left open.[4]

The proclamation failed to achieve its immediate objectives. Noticeably lacking throughout the preparations had been any significant participation by Polish leaders. Von Beseler had apparently consulted Lempicki, Wladyslaw Studnicki, and a few others, but no major Polish political groups had entered into the talks. Instead of the mass of volunteers which the Germans had hoped for, only a few hundred persons

1. *L'All. et la paix,* pp. 429ff.
2. *PSS,* 30:184–92.
3. *L'All. et la paix,* pp. 492–508, 512.
4. Text in Malbone W. Graham, *New Governments of Eastern Europe* (London, 1928), pp. 751–52.

answered the call to arms. The uncertainties, such as the lack of frontiers and even the absence of any provision for a Polish administration, dampened enthusiasm for the cause of the Central Powers.[5]

Within the Russian government, the proclamation crushed whatever sentiments for a separate peace may have existed but at the same time contributed to increased tension between Russia and its allies. In October, a Polish specialist connected with the Russian embassy in Rome had already reported that the Russian government had lost control of the Polish question. The idea of autonomy no longer had a place in "general Polish political activity." Almost the whole of Polish society demanded independence; only a few Poles, such as Piltz and Wielopolski, supported even the idea of "self-sufficiency" *(samostoiatel'nost')*, that is, a Poland in personal union with Russia. Russian prestige had fallen because the government had done nothing to realize the promises made in 1914 by Grand Duke Nikolai Nikolaevich.

The report went on to attribute these developments to the "well organized Austro-German propaganda" in the occupied territories and in Switzerland; to the lack of a fitting Russian response to this propaganda; and to the Tsarist government's military misfortunes and administrative mistakes. At best, Russia could only hope that the demand for independence represented a "transitional stage" in the Polish question.[6]

On November 15, every Russian ambassador formally protested the Central Powers' proclamation and reaffirmed Russia's promises to unite Poland under the rule of the Tsar. The inhabitants of Poland still maintained their allegiance to "His Imperial Majesty My Most August Monarch." To the discomfort of the Russians, France, England, and even Italy took formal note of the Russian declaration and announced their support of the Russian position. This "amounted to the 'internationalization' of the issue which Polish leaders had long urged."[7]

In the Russian Duma on November 15, a Polish deputy arose to

5. See Fritz Fischer, "Deutsche Kriegsziele: Revolutionierung und Separatfrieden im Osten 1914–1918," *Historische Zeitschrift* 188:294; Fischer, *Griff nach der Weltmacht* (Dusseldorf, 1964), pp. 346–49; Leon Grosfeld, *Polityka państw centralnych wobec sprawy polskiej w latach 1914–1918* (Warsaw, 1962), pp. 81–187; Titus Komarnicki, *Rebirth of the Polish Republic* (London, 1957), pp. 91–97.

6. Report by Ts. Ianushovskii, Oct. 16, 1916, OAr, IIf, f. 21. See also Henryk Wereszycki, "L'Opinion publique en Pologne devant la chute du tsarisme," *Revue d'histoire moderne et contemporaine* 15, 24–38.

7. Alexander Dallin, "The Future of Poland," in *Russian Diplomacy and Eastern Europe 1914–1917* (New York, 1963), p. 68.

denounce the German proclamation. For this he received loud cheers, but he went on to complain that the Russian government had done "nothing to strengthen the belief that Russia's decision, expressed in the historic appeal to the Polish nation, is unalterable and that a return to the past is impossible." Germany was exploiting Russia's silence, he charged. Another deputy then retorted, "In time of war, no government in the world could do more for a land than the Russian government has done for Poland." In the State Council, the chairman of the Council of Ministers, Boris Stürmer, left the hall when a Polish representative mounted the podium to speak.[8]

The news of the Central Powers' proclamation aroused a storm of comment among the political emigrés in Switzerland, although the discussion became complicated by reactions to two coincidental deaths. On October 19, the Russian minister in Bern, Vasily Romanovich Bakherakht, died, and on November 16, the Polish writer Henryk Sienkiewicz died.

Bakherakht had served as Russia's "Envoy Extraordinary and Minister Plenipotentiary" since the summer of 1906. Before that he had been secretary of the legation in Bern and he had extensive ties in Swiss society. At the time of his death, he was the doyen of the Bernese diplomatic corps, and the Austrian minister called him an "uncommonly congenial person." On September 12 he had gone on leave for reasons of health, and in the night of October 18 and 19 he died. He was buried in Vevey, and the diplomatic corps of the Entente powers and of neutral states participated in the service.[9] Mikhail M. Bibikov acted as temporary Russian chargé d'affaires.

Sienkiewicz's death on November 16 added to the controversy surrounding the creation of the Polish Kingdom, and at the same time it reflected the development of the Polish question. As one eulogist declared, Sienkiewicz had spoken his piece as an artist, but as "a generally recognized representative of Poland he had not completed his role. We still awaited his words."[10] Throughout the war, Sienkiewicz had straddled the political fence; supporters of both warring camps claimed his sympathies. He refused to commit himself, declaring that his first task was to work for war relief in Poland.

---

8. *Kievskaia Mysl'*, Nov. 15, 1916.
9. See *Der Bund*, Oct. 23, 1916; Pleasant A. Stovall, *Switzerland and the World War* (Savannah, 1939), p. 206; HHSAr, Pa, XXVII/55/Ber/288.
10. *Kievskaia Mysl'*, Nov. 22, 1916.

On August 21, 1916, the councillor of the Austrian mission in Bern, Wladyslaw Skrzyński, visited Sienkiewicz and came away with the impression that the novelist objected to the policies of the pro-Russian camp among the Poles: "For the Russophiles, Polish history appears to have begun with 1863." The whole policy of the pro-Russians consisted in "ingratiating themselves so as to avoid the whip." They wanted to know nothing of the "greatness of the former kingdom." The Austrian diplomat thought that any positive action by the Central Powers could bring Sienkiewicz off the fence. For the moment, however, Sienkiewicz loftily dismissed the thought of supporting Austria: "Tell me, how can one, even with the best will, be for something when one has no idea where it is going?"[11]

The pro-Entente press agency in Lausanne attempted to organize a mass protest by Poles against the proclamation of the Polish Kingdom, but Sienkiewicz refused to sign, despite considerable political pressure: "That was his last political act; two or three days after that he no longer lived."[12] After his death, all factions sought to claim him. The Austrian minister requested and received permission from Vienna to send a wreath to the funeral. The Austrian government invited Sienkiewicz's widow to return to the Austrian part of Poland.

In some respects Sienkiewicz's funeral, also held in Vevey, surpassed Bakherakht's. The French, English, and Russian consuls in Lausanne attended the requiem mass, together with representatives of all Polish organizations in Switzerland. When the funeral party proceeded to the burial plot, representatives of the Austrian and German missions in Bern arrived. Sienkiewicz's casket was draped with the Polish flag, and the Austrian minister commented on the "piquancy" of seeing Russian, German, and Austrian officials all attending a ceremony marked by the singing of the Polish national anthem.[13]

By this point in the war, the Polish conflict had run far beyond the control of any one of the partitioning powers. Austrian officials in Switzerland hailed the proclamation of the Polish Kingdom as a "great

---

11. HHSAr, PA, XXVII/56/Varia/23. On Skrzyński, see Janusz Pajewski, *Wokół sprawy polskiej: Paryż-Lozanna-Londyn 1914–1918* (Poznań, 1970), p. 136–41.

12. Henryk Korybut-Woroniecki, "Stowarzyszenie 'La Pologne et la Guerre' w Szwajcarii," *Niepodleglosc,* no. 41, p. 398. See also Pajewski, *Wokół sprawy polskiej,* pp. 132–36.

13. HHSAr, PA, XXVII/56/Ber/105.

step on the way to the solution of the Polish question," but they still viewed it as a defeat for Austrian policies. At the same time, they insisted that the proclamation would push the Western powers toward a stronger stand, possibly forcing the Russians themselves to accept the idea of Polish independence.[14]

The protest of the pro-Entente Poles, published on November 14, attacked the thought of giving independence only to one part of Poland: "The Polish nation, one and indivisible, seeks the creation of a Polish state from the three parts of Poland." In their further statements as individuals, the pro-Entente Poles indeed spoke more freely of independence. The proclamation had raised the Polish question to a matter of official international politics, and even the Russians could no longer maintain that Poland was solely a domestic issue. Dmowski, for one, declared that the act of November 5, which "fell on the Allied governments a little like thunder from a clear sky," nevertheless "did us a great service in relationship to the Western governments."[15]

At best, supporters of the Entente admitted that "it is not possible for a European liberal to be an admirer of Russia," but warned that the minority nationalities must not deceive themselves by seeking freedom and unity from foreign hands.[16] According to one pro-Russian observer, Kucharzewski's line of advocating independence without leaning on one or another warring camp now proved to be the most successful. "Founded on barely more than a utopia," this program was in the best position to exploit the new situation. Kucharzewski soon left Switzerland to work in Poland, leaving La Pologne et la Guerre to the direction of the historian Szymon Askenazy.[17]

Socialist circles in Switzerland generally treated the proclamation of the Polish Kingdom with scorn. Robert Grimm set the basic tone in declaring, "There can be no more horrible deception for Polish nationalists than this manner of 'resolving' the Polish question." Poland would probably receive Prince Leopold of Bavaria as its king and thereby become essentially a German province. The Germans and the Austrians

14. HHSAr, PA, XXVII/56/Ber/89 and 97.
15. Dmowski, *Polityka polska i odbudowanie Panstwa* (Warsaw, 1926), p. 242. Cf. "Das polnische Königreich und die Polen. Unterredungen mit polnischen Politikern in der Schweiz," *Neue Zürcher Zeitung*, Nov. 11, 1916.
16. Georges Lorand, "Aux amis de Russie," *Journal de Genève*, Jan. 25, 1917.
17. See memorandum by Ts. Ianushovskii, May 14/27, 1917, OAr, IIf, f. 21; Askenazy, *Uwagi* (Warsaw, 1924), pp. 81ff.

sought only "cannon fodder . . . The new petty kingdom [*Zaunkönig-reich*] of Poland by the grace of the Habsburgs and Hohenzollerns is a further bloody satire of the 'liberating mission' of the predatory imperialist states which now have waged war with each other for two and one-half years."[18]

In Paris, *Nachalo* described the proclamation as being "permeated with fear of the vitality of the Polish nation" and as "a deception in relation to the aims of this nation." Mensheviks in Switzerland noted that the Entente powers, who had most loudly advocated "the liberty of nationalities," had as yet said nothing about Poland. Germany had now shown itself to have more initiative and daring, to be more ready to break with the past. The proclamation therefore represented a "very great moral blow" to the Entente. The Poles, however, had still received nothing.[19]

According to the Bund, the proclamation had the "mark of a vulgar, naked deception." No small state could hope for real independence under such circumstances; Poland's future in fact still depended on the course of the war. Nevertheless, the proclamation had a historical significance for the proletariat. Without giving anything substantial to the Polish people, the proclamation brought a new complication, with new conflicts, into the international imperialist order. The proclamation would probably only sharpen national antagonisms within Poland, and the "Polish ruling classes" could be expected to intensify their oppressive policies toward the Jews. Speaking in Geneva, Kosovsky warned of "Polish anti-Semitism" and declared that Social Democrats must oppose the formation of new national states which would be only "new tools for national oppression."[20]

The proclamation succeeded in drawing together the two wings of the SDKPiL and the PPS-Lewica, which issued a joint declaration entitled "The 'Liberation' of Poland by the Central Powers." Poland, the declaration asserted, had been "degraded, under the pretext of liberation, to the role of a Senegal, providing Austria and Prussia with colonial regiments." Nevertheless, the Central Powers had dealt the Western democracies "a stunning moral defeat." Speaking in Zurich,

18. *Berner Tagwacht,* Nov. 6, 1916.

19. *Nachalo,* Nov. 8, 1916; *Izvestiia ZSOK,* Dec. 14, 1916.

20. Okhrana report no. 1293, Dec. 26, 1916/Jan. 8, 1917, OAr, XIIIb(1), 1916; *Berner Tagwacht,* Dec. 29, 1916.

Kon reiterated that the "liberation of Poland can be realized only by its toiling masses, and chiefly by its self-conscious proletariat." Radek denounced the proclamation as a "cynicism": socialists must oppose the formation of national states which would themselves only become imperialistic.[21]

The Central Powers received unreserved praise only from their allies and paid agents. The League of Alien Peoples of Russia publicly rejoiced: "Our plea to the President of the United States in May died away unheard. In vain we awaited an answer. But now from another side it is demonstrated that among the great powers humanity and justice still live, that the principle of national freedom, despite war and suffering, has not vanished from the earth." Voicing its congratulations to "you, the Polish people," the league proclaimed: "Remember the call directed to the president of our league, Michael Lempicki, at the Conference of Nationalities in Lausanne, 'Poland, lead on. We will follow.' "[22]

The Polish Press Bureau in Bern decried the protests against the proclamation, which "can mislead European public opinion." Poland needed the help of the entire nation. The "basically disapproving stand and exclusively negative view" of some circles showed only that these emigrés had lost touch with their homeland. On November 19, Stanislaw Zielinski organized a celebration in Rapperswil of Poles from German-speaking Switzerland. Besides depositing a wreath at the mausoleum of Tadeusz Kosciuszko, the gathering expressed thanks to Switzerland for its hospitality.[23]

However happy Berlin's Polish friends might have been, however, the proclamation only brought new problems to Romberg in Bern. On the one hand, his Ukrainian and Lithuanian friends began to raise difficult questions about German intentions toward their nations, and on the other, Berlin, paying more serious attention to the nationalities of Russia, began to challenge the work of Romberg's agents.

Stepankowski summarized the impact of the proclamation as an enormous political gain for Germany. It had brought disarray among the Russians; both Toporov and Sviatkovsky agreed that the Franco-

---

21. Okhrana report no. 1185, Nov. 23/Dec. 6, 1916, OAr, XIIIb(1); report of Nov. 14/27, 1916, OAr, XIX, f. 6; *Volksrecht*, Nov. 11, 14, 1916; Feliks Tych, *PPS-Lewica w latach wojny 1914–1918* (Warsaw, 1960), pp. 114–15.

22. *Internationale Korrespondenz*, Nov. 21, 1916.

23. *Der Bund*, Nov. 17, 21, 1916.

Russian alliance had been prejudiced by this development in the Polish question. The Entente powers, Stepankowski declared, had now changed their attitudes toward the Ukrainians and the Lithuanians. Germany and Austria must now supplement their proclamation on Poland with proclamations of Lithuanian and Ukrainian independence; such action was necessary in order to limit the scope and ambitions of "Polish imperialism." Gabrys informed Romberg that Sviatkovsky had advised his government to take some definite action on the national question.[24]

As early as August 1916, Gabrys had questioned Romberg about Germany's reported plans for Poland. The Lithuanians, he warned, viewed the idea of Polish independence with suspicion. In November, Gabrys apparently inspired press reports protesting both the proclamation on Poland and the recruitment of Lithuanians for the German armed forces.[25]

When Gabrys published a pro-Russian declaration by Yčas, Romberg protested, but Gabrys insisted that his compatriots had forced him to do so. Schubert attempted to assure the Lithuanian that the boundaries of the new Polish state would remain open, and he told Berlin that the Lithuanians in Switzerland could probably be satisfied by "very vague promises which say nothing." Romberg and Schubert nevertheless found it impossible to deliver even these small crumbs, and in February 1917, von der Ropp reported that Gabrys was very disappointed by German inaction on the Lithuanian question. At the same time, von der Ropp expressed the dilemma of the Germans as he complained about the necessity of always seeming "to conspire with these national enthusiasts."[26]

The decision of the League of Alien Peoples to open an information bureau in Bern brought a whole new battery of problems for Romberg. Von der Ropp and Uexküll, after considerable effort, obtained permission from the Austrian government for Dontsov to leave the Dual Monarchy for Switzerland. In Bern, friction immediately developed between Dontsov and Stepankowski. The league had directed Dontsov to handle the financial affairs of the new bureau, but Stepankowski and Romberg complained that Dontsov should know as little as possible

24. AAM, T120/4820/L243316, L243321.
25. AAM, T120/4820/L244900; *Rech'*, Dec. 9, 1916; *Kievskaia Mysl'*, Nov. 13, 1916.
26. Correspondence in AAM, T136/22.

about the connection between the league and the German mission in Bern. Somehow or other, the Germans wanted to believe that Dontsov knew nothing of Romberg's relationship with Stepankowski and that Stepankowski knew nothing of the relationship between the League of Alien Peoples and the Auswärtiges Amt. (Von der Ropp told Gabrys that the league received its funds from the German industrialist Albert Ballin and not from the German government.)

Uexküll explained that the league, and its sponsor the Auswärtiges Amt, could no longer put up with the sloppy financial records and profligate ways which had thus far marked the work of Stepankowski and Gabrys. Romberg replied that the Bern mission provided more money to the league's office than did Berlin; in any case, Gabrys seemed to be the one who could not keep his books straight, not Stepankowski. Romberg finally won the argument, since Dontsov only directed publications and Stepankowski handled the money.[27]

The appearance of the first issue of Dontsov's new publication, *Bulletin of the Nationalities of Russia,* brought a storm of protests from Berlin. Lempicki had had his doubts about putting Ukrainians in charge of the Bern office, and the Auswärtiges Amt now reported, "Our Poles are *furious* about the compilation of Polish reports and they even demand that the league officially deny that it has any connection with this *Bulletin.*" The report on Lithuania, moreover, was "much too pro-Russian," the printing was bad, and the newspaper was generally "uninteresting." Uexküll warned the German mission, "It serves no purpose to expend any work and funds on such a sheet."[28]

In anguish, Romberg wrote directly to the Chancellor, defending both Stepankowski and Dontsov. Dontsov, he asserted, had understood that he was to have a free hand in his editorial policies; the task of the journal certainly did not lie in just adding to the "countless" Polish publications already in circulation. Von der Ropp and Uexküll simply understood nothing of the problems of propaganda work in Switzerland.[29] Again Romberg emerged victorious as the Germans continued to support the publication until March 1917.

Another target of bitter criticism from Berlin was Gabrys's work in

27. See Romberg's summary, Oct. 11, 1916 and his dispatch, Nov. 28, 1916, AAM, T136/22.
28. AAM, T120/5224/K490001.
29. Romberg to Berlin, Oct. 11, 1916, AAM, T136/22.

preparing the full protocol of the Conference of Nationalities. On September 10, Wesendonck singled out the grant of 20,000 marks to Gabrys as an especially dubious venture. Von der Ropp even dispatched a letter to Gabrys by diplomatic pouch, declaring that the work on the protocol had dragged on for so long that it had no more interest. He directed Gabrys to stop the project and to return the advance which he had received. Uexküll complained to Schubert that the league could not continue "to give out money in Gabrys's gallop tempo," and Arthur Zimmermann informed Romberg of his own view that Gabrys's work was too "costly."[30]

Romberg and Schubert both protested against these attacks, and the mission even refused to deliver von der Ropp's order that Gabrys stop work on the protocol. Gabrys in fact claimed to have spent the entire advance, and he now requested another 15,000 to 20,000 francs of the Germans. He attributed the delay in publication entirely to the fact that the Estonian delegate to the conference, his old antagonist Keskūla, had not yet delivered the text of the Estonian statement. Romberg defended Gabrys against all the charges; he insisted that the Lithuanian had put a great deal of time into his work, he had allegedly received an offer of 10,000 francs per month to relocate his work again in Paris, and the Auswärtiges Amt should take note of the high costs of printing in Switzerland. Romberg argued that Gabrys had provided the Germans with valuable service virtually without personal profit, because he believed that Germany would determine Lithuania's future.[31]

In the fall of 1916, both Uexküll and von der Ropp visited Switzerland to investigate the situation. Stepankowski and Gabrys, with Romberg's assistance, succeeded in justifying themselves and in convincing the Germans of the value of their work. In Gabrys's case, Uexküll agreed to the request for another 20,000 francs, but since the league lacked funds itself he could only give an indefinite promise. Romberg, meanwhile, obtained permission from the Auswärtiges Amt to give Gabrys the money from his own secret fund. The league was to know nothing of this subvention.[32]

Romberg had become generous to a fault in his support of Russian emigrés. In August 1916, when a Russian Socialist Revolutionary,

30. Wesendonck to Warburg, Sept. 10, 1916, von der Ropp to Gabrys, Oct. 4, 1916, and Uexküll to Schubert, Oct. 9, 1916, in AAM, T136/22; Zimmermann to Romberg, AAM, T120/4820/L245030.

31. Romberg's letters of Oct. 11, 13, Nov. 28, 1916, AAM, T136/22.

32. Romberg to Berlin, Nov. 28, 1916, AAM, T136/22.

Alexander Evgenievich Tsivin (Zivin), came to him with a recommendation from the Austro-Hungarian military attaché, Romberg immediately took up his cause. For about a year, Tsivin had cooperated with the Austrians. He had visited prisoner of war camps with the aim of recruiting agents for work in Russia, but because of a lack of time, he had had to give up the project. He nevertheless claimed to have sent other agents into Russia for purposes of antiwar propaganda.

The Austrian High Command had now decided, however, that Tsivin's work had shown insufficient tangible results, and it refused to support him any longer. The Austrian mission in Bern lacked funds of its own to maintain him, and Tsivin claimed to find himself in an awkward situation. In expectation of financial aid, he had entered into new obligations. He was considering moving to Sweden, but he preferred to remain in Switzerland.

Tsivin made "a not unfavorable impression" on Romberg. He argued that his party sought the quickest possible end to the war so that it could put its revolutionary program into effect. He claimed to have a well-functioning organization which he did not want to dissolve. He asked Romberg only for a visa to travel to Scandinavia, but when the diplomat asked how much money he needed, he replied 25,000 francs, to cover the expenses of the next month. (The Austrians had given him 140,000 francs in eleven months.)

In relaying this request to Berlin, Romberg declared, "I do not know whether we have connections with the Russian socialists, and I am therefore not in a position to judge whether a connection with M. Tsivin would be desirable." Nevertheless, he requested authorization to give Tsivin money on a probationary basis: "It would certainly be a pity if the whole apparatus which has been built up with Austrian funds were to be wasted and not used."[33]

Tsivin had already drawn the attention of Okhrana agents, who had reported his dealings with the Austrians. A member of the Socialist Revolutionary Committee for Intellectual Aid to Prisoners of War in Austria and Germany and a member of the editorial board of *Na Chuzhbine,* Tsivin may have been one of the two unidentified Socialist Revolutionaries who attended the Kiental conference.[34] Tsivin stood in

---

33. AAB, Wk 11c geh., Bd. 15. Romberg's report reprinted in Z. A. B. Zeman, *Germany and Revolution in Russia 1915–1918* (London, 1958), pp. 18–23.

34. He may have been the man whom the Austrian military attaché in Bern claimed to have sent as his agent. See Clemens von Walzel, *Kundschaftsdienst oder Spionage?* (Leipzig, 1934), p. 102.

the inner circles of the local party groups, but he undoubtedly overestimated his own importance in telling Romberg that in the party hierarchy he was second to Natanson.

The Auswärtiges Amt accepted Romberg's recommendation, and in the next three to four months Tsivin received a total of 100,000 francs in support of his efforts. Although some historians have attempted to depict him as an important agent, possibly even as one who gave Romberg entry into Leninist circles, in fact the Socialist Revolutionary emigré offered Romberg little more than fragmentary reports on events in Russia, combined with intelligent speculation and interpretation. Romberg's reports to Berlin gave no indication that Tsivin had offered information about emigré groups other than the Socialist Revolutionaries.

After many delays, Tsivin travelled to Scandinavia in January 1917, allegedly to set up a network for communications between Russia and Switzerland. All parties concerned agreed that his mission was a failure. The Auswärtiges Amt cut off his pay, asserting that he had failed to demonstrate any really worthwhile activity. Tsivin apparently decided then that he had been asking for too little. He returned to ask Romberg and Schubert for from 450,000 to 500,000 francs with which to carry out a revolution in Russia in April. Schubert declared that there was little possibility that the Auswärtiges Amt would agree, but, impressed by the scope of Tsivin's plan, he asked Berlin to verify whether the Socialist Revolutionary Party was really so strong as Tsivin claimed, whether Russia was indeed experiencing a serious strike movement, and whether the Socialist Revolutionary movement was in fact directed from Switzerland.

After the collapse of the Tsarist government in March, Romberg resumed payments to Tsivin, giving him at least 60,000 francs more. Nevertheless, Tsivin represented no significant change in Romberg's basic concern with the nationalities of Russia rather than with the socialist emigrés. Romberg could show very little for his investment in this case, and the main thrust of his work remained directed toward the national question in Tsarist Russia.[35]

By the fall of 1916, the Entente agents in Switzerland had also turned their attention to the national question. The League of Alien Peoples, and indirectly the German mission, suffered a demoralizing blow in

35. See AAB, Wk 11c geh., Bd. 15–19.

November when first the Swiss press, and subsequently the British and French press, carried reports that von der Ropp had spoken critically of the German military and demeaningly of the Kaiser during a speech in Zurich. He had reportedly declared that Hindenburg "outshines William as the sun outshines the moon." Hindenburg, he asserted, held the real reins of power in Germany.

The ensuing scandal threatened the existence of the league. Von der Ropp had repeatedly made clear his own dislike of the military leadership, and now the High Command inquired of the Auswärtiges Amt whether von der Ropp had really spoken so "disagreeably" about the army. Von der Ropp vigorously denied the report, and in Switzerland Romberg eventually attributed the whole incident to an intrigue by Sviatkovsky. Von der Ropp, in the company of Stepankowski, had met the Russian agent in November, and Sviatkovsky had apparently decided to upset the league's work.[36]

The league in turn scored a small success when the Russian Duma excluded Lempicki from its membership on the charge of cooperating with the Germans. D. Z. Manuilsky rose to Lempicki's defense, describing in emotional terms Lempicki's decision to remain in Poland in 1915, "in his own land, among the ravaged, hungry population." While declaring that he did not mean to attack or to defend Lempicki's political activities, Manuilsky directed his comments against the Russian liberals, accusing them of hypocrisy in the national question.[37]

By the time of the revolution in Russia in March 1917, Romberg's network of informants was beginning to feel great strains. So long as Berlin had no definite policy toward the national question in Eastern Europe, Romberg had had a considerable freedom of action. Now his freedom was limited; the emigrés were posing demands which he could not hope to meet. His effort to work with Tsivin had been a fiasco. On the other hand, he was always ready to follow up any new and promising lead.

36. AAM, T120/4820/L243364.
37. *Nachalo,* Jan. 28, 1917.

16

Splitting the Swiss

In the fall of 1916, as the national question in the Tsarist Empire expanded to new dimensions, Lenin alone among the Russian socialist émigrés demonstrated fresh initiative. He had internationalized Russian socialist politics by his attacks on the Mensheviks at Kiental; he had developed his own activity on the international level by challenging Grimm's leadership of the International Socialist Commission; now he carried his offensive into the ranks of the Swiss Socialist Party. He had long advocated splitting; under the banner of the Zimmerwald Left, he proceeded to organize an anti-Grimm faction within the Swiss Socialist Party.

However disorganized the Zimmerwald Left may have been, it still constituted a stronger force than any other Russians could exercise. According to Martov, the Menshevik groups in Switzerland now lay in a state of disarray: "In Geneva our people expect nothing, since the party is negligible, torn by internal struggle."[1] Attacked by the Bolsheviks, by the *Vperëd* group, and by *Nashe Slovo*, the Mensheviks had trouble even in organizing meetings.

To a degree, developments in the emigré colonies in London and Paris served to demoralize the emigrés in Switzerland. In July 1916 British authorities announced their intention to deport all Russian citizens of military age who refused to enlist in the British army and who could not prove that they were political emigrés. The fact of being Jew-

---

1. *Pis'ma P. B. Aksel'roda i Iu. O. Martova* (Berlin, 1924), p. 357.

ish would not of itself constitute proof of being a political emigré. A storm of protests arose, denouncing the plan as being aimed primarily against the Jews. In the words of the *Manchester Guardian* of July 28, this action would "tear up by the roots the proud British tradition of offering asylum."

Reports reaching Switzerland spoke of 25,000 Jews in London being put under police surveillance and facing the decision whether to enlist or to accept deportation to Russia. The Russian government could thereby expand its army at the same time that it undermined its political opposition. Protest meetings asked for aid from Swiss socialists and denounced the subservience which the Western powers seemed to be showing toward Russia.

Still more disturbing came the news that on September 15, French authorities had suppressed *Nashe Slovo* on the charge of inciting mutiny among an expeditionary force of Russian soldiers in southern France. At the same time, the French government ordered Trotsky's deportation. After some talk of possibly reviving the paper in Switzerland, the emigrés in Paris began the publication of *Nachalo* (*The Beginning*) on September 30. The connection between the two papers was unmistakable, as the editor of *Nachalo*, V. N. Meshcheriakov, shared an apartment with Dridzo-Lozovsky, the former editor of *Nashe Slovo*.

For six weeks Trotsky fought the deportation order, seeking at least the opportunity to go to Switzerland. The Swiss government refused, however, at first saying that the French had not explicitly ordered him to Switzerland. Trotsky bombarded Grimm and Riazanov with telegrams, and Grimm carried his protest directly to the Swiss Foreign Office. For a time, success seemed at hand, but the Swiss consul in Paris continued to refuse the visa, declaring that he was acting on orders. At the end of October, French authorities expelled Trotsky to Spain, and from there, after renewed efforts for a Swiss visa had failed, Trotsky made his way to the United States.[2]

Grimm called the Swiss government's inaction "a brutal violation of the rights of asylum." The Swiss authorities, he asserted, recognized that "Comrade Trotsky is a very respectable person," but they had submitted to diplomatic pressure: "If now the government of so great a state as

2. Leon Trotsky, *My Life* (New York, 1960), pp. 252–57; Isaac Deutscher, *The Prophet Armed* (New York, 1965), pp. 238–41; Okhrana report, Oct. 21/Nov. 3, 1916, OAr, XVIIc, f. 2.

France has yielded to the pressure of Russia, then Switzerland cannot resist." The affair, he concluded, inevitably shed a new light on the discussions of Swiss national defense.[3]

Lenin took virtually no note of Trotsky's misfortune, or even of the action of the Swiss government. Lenin's writings of this period and his published correspondence recorded nothing of these events, as he continued only to attack Trotsky as a "Kautskyite." The supression of *Nashe Slovo*, however, removed one of Lenin's sharpest critics from the political arena. Besides the Mensheviks, only the *Vperëd* group remained, and Lenin summarily dismissed Manuilsky and Lunacharsky as a "public without a head."[4] The Swiss socialist movement seemed to occupy more of his attention at this moment than did the Russian.

The Swiss Socialists had now begun a bitter debate on the question of national defense. The Kiental conference had called for the denial of all military credits in the warring countries; could a Swiss adherent of the movement tolerate Swiss militarism? As some questioned whether Switzerland could maintain its neutrality, others raised the idea of disarmament, arguing that if attacked, Switzerland in any case could not defend itself.

Lenin urged his followers to oppose both the idea of "defense of the fatherland" and the idea of disarmament, which he called a pacifist and a "papist" slogan.[5] In July, while Lenin was on vacation, Platten, Nobs, and Kharitonov carried the offensive into a conference of the Socialist Party of the City of Zurich, criticizing the actions of Socialist deputies in the Nationalrat. Nobs introduced a resolution demanding that the next party congress consider the question of defense, the military budget, and demobilization. Platten offered another resolution directing the deputies from Zurich to form a unified and determined front, and Kharitonov added an amendment specifically calling for the faction to adhere strictly to the decisions of the Zimmerwald and Kiental conferences.

Grimm, who represented Zurich in the Nationalrat, responded that the faction in fact represented the indecision and confusion which permeated the party. In response to Platten's resolution, he argued that only a national party congress could commit the deputies on issues of national significance, and he warned, "Radicalism by the leaders, from which

3. *Berner Tagwacht,* Nov. 4, 1916.
4. *PSS,* 49:317.
5. M. M. Kharitonov, "Iz vospominanii," *Zapiski Instituta Lenina,* 2:136–37.

the masses are not capable of drawing the consequences, has no worth." Nevertheless, the Zurich city party organization, on July 24, endorsed both Nobs's and Platten's resolutions, together with Kharitonov's amendment.[6]

Grimm threw his personal prestige into the battle by threatening to resign, even though almost all concerned had attempted to make clear that the resolution had not been aimed at him personally. On September 11 the city leadership, the Vorstand, singled out Grimm as the deputy best representing the views of Socialists in Zurich. On September 14 Grimm, Nobs, and Alfred Bucher (a member of the Jungburschen, the Vorstand, and the Kegelklub), agreed on the need for a new orientation in the program of the Socialist Party and called for a discussion of the question of defense of the fatherland.

Despite Grimm's victory, however, the radical tone in Zurich continued to grow. On August 1, Münzenberg's youth group, the Jungburschen, came to blows with the Zurich police. Against the advice of the leadership of the Socialist Party, the youths then scheduled mass protest demonstrations throughout Switzerland on September 3. These, however, passed generally peacefully, as the Bundesrat debated deporting Münzenberg.[7]

When Lenin returned to Zurich in the middle of September, the Zimmerwald Left displayed new energy. Lenin's work, particularly with Münzenberg's group, exhilarated him. As he wrote to Inessa Armand, "Here we have just begun to become a bit acquainted with the youth, and we regret very much that we have no full control of a single language."[8]

For the youth, anarchism and disrespect for authority was a tradition, and they delighted in embarrassing older socialists who dared to address them.[9] Lenin disapproved of the group's anarchism, which he attributed to Brupbacher, but he welcomed their youthful enthusiasm. For their elders who might have similar views he had only scorn; with the Jung-

---

6. Unless otherwise noted, all references to the meetings of the Socialist Party of the City of Zurich or of its leadership, the Vorstand, are taken from the manuscript protocols of the party, to be found in Zurich.

7. See Markus Mattmüller, *Leonhard Ragaz*, 2 vols. (Zurich, 1957–1968), 2:187–88. Zurich police officials found no Russian influences behind the demonstrations. See the reports in ZStAr, P239.13.

8. *PSS*, 49:295.

9. See W. Münzenberg, *S Libknekhtom i Leninym* (Moscow, 1930), pp. 36ff.

burschen he was ready to sit and argue. The youth in turn felt flattered:
"He took us young people seriously."[10]

The Zimmerwald Left in Zurich regarded *Volksrecht,* edited by Ernst
Nobs, as its organ. In later years, Nobs repeatedly denied that he had
been a member of the Zimmerwald Left and that Lenin had had any
influence on the newspaper's editorial policies. He even claimed to have
rejected an article by Lenin. Nevertheless, the Zimmerwald Left expressed itself through the newspaper, and *Volksrecht* played an important role in Lenin's offensive against Grimm and the national leadership
of the Swiss Socialist Party. Nobs himself seemed to go along with the
left in the summer of 1916—he had in fact voted with Lenin at Kiental—but there is no evidence that he belonged to the inner circle of
Lenin's supporters. By 1917, he already stood among Lenin's major
opponents.[11]

For Lenin, the military and national questions were the most important of the day. When the Bolshevik Party's new publication, *Sbornik
Sotsial'demokrata,* appeared in October, it carried articles by Lenin on
both subjects.

In discussing national self-determination, Lenin argued that wars of
national liberation must yet be considered progressive and that even
Europe, under certain circumstances, could still see legitimate national
wars. National repression, however, would only end with the victory of
socialism. While both the Dutch and the Polish Marxists were among
"the best revolutionary and internationalist elements in international
Social Democracy," they had proven unable to rise in theory above the
"specific conditions" of their own "small and helpless" countries. Radek's
interpretation of the Irish rebellion as an urban, petty bourgeois putsch
was "monstrously doctrinaire and pedantic." Nevertheless, the Dutch
and the Poles, Lenin added, were more sincere and "closer to us" than
those "who recognize self-determination hypocritically and wordily as
Kautsky among the Germans and Trotsky and Martov with us."[12]

10. See Ferdinand Böhny, "Die sozialistische Jugendbewegung des Ersten
Weltkrieges als politischer Faktor," *Der öffentliche Dienst VPOD,* Nov. 20, 1964.
11. See Ernst Nobs, "Lenin und die Schweizer Sozialdemokraten," *Rote Revue*
33:49–64; Willi Gautschi, *Der Landesstreik 1918* (Zurich, 1968), pp. 53, 55–56;
Bericht Brunner, p. 34; Fritz Brupbacher, *Zürich während Krieg und Landesstreik*
(Zurich, 1928), pp. 57ff.; Münzenberg, *S Libknekhtom i Leninym,* p. 107.
12. "O broshiure Iuniusa," and "Itogi diskussii o samoopredelenii," *PSS,*
30:1–58.

Turning to the military question, Lenin explained that while socialists favored disarmament in a socialist society, the slogan of disarmament in a capitalist society constituted only a deception. Such a call is tantamount to abandoning class struggle and renouncing revolution: "Only after the proletariat has disarmed the bourgeoisie will it be able, without betraying its world historical mission, to consign all armaments to the scrap heap." As a positive program for Switzerland, he proposed the formation of "voluntary military-training associations" of perhaps one hundred members, "with free election of instructors paid by the state."[13]

In order to reach a German-speaking audience in Switzerland, Lenin also prepared a German text of his article on the military question, modifying it only slightly. Although the work reached print only in the fall of 1917, it nevertheless reflected Lenin's concerns in October 1916 about the development of a Swiss following. He also spent time studying Swiss history and considering how to exploit the Swiss institutions of initiative and referendum to advance the cause of social revolution.

The assassination on October 21 of the Austrian Prime Minister, Count Stürgkh, by the Austrian Socialist Friedrich Adler aroused a new storm of ideological declarations among the Russian emigrés as well as among socialists in general. As Radek noted, Western and Central European Social Democrats, since the days of the First International, had opposed the tactic of political assassination. Terror alone could not alter the existing political structure of capitalism. Like most other emigrés, Radek declared of Adler, "We would follow him in his burning devotion to the cause, in the spirit of sacrifice, but not in the method, which does not lead to the goal."[14]

Lenin viewed the act as the result of desperation on Adler's part, stemming from his inability to win a significant internationalist following within the Austrian Socialist Party. As his own philosophy, Lenin declared that although "we are *not at all against* political killing," he considered "individual assassinations inexpedient and harmful as a revolutionary tactic." Such individual action was useful only in the context of a mass movement. Adler should better have turned to "illegal propaganda and agitation," even at the cost of splitting his party.[15]

With the Swiss Socialist Party's annual congress scheduled for Zurich

13. *PSS,* 30:151–62.
14. "Zimmerwald und der politische Terror," *Berner Tagwacht,* Oct. 26, 1916.
15. *PSS,* 49:311–14.

on November 4 and 5, Lenin prepared in the same way as he had for Zimmerwald. On the eve of the meeting, he met with the Swiss party's left wing, including Platten, Nobs, and Münzenberg. On the afternoon of Saturday, November 4, even after the congress had opened, Lenin met again with Münzenberg's youth group, to whom Radek presented the resolution of the Zimmerwald Left on the Nationalrat faction. The group accepted the resolution and carried it into congress. At the same time, however, friends of Grimm attended the meeting, uninvited. When informed of the proceedings, Grimm publicly complained about foreign intervention in the affairs of the Swiss party.[16]

Both Radek and Lenin attended the congress as foreign observers. When the Zimmerwald Left opened its offensive against the Nationalrat faction, Herman Greulich sarcastically commented that Grimm spent so much time answering complaints from Zurich that he often missed important votes: "If you send a radical delegation to Bern, then it can happen that at a crucial moment they are playing Jass or else at a bowling alley (*Kegelbahn*)." (The reference to Jass, a card game, was apparently directed toward Platten.) Grimm took a middle position, dissociating himself from Greulich's attack on the "Kegelklub of the radicals" but claiming that the Zurich resolution in fact criticized just such action for which it praised Liebknecht. Naine, in turn, noted the initiative of the youth: "One can rejoice that the young generation brings new ideas; they must also choose their parliamentary representatives from those who share their new ideas."

Nobs and Platten seem to have received the most enthusiastic applause from the delegates. Platten insisted that the party's deputies should demand "the unconditional rejection of all military requests." This would show the military that it had to deal "not just with a parliamentary opposition but with the utmost resistance of the masses."

Ultimately, the congress unanimously adopted an amended version of the Zurich resolution. The text criticized the lack of discipline within the Socialist faction of the Nationalrat and promised that the local party organizations hereafter would propose as candidates for the Nationalrat only those who "pledge themselves to act in parliament in the spirit of party decisions." Grimm called the resolution in essence a collection of

16. See *PSS*, 49:318–19, 322–23. On Lenin's lobbying, see Jacques Schmid, *Unterwegs 1900–1950* (Olten, 1950), pp. 90–91.

banalities. The congress made no statement on Kiental or on the question of national defense; the party scheduled a special congress to meet in February 1917 to discuss problems arising from the war.[17]

Lenin felt that the work of the congress had gone satisfactorily. In addressing the group himself, he had hailed the Swiss party for earning an attack from the Danes on the charge of having fostered "pernicious splitting activities" within the International. (Despite the variety of attacks on it, the Swiss Socialist Party stood alone as the only official party to endorse the Zimmerwald manifesto at a party congress.) Splitting, Lenin pointed out, was a phenomenon occurring within virtually all major socialist parties.[18]

The Swiss themselves completed a major split at Zurich by declaring that membership in the Grütliverein (Grütli Society) was incompatible with membership in the Swiss Socialist Party. Founded in 1838 and at one time the dominant element in the organization, the Grütliverein had taken a defensist attitude toward the war. Now the party was to have no autonomous units, but when the Zurich faction offered a new party statute, the congress voted instead to entrust a seven-man commission with the task of preparing recommendations on party statutes for another meeting.

The one point of the Leninist program which seems to have entered the final decisions of the congress lay concealed in a resolution offered by Nobs expressing solidarity with political prisoners in various warring countries, including the Bolshevik Duma deputies, Karl Liebknecht, Rosa Luxemburg, and Fritz Adler. In its conclusion, the resolution called upon the party leadership to organize "mass collections of money for the support of the struggle of socialists against the war." As Lenin had earlier noted, "If twenty thousand Swiss party members contributed two centimes weekly as a sort of 'extra war tax,' we would receive twenty thousand francs annually, more than enough . . . to publish periodically in three languages and distribute among the workers and soldiers of the belligerent countries the whole truth about the incipient revolt of the workers."[19]

In all, the party congress exuded an entirely new spirit; in Grimm's

17. *Berner Tagwacht*, Nov. 6, 7, 1916; *Protokoll über die Verhandlungen des Parteitages vom 4. und 5. November 1916* (Lucerne, 1917).
18. *PSS*, 30:180–83.
19. *Berner Tagwacht*, Nov. 6, 1916; *PSS*, 30:143.

words, "fresh life pulsates in the party." At the same time, however, Grimm expressed considerable concern about the tendencies within the group. Naine had already noted the role of a younger generation; now Grimm commented, "The party comrades must undertake to think themselves, instead of allowing others to think for them."[20]

Lenin intensified his work among the Swiss in the weeks after the congress, but he apparently found his work frustating at times. As a group, the Swiss hesitated to oppose Grimm: "It is difficult for them, since everything is explicitly a war with Grimm, and they have too little strength. We will wait and see." The key issue in the months to come lay in the decision of the party congress to hold a special meeting on the military question. Lenin's followers demanded the immediate convening of the session. The party leadership, now supported by Nobs, hesitated, fearing that the Swiss workers harbored patriotic feelings and that only the Grütliverein could profit by a public debate of the question at just this time.[21]

In a series of theses under the title "Tasks of the Left Zimmerwaldists in the Swiss Social Democratic Party," Lenin declared that the Swiss government was completely dependent on the "bourgeoisie of the imperialist great powers." Should Switzerland enter the war, the proletariat must not "defend the fatherland"; it should accept arms but turn them against its own bourgeoisie. To expose the costs of war, socialists must oppose all proposals to establish indirect taxation; they must propose progressive property and income tax scales. A maximum salary must be set for all salaried employees and officials.

Socialists should exploit the parliamentary institutions of Switzerland to advance the cause of social revolution, not to "advocate reforms 'acceptable' to the bourgeoisie." Women should receive complete political equality with men. Every foreigner should become a Swiss citizen after living in the country for three months and at no cost: "the disfranchisement and alienation of foreign workers serve to increase political reaction, which is already mounting, and weaken international proletarian solidarity."

The party should organize a broader campaign for publishing revolutionary literature and should expand its propaganda among the military. It should "create a united internationalist trend among the German,

20. *Berner Tagwacht,* Nov. 7, 1916.
21. *PSS,* 49:324; Mattmüller, *Ragaz,* 2:191.

French, and Italian workers of Switzerland," who were being increasingly exploited by the Swiss bourgeoisie.[22]

The theses, which Lenin circulated in eleven typescript copies, had their own fate. Lenin sent a French text, prepared by Inessa Armand, to Guilbeaux for publication in western Switzerland. In 1917 Swiss authorities seized it when they arrested Guilbeaux. Fritz Brupbacher later declared, "We Communists will take it into our hands after the conquest of power and we will present it as our first gift to the Soviet Republic."[23]

Lenin's Swiss followers proved incapable of absorbing all his teachings. At one point he complained, "I think Switzerland must have bacilli of petty bourgeois (and petty state) stupidity, Tolstoyism, and pacifism, which destroy the best people. It really must!" Describing a session with the Zimmerwald Left, he exclaimed, "These conversations made it especially clear to me: (1) how devilishly weak the Swiss left are (in *all* relations); (2) how bad Bronski's and Radek's system is in writing about the left in other countries."[24]

Lenin's cooperation with Radek at the Swiss party congress had not meant a complete reconciliation between the two. The echoes of his earlier conflict continued to ring in his writing and correspondence throughout the winter of 1916–17. His reconciliation, he insisted, had served a useful purpose in the campaign of the Zimmerwald Left against Grimm. His disagreement with Radek, in any case, had not been a total one, but only in a "specific sphere," that of Russo-Polish affairs and the problem of *Kommunist*, which he called "group stupidity." Lenin still considered Radek either a fool or a scoundrel, or possibly both. All that their common front at Zurich represented, he explained, was that "I succeeded in separating the questions—this was not easy; the international onslaught against the Kautskyites (including Grimm) is not weakened by an iota and at the same time I have not been subjected to 'equality' with Radekist stupidity."

Lenin viewed his alliance with Radek and the Zimmerwald Left as "a conditional thing." In no way would he allow himself to be controlled by any group: "We had to take what was necessary from Radek and E. B.

22. *PSS*, 30:196–208, 376–79.
23. Fritz Brupbacher, "Lenins Eingabe um Aufenthaltsbewilligung in Zürich," *Die Aktion* 18:121. See also Heinz Egger, *Die Entstehung der Kommunistischen Partei der Schweiz* (Zurich, 1952), pp. 80–85.
24. *PSS*, 49:341, 352.

and Co., without allowing our hands to be tied. I think that I succeeded."
Even in the winter of 1916–17, Lenin charged that Radek and Bukharin
were still following "the true policy of riff-raff and scum; impotent to
argue with *us* directly, turning to intrigues, fouls, and infamy."[25]

There were times when Lenin's troubles seemed to weigh even more
heavily on him. A threatened scandal about financial matters in Bern
shocked him, and in a letter to Inessa Armand, he paused to reflect on
the past: "Look at my fate. One militant campaign after another—
against political stupidities, banalities, opportunism, etc. This since 1893.
And the hatred of the vulgar people in payment. But I still would not
exchange this fate for 'peace' with the vulgarizers."[26]

At the beginning of 1917, Lenin seemed both physically and emotion-
ally tired. He refused an invitation to lecture in Geneva: "I am not well,
my nerves are not good. I *am afraid* of lectures." In February he wrote
to Armand, "I am tired of meetings; my nerves are weak, my head aches;
I am absolutely tired."[27]

When the Zurich youth group invited Lenin to address it on the anniversary of Bloody Sunday in Russia, Lenin prepared a detailed account
of the revolution of 1905. He even practiced delivering the talk in German. In its concluding comments, his reflective and even depressed
mood manifested itself. Declaring, "We must not be deceived by the
present grave-like stillness in Europe," he reiterated his confidence in
the coming of revolution. Nevertheless he identified himself with an older
generation: "We old people may not live to see the decisive struggles of
this coming revolution. But I can, I believe, confidently express the hope
that the youth which is working so splendidly in the socialist movement
of Switzerland and of the world will be fortunate enough not only to
fight, but also to win, in the coming proletarian revolution."[28]

Lenin's pauses for reflection, however, did not dull his campaign
among the Swiss. In preparation for the planned Swiss party congress in
February, he worked with Bronski and Platten to prepare theses on the
military question in Switzerland. When the Swiss party's Central Com-

25. *PSS*, 49:330–33, 341. See also Semkovsky's criticism of Lenin and Radek
in *Izvestiia ZSOK*, Dec. 14, 1916.

26. *PSS*, 49:340.

27. *PSS*, 49:361, 383. See also G. Zinoviev, "Die Ankunft Lenins in Russland," in Fritz Platten, ed., *Die Reise Lenins durch Russland im plombierten
Wagen* (Berlin, 1924), p. 68.

28. *PSS*, 30:327–28.

mittee, on January 7, 1917, decided to postpone the special congress, Lenin's anger knew no bounds: "That villain Grimm, at the head of all the rightists, carried through the decision (against Nobs, Platten, Münzenberg, *and Naine*)."[29]

Lenin now turned his attention to the Socialist Party of the City of Zurich. Bronski, Platten and Bucher served as his agents, but he ran afoul of Nobs, who put the unity of the party above the interests of the Zimmerwald Left. As president of the Zurich party organization, Nobs effectively blocked and even nullified Lenin's tactical maneuvers.

Lenin, to be sure, won the first battle, when at the beginning of January Platten and Bronski came to Nobs to urge a meeting of the full membership of the city party organization to consider President Woodrow Wilson's recent declarations on the problem of European peace. Nobs agreed that the problem was urgent, and at his insistence the Vorstand, which included Bucher, agreed to hold the meeting on January 5. Platten was to offer a report on "The Proletariat and the Peace Notes."

Although called on very short notice, the meeting drew a large audience. When Platten had finished his talk, Bronski took the floor with a prepared resolution. The diplomatic maneuvering, he argued, had actually expanded the arena of the war, and neutral countries such as Switzerland faced the danger of being drawn into armed conflict. The Swiss Socialists must therefore move quickly to declare themselves on fundamental issues of war and peace. The workers must declare that they want a "party of struggle and not an electoral apparatus which is ready when necessary to work for the interests of the ruling classes."

Bronski's resolution came out against national defense and criticized the central party leadership for its delays in considering the military question. After a heated debate, the assembly endorsed the resolution by a vote of two hundred seventeen to three, with almost half of those present abstaining.[30]

A storm immediately broke over the heads of the Vorstand and of Nobs personally as unhappy party members even charged that the Vorstand had called the meeting under false pretenses, intending all along to pass a resolution on questions not specifically included in the agenda. The Vorstand responded with a declaration asserting that it had had no

---

29. *PSS,* 49:357.
30. See Mattmüller, *Ragaz,* 2:192; manuscript protocol of the meeting, Socialist Party of the City of Zurich.

intention of sponsoring a discussion of the military question, but that any party assembly had the full autonomous right to take a stand on any question, whether or not it had a place on the prepared agenda. To clarify its position, the Vorstand established a special commission to examine the question of whether either Nobs or Platten had acted improperly. In a general meeting on February 6, Nobs read the Vorstand's declaration—which Bronski criticized as senseless. On February 27, the special commission reported that it had found no evidence of wrongdoing; Bronski called the commission's report "comical."

Bronski now became the focus of the struggle between Lenin and the regular party leadership. (Bronski had gained considerable note in Zurich through his work in the Eintracht Society and through his lectures to youth groups.) On January 15, the city Vorstand adamantly rejected a request by the remnants of the Eintracht group that it sponsor a special seminar by Bronski. Only Bucher supported the request.

Bucher gained national note by initiating a petition calling for a party congress in April. Grimm angrily warned the comrades in Zurich against becoming "knowing or unknowing tools" of a "clique." Lenin countered by charging that at the Central Committee's meeting of January 7, Grimm had shouted "the most vile things against the 'foreigners,' against the *youth*, accusing them of a split and so on." Grimm, he declared, was "playing a disgraceful, unscrupulous game."[31]

Lenin pressed his Swiss supporters to break openly with Grimm. At a meeting early in February, in Münzenberg's apartment, Platten still hesitated, while Münzenberg eagerly agreed. Eventually the group accepted Lenin's demand, and Karl Radek stayed up through the night writing an attack.[32] The Zimmerwald Left then carried its campaign back into the Zurich cantonal party organization, which held a special congress of its own on February 11 and 12, 1917, but Lenin found that his task was just as frustrating as before. Nobs and Platten, he complained, were frightened by Grimm, and they in turn "frightened our young ones": "Such warriors! Such leftists!" The Swiss were "almost hopeless."[33]

Alfred Bucher represented the Zimmerwald Left at the cantonal party

31. See *Berner Tagwacht*, Jan. 22, 1917; *PSS*, 30:286–95, 49:358–60; Rudolf Martin Hogger, *Charles Naine* (Zurich, 1966), pp. 159–60; *Bericht Brunner*, p. 33.
32. Münzenberg, *S Libknekhtom i Leninym*, p. 139.
33. *PSS*, 49:373, 380, 383–84.

congress, offering a resolution obliging the Socialist parliamentary deputies to oppose all military requests and credits and to demand demobilization of the armed forces. The resolution added a call for the support "of all revolutionary movements and struggles against the war and against one's own government in all warring countries." Within Switzerland, the party should put all its effort into organizing "revolutionary mass struggles" aimed at the "socialist reorganization" of the country.

Platten spoke in support of the resolution, declaring that Switzerland was in fact too small to be able to defend itself if war came. When an opponent of the proposal raised the question of what would happen if revolution occurred in Russia and the German army intervened on behalf of the Tsar, Bronski shouted, "Then we would transplant the revolution to Germany." The assembly rejected the resolution by a vote of eighty-two to thirty-two.[34]

Lenin suffered a more serious setback in the defeat of Bronski's candidacy for membership in the city Vorstand. At a general city meeting on February 6, Nobs had called for the election, and Bronski had been nominated from the floor. In the vote which immediately followed, Nobs received the most votes, Bucher the second most, and Bronski, too, won a place on the nine-member executive group. Four of the winners, however, immediately declared their refusal to serve with Bronski. Although Bucher claimed that their action was indeed aimed against him— he offered to resign—Bronski loftily dismissed the squabble as being aimed not against him personally but against the political program which he represented. He insisted on his right to serve. Nobs eventually settled the argument by proposing to annul the election results and to hold a new ballot at a later meeting. The assembly concurred.

On February 19 the Vorstand met with its old membership. Nobs criticized Bucher's actions and explained that Bronski's supporters had used a "bullet ballot"; that is, that instead of voting for a full slate of candidates they had cast their ballots only for Bronski—and presumably Bucher. (This was not of itself unusual; the Jungburschen had apparently indulged in such practices before in order to elect Bucher.) Members of the Vorstand still expressed opposition to Bronski, but all agreed on holding another election, even at the risk that Bronski might again win a place.

On February 27, another general assembly of the city party organiza-

34. *Volksrecht*, Feb. 13, 14, 1917.

tion took up the election, and Bronski again was nominated from the floor. Speakers arose to attack him personally, but Bronski defended himself in his typical sarcastic fashion. This time, however, he failed to win a seat. Lenin and other members of the Zimmerwald Left could never forgive Nobs for his role in undoing their apparent victory.[35]

Despite such troubles, Lenin had succeeded in organizing a faction within the Swiss Socialist Party. This in turn served eventually as the seedbed of the Communist Party of Switzerland. Largely limited to Zurich, the group hesitated to move openly against Grimm; it refused to split with the party. Nevertheless it carried Lenin's ideas into the discussions of the party.

Some historians have attempted to argue that Lenin had despaired of ever returning to Russia and that he had turned to the Swiss left with the hope of winning himself a following and a home. Apart from his one call for less stringent conditions of citizenship, there is no indication that Lenin was ever concerned with such ideas. His work among the Swiss reflected rather his irritation and disgust with Grimm's control of the Zimmerwald movement; he had decided to carry the struggle into Grimm's own yard.

35. Cf. *PSS*, 49:383–84; Mattmüller, *Ragaz*, 2:193.

17

The Coming of Revolution

On March 13, 1917—February 28 by the Russian calendar—the Tsarist regime in Russia collapsed. Tsar Nicholas abdicated the throne, and his brother Michael refused to accept it. A Provisional Government, organized by the Progressive Bloc of the State Duma, formally assumed power in Petrograd, but at the same time, a Soviet, or council, of Workers' Deputies was formed by a group of socialist intellectuals and workingmen. Subsequently, as it added representatives of soldiers' and peasants' soviets, the Petrograd Soviet claimed to represent the working people of all Russia.

The relationship between the Provisional Government, led by the Kadets, and the Petrograd Soviet, dominated by Socialist Revolutionaries and Mensheviks, was an uneasy one. The socialists, convinced that their hour had not yet struck, insisted that the revolution had a bourgeois character; they could not participate in the Provisional Government. When a socialist, Alexander Kerensky, agreed to take the post of Minister of Justice, the leadership of the Soviet feared that the Provisional Government had in fact captured a hostage.

Among the major points of difference between the Soviet and the Provisional Government stood the question of their respective attitudes toward the war; closely related to this was the problem of their respective attitudes toward Russian political emigrés. As one of its first acts, the new government proclaimed a political amnesty. Bolstered by the return of political activists from Siberia, the Soviet opposed the intentions of the Provisional Government to continue the war effort. At most, in view of the presence of German troops on Russian territory, it could accept a defensive war, fought under the slogan of "No annexations and no indemnities," but at the same time the government should be seeking a general peace. The Provisional Government, both out of conviction and out of fear of reprisal from the other Entente powers, favored a continuation and even an intensification of the struggle. As part of this program, the government refused to do anything to facilitate the return of the political emigrés in the West who had taken outspoken positions against the war. Miliukov, now Foreign Minister, distrusted them.

In the first months of 1917, the emigrés had maintained and even intensified their old disputes. The most pressing topic of the day—before the Tsarist collapse—seemed to be a debate over the position to be taken toward an upcoming conference of socialists from the Entente countries. On February 1, Zinoviev, Radek, Martov, Manuilsky, Balabanova, and Grimm met in Bern to discuss the matter, and while they generally agreed that the Russian and Polish socialists should not attend the meeting, they could not draw up a manifesto on the question to which they could all subscribe.[1]

The defensists too had split over the appearance of a new publication, *Russkaia volia* (*The Russian Will*), edited by Amfiteatrov and supported by funds given by Protopopov, now Russian Minister of the Interior. (Protopopov had already been considering such a newspaper when he had travelled in Western Europe as a member of the Russian parliamentary delegation.) The combined Socialist Revolutionary and Social Democratic group in Zurich, which supported *Prizyv*, demanded Alexinsky's expulsion from *Prizyv*'s editorial board because of his cooperation in the publication of *Russkaia volia*.[2]

The emigrés found some cheer, on the other hand, in the arrest of Henry Bint, the Okhrana agent, by Swiss authorities. In the fall of 1916, the Swiss government had indicated that it would no longer tolerate the activities of foreign agents. The Federal Criminal Court (Bundesstrafgericht) announced, "The surveillance of foreigners by foreigners is subject to punishment."[3] Bint had made fourteen trips to Switzerland during the war, each trip lasting from four to fourteen days. Now, on his fifteenth trip, he became the first major victim of the Swiss crackdown.

Lausanne police arrested him on February 2, and investigation led to

---

1. Okhrana report, Feb. 24/Mar. 9, 1917, OAr, XVIb(2), 101; Henri Guilbeaux, *Du Kremlin au Cherche-Midi* (Paris, 1933), p. 127; *PSS*, 49:379.
2. Okhrana report, Jan. 28/Feb. 10, 1917, XVIb, f. 5.
3. *Der Bund*, Nov. 22, 1916.

further arrests of his resident agents in Zurich, Lausanne, and Geneva. For 150 francs a month each his agents had been providing him with police registration records of Russian emigrés in their cities. The Okhrana attempted to free Bint quickly through the intervention of the Russian mission in Bern, but when the Swiss discovered that they had deported Bint in 1903, they decided to hold him for having illegally entered the country.

The Okhrana then approached a Parisian lawyer, asking him, in the name of Bint's wife, to go to Lausanne. In 1916, Bint had begun to collect intelligence from within Germany; the Okhrana wanted him to confess only to having watched Russian emigrés. Swiss authorities would most likely simply deport him for such an offense.

Sitting in prison in Lausanne, Bint felt that his employers had deserted him. He was a veteran of the Franco-Prussian war of 1870 and he was now sixty-five years old; prison life wore heavily on him. On March 14, writing to his contact in the Okhrana office, he complained that six weeks had passed without any action: "I am sick." On March 17, he reported hearing "what a terrible thing" had occurred in Petrograd; the news had affected his health. On April 5, he protested against having a Parisian lawyer. This might prejudice his case, and the lawyer probably knew nothing of Swiss law. He again complained of sitting alone in jail and of stomach pains; day and night he lay on his bed; his captors, he said, had "no pity" for his age or for his suffering.

On April 12, a Swiss court released Bint on bond of 3,000 francs. He had only 2,500 francs with him; he requested money from Paris and borrowed 900 francs in the meantime from his Swiss lawyer. By the end of the month he had left Switzerland. When his case came to trial in May, he did not appear. To his dismay, the Swiss government kept the bail money.[4]

Bint reported reading of the revolution on March 17. The news of the events in Russia had crept slowly into Switzerland. After several days of confused, vague reports of civil disturbances, the picture became clear only in the course of March 15 and 16. On the fifteenth, the Russian mission in Bern publicly denounced the reports as fabrications. The newspapers of the sixteenth finally proclaimed the fact of Tsar Nicholas's abdication.

The news shocked the emigrés. Zinoviev in Bern first read of it in a

---

4. Bint's correspondence in OAr, IIIe, VIk, f. 6. See also Bint's file in the archives of the Swiss Fremdenpolizei, BBAr, Pd, Sch. 243.

newspaper: "My head spun in the spring sun. I hurried home with the paper, which was not yet dry. There I found already a telegram from Vladimir Ilich [Lenin], ordering me to come 'immediately' to Zurich." Lenin had received the news from Bronski, who had come to his apartment. Krupskaya described Lenin as breathless: "When Bronski had left and we had come to our senses, we went to the lake, where all Swiss newspapers were posted daily under a roof. Yes, the telegrams spoke of a revolution in Russia."[5]

Throughout Switzerland, local emigré colonies organized meetings. In Geneva some ten speakers, including Lunacharsky, Balabanova, Kon, and Sokolnikov, addressed an enthusiastic gathering which organized a bureau to prepare for the emigrés' return home. In a telegram to the Petrograd Soviet, the group demanded the immediate recall of the Russian consul in Geneva, Gornostaev. Swiss police responded by putting guards around the Russian consulate, Gornostaev's home, and even the Geneva office of the Bank of Petrograd. In Davos, the Russian consul organized a celebration with "members of the Relief Society and even ultraradical elements" although he privately declared his opposition to the revolution as representing a catastrophe for Russia.[6]

The emigrés now found the path through England and France blocked, however, and their feelings of frustration quickly grew as news came that defensists such as Plekhanov, Alexinsky, Fondaminsky, and Kropotkin were returning without difficulty. They had to consider other possibilities.

On March 19, the International Socialist Commission in Bern sponsored a meeting of Russian and Polish emigrés adhering to the Zimmerwald movement. At that time, Martov raised the possibility of travelling through Germany to Stockholm under an agreement whereby the Russian government would allow German civil internees to return home. After the general meeting, a smaller committee consisting of Martov, Natanson, Kosovsky, and Zinoviev formally approved this plan; the emigrés thereupon turned to the problem of seeking the agreement of the Provisional Government.[7]

5. G. Zinoviev, "Die Ankunft W. I. Lenins in Russland," and N. K. Krupskaya, "Aus der Emigration nach Petersburg," both in Fritz Platten, *Die Reise Lenins durch Deutschland im plombierten Wagen* (Berlin, 1924), pp. 59, 67.

6. See *Journal de Genève*, Mar. 25, 26, 1917; HHSAr, PA, XXVII/57/Ber/601.

7. See *PSS*, 49:406; *Leninskii Sbornik*, 2:385; Israel Getzler, *Martov* (Cambridge, 1967), pp. 147–50.

Proclaiming itself the "legal center of the entire political emigration in Switzerland," the Central Secretariat of Emigré Funds established a Central Swiss Committee for the Return of Political Emigrés to Russia, located in Zurich. The group included representatives of the League of Swiss Relief Societies, the Krakauer Verband, and the Vera Figner Committee, as well as representatives of party groups: The Bolshevik Central Committee, the Menshevik Organizational Committee, the Internationalist Socialist Revolutionaries, the Swiss Center of Socialist Revolutionary Patriots, the Central Bureau of the *partiitsy*, *Prizyv*, the Bund, *Vperëd*, *Nashe Slovo*, PPS-Lewica, both the Central Committee and the National Committee of the SDKPiL, the Swiss Center of Anarcho-Communists, the Armenian *Droshak*, and the Zionist Poalei-Tsion.

The Executive Commission of the Emigré Committee at first consisted of five members: Pinkus Iofe of the Central Secretariat of Emigré Funds, Ustinov of the Vera Figner Committee, Bagocki of the Krakauer Verband, Bolotin of the League of Swiss Relief Societies, and Semkovsky of the Organizational Committee. Bagocki served as secretary of the Executive Commission, and Semkovsky as the president. The commission subsequently coopted other members, including Balabanova, Kon, and Reichesberg.

On April 4, the Executive Commission directed a telegram to the Petrograd Soviet and to Minister of Justice Kerensky complaining that not one emigré had yet been able to return from Switzerland through England and France: "Weeks pass, months will go by, and the political amnesty remains for us a fiction." The only solution, the commission argued, lay in an agreement between Russia and Germany, modelled after agreements for the exchange of civilians made during the first months of the war: "We strongly ask for immediate, firm steps in this direction." On April 5 Axelrod, Lunacharsky, Martynov, Natanson, Riazanov, and others signed another telegram to Petrograd, affirming their personal support of the plan advanced by the Emigré Committee.

At the same time, the Emigré Committee experienced division within its own ranks. The defensists eventually split off to form their own organization, and the Bolsheviks began to question the committee's concern for winning the agreement of the Russian Provisional Government. Referring without name to the Bolsheviks, the Emigré Committee requested groups in Switzerland "not to bring disorganization into the matter of the return of the political emigration and to await the result of the steps taken by the Central [Emigré] Committee as the organ of the entire political emigration." The committee distributed application forms to all emigrés wanting to return to Russia, and it asked the Russian mission in Bern for aid in obtaining passports and funds. The mission promised to do what it could.[8]

The way through Germany opened up quickly. Grimm acted as the intermediary for the Emigré Committee in taking their request to the Swiss Foreign Minister, Hoffmann. After Hoffmann had spoken with Romberg, the Auswärtiges Amt in turn obtained the permission of the High Command, which had already discussed with Parvus the possibility of allowing Russian emigrés to travel through Germany. On March 26, Romberg received news of the approval of the idea.[9]

For the Auswärtiges Amt, the decision represented an effort to bring about a quick, separate peace with Russia. In Bern, Romberg received many unsolicited opinions opposing the idea, but he drew heart from Stepankowski's reports that the English were worried by the spirit of the emigrés. The Germans feared only that they might appear excessively enthusiastic about the plan and thereby undermine it.

Romberg passed on the news of the army's decision, but on April 3, he complained that no one had yet contacted him. He had been led to expect visitors several times, but the Russians seemed to be holding back, "apparently from fear of compromising themselves in St. Petersburg." In Russia, Miliukov had announced that any Russian citizens travelling through Germany would be subject to legal action.[10]

On April 4 Romberg finally received a visitor, Platten, who came on behalf of the Zimmerwald Left, "a number of the most prominent emigrés, twenty to at the most sixty persons." The group would accept any conditions which the Germans might pose, on the assurance that it could travel together without any hindrance. Romberg immediately requested authorization from Berlin, emphasizing that the German government here had a chance to show its "trust" in the Swiss Socialists by accepting "their guarantee as sufficient." On April 5, the Auswärtiges Amt reported the approval of the military.[11]

8. On the work of the Emigré Committee, see *Biulleten' ispolnitel'noi komissii,* Apr. 10, 1917.

9. See Werner Hahlweg, *Lenins Rückkehr nach Russland 1917* (Leiden, 1957), p. 67; Z. A. B. Zeman, *Germany and the Revolution in Russia, 1915–1918* (London, 1958), pp. 25–30.

10. Hahlweg, *Lenins Rückkehr,* pp. 76–77.

11. *Ibid.,* pp. 77–79; Zeman, *Germany and the Revolution,* pp. 35–36.

Despite the warnings of the Emigré Committee, Lenin had chosen to break with the united front and to push ahead on his own. Angelica Balabanova later speculated that Lenin's decision to negotiate directly with the Germans stemmed from his desire to win a tactical advantage over other emigré leaders.[12] For Lenin, however, the revolution in Russia represented only a "first stage," not an accomplishment. Also weighing on his mind must have been the memory that in 1905 he had been relatively slow in returning to Russia from abroad. He considered a number of alternatives for returning: attempting to fly over Germany, using another emigré's papers, and even travelling as a deaf and dumb Swedish sailor. (He dropped the last idea when Krupskaya warned him that he might fall asleep, dream of Mensheviks, and give himself away by screaming insults.) He rejected an offer from Parvus, arranged apparently through Hanecki and Bronski, for permission to travel through Germany by himself.[13]

Lenin enthusiastically endorsed Martov's proposal for an exchange between the German and Russian governments. On March 30 he declared that the "only hope to get out of here is an exchange of Swiss emigrés for German internees." On March 31, angered by the Emigré Committee's lack of progress, he announced his own readiness to act, and he invited any of his followers who wished to return to contact him.[14]

On April 3, meeting with Zinoviev, Platten, and Münzenberg in Zurich, Lenin decided to open direct talks with Romberg: "We unanimously came to the conclusion that Grimm was consciously blocking the speedy return to Russia of the Bolshevik group." Lenin declared, "We must go at any cost, even through hell." Münzenberg refused to serve as Lenin's agent because he himself was a foreigner in Switzerland, and, after some deliberation, Platten finally agreed to undertake the task. (From Platten's viewpoint, this involved a certain risk to his own position within the Swiss Socialist Party.) The group left immediately for Bern, where Grimm vainly opposed their initiative, but Lenin insisted all the more strongly.[15]

---

12. Angelica Balabanova, *My Life as a Rebel* (London, 1938), pp. 164–67.
13. On Lenin's considerations about returning, see *PSS*, 49:403ff. For a day-by-day account, combined with speculation, see Nicolaus Fritz Platten, "Von der Spiegelgasse in den Kreml," *Volksrecht*, serialized Mar. 15–Apr. 17, 1967.
14. *PSS*, 31:83–84; 49:418; *Leninskii Sbornik*, 2:376–77.
15. See Willi Münzenberg, *S Libknekhtom i Leninym* (Leningrad, 1930), pp. 147–48; Platten, *Die Reise Lenins*, pp. 28–29; M. M. Kharitonov, "Iz vospominanii," *Zapiski Instituta Lenina*, 2:144.

Platten's proposal to Romberg took upon himself all responsibility for the emigrés while in transit through Germany. Although Platten insisted that he was acting in a personal capacity, Romberg clearly identified his effort as having the backing of the Swiss Socialists. The train must enjoy extraterritorial privileges, Platten declared, and German authorities were to take no action toward any of the travellers. Platten agreed to pay regular prices for the train tickets. In a move to assure a seat for Radek, who was an Austrian citizen, Platten's proposal spoke only of "political emigrés and legals," without specifying nationality. Romberg ignored the omission but questioned the meaning of "legals." Platten's explanation that some emigrés had legitimate identification papers then satisfied him. The Germans agreed not to examine the list of names of the travellers.[16]

Now more than ever, Lenin insisted on maintaining the identity of the Bolsheviks as a distinct political force. On March 16 he declared, "All our slogans remain the same." The illegal organization of the party must continue. On March 17, he drew up a set of theses declaring that the Tsar had gone into hiding and speculating that "in order to deceive the people" the Tsar might yet emerge with a proclamation of a separate peace with Germany. The Provisional Government, Lenin asserted, could give Russia neither peace, bread, nor freedom; the revolutionary proletariat must continue the struggle for socialism; it must not yield to the new calls for national defense.[17]

Lenin demonstratively refused to appear on the same platform with Martynov of the Organizational Committee, in order to emphasize the fact that the Bolsheviks were by no means ready to gloss over past differences. When Lunacharsky once again came forth with a plan for the unity of all Russian internationalists, Zinoviev was inclined to accept the idea of a conference, but Lenin overruled him and rejected the idea.[18]

In a two and one-half hour speech in Zurich at the end of March, Lenin declared, "The transformation of the imperialist war into a civil war has begun." The worst thing anyone could do would be to support the new Russian government. Echoing his theses of 1915, he offered his

16. Platten, *Die Reise Lenins*, pp. 29–33.
17. *PSS*, 31:1–6, 49:399; *Leninskii Sbornik*, 2:319–23.
18. Kharitonov, "Iz vospominanii," p. 141; Vperiod Ar.; Yves Collart, "À propos de deux lettres d'Anatole Lounatcharski," in Jacques Freymond, ed., *Contributions à l'histoire du Comintern* (Geneva, 1965), pp. 135–39.

own terms for an end to the war: the renunciation of all secret treaties and their publication, a proposal for an immediate armistice, freedom for all colonies and oppressed peoples, a declaration of distrust of all bourgeois governments together with an appeal to the working class for the overthrow of these governments, and a proposal that the capitalists alone pay the war debts. Such peace proposals could then justify a "revolutionary war," in which "we could count on the help of the revolutionary proletariat."[19]

Just before leaving Switzerland, Lenin published his "Farewell Letter to the Swiss Workers," wherein he took a parting shot at those who complained of the "unwholesome effect" of foreigners in the Swiss workers' movement. Hardly more than ten or fifteen Swiss Socialists, he noted, had joined the ranks of the Bolsheviks, but these had struggled not only against social patriotism but also against the "so-called center." He praised the "brave, youthful vanguard." Now he had to leave for Russia, where the Russian proletariat faced the task of "beginning a series of revolutions." His words to the Swiss, he hoped, would pass on to the Germans, the French, and the Italians.[20]

The final days before departure saw hurried preparations and strenuous efforts to win a degree of international backing. Zinoviev urged Karpinsky in Geneva to seek the support of French and Swiss intellectuals for Lenin's decision to travel through Germany. The Bolsheviks considered declarations of support from French internationalists to be especially important.[21] Romain Rolland, however, warned that the Bolsheviks were risking becoming "the instruments of the enemy."[22]

Among the Russians, Lenin particularly regretted that he could not win Lunacharsky's support. As late as February 1, in *Vperëd*, Lunacharsky had attacked him, but after hearing the news of the revolution, the *Vperëd* group had decided to seek unity with the Bolsheviks. Lunacharsky, however, expressed concern because the Germans had granted transit "even too enthusiastically," and he vainly advised Lenin to wait for another two weeks for a statement from Petrograd.[23]

19. *PSS*, 31:72–78; *Volksrecht*, Mar. 31, Apr. 2, 1917.

20. *PSS*, 31:87–94; Platten, *Die Reise Lenins*, pp. 7–13.

21. *Leninskii Sbornik*, 2:380–81; Henri Guilbeaux, *Vladimir Il'ich Lenin* (Leningrad, 1925), pp. 157–60.

22. Guilbeaux, *Lenin*, p. 160; Romain Rolland, *Journal des années de guerre* 1914–1919 (Paris, 1952), pp. 1129–30.

23. Rolland, *Journal*, pp. 1139–40; Vperiod Ar.; Kharitonov, "Iz vospominanii," pp. 144–45.

In the night of April 6 and 7, in Radek's quarters in Bern, Lenin met with Guilbeaux, Zinoviev, Armand, Paul Levi, a German, and Fernand Loriot, a French Socialist, to draw up a protocol explaining and justifying the return through Germany. Summarizing the entire course of the negotiations on the return of the emigrés, the document insisted that the Provisional Government planned to allow no internationalist emigrés to return to Russia. Therefore the transit through Germany remained the only possible course for a quick return. Having reached agreement with the Germans, the Bolsheviks had vainly invited other groups to join them. The protocol concluded with a declaration of support for the Bolsheviks' decision, asserting, "The Russian comrades have not only the right but the obligation to exploit this opportunity to return to Russia which has been offered them." The signatures, many of them by proxy, included Guilbeaux, Bronski, Platten, Burgomeister Lindhagen of Stockholm, and Ture Nerman.[24]

Platten had obtained permission for sixty emigrés to make the trip. In the end, only thirty-two went. The participants signed a declaration accepting the conditions agreed upon by Platten and Romberg, agreeing to follow Platten's directions during the journey, and acknowledging that they knew of the opposition of the Russian government toward the venture. The signers included Lenin, Krupskaya, Zinoviev, with his wife and son, Sokolnikov, Kharitonov, Mikha Tskhakaia, and Olga Ravich. Radek made the trip without signing the declaration.[25]

The travellers met for lunch on April 9, Easter Monday, at the restaurant Zähringerhof in Zurich. By midafternoon, when the group assembled in the Bahnhof, the presence of some one hundred curiosity seekers, friends, critics, and secret agents contributed to a generally chaotic scene. One emigré, Oscar Blum, was forcibly removed from the train after Lenin and Zinoviev had challenged his presence. At 3:10 the train pulled out; it passed over the Swiss frontier at Gottmadingen that same evening. With only minor incidents, the Russians passed through Frankfort, Stuttgart, and Berlin on their way to Sweden, where the German government had assured their safe entry. Officials at the Russian frontier eventually refused entry to Platten, who returned to Switzerland, and Lenin arrived at the Finland Station in Petrograd on April 19.[26]

24. *Leninskii Sbornik,* 2:383–93; Guilbeaux, *Lenin,* pp. 161ff.
25. *Leninskii Sbornik,* 2:405–6.
26. See the descriptions of the departure in Hahlweg, *Lenins Rückkehr,* pp. 96–98; Platten, *Die Reise Lenins,* pp. 33–35; Kharitonov, "Iz vospominanii," p. 145;

The subsequent polemics surrounding Lenin's trip lie rather beyond the boundaries of this study. The legends of Lenin's activities in Switzerland began to grow in the summer of 1917, and Alexinsky had already laid the groundwork for the charge that Lenin was working as a German agent. Yet another important factor in the picture—all too often ignored —was the fact that many Western diplomats, and indeed many intelligence agents, first learned Lenin's name on the occasion of his departure from Switzerland. For them, Lenin's name was associated with the Germans from the beginning. An investigation conducted by the emigré groups themselves, on the other hand, concluded that Lenin could only be accused of breaking the united front of the emigrés in dealing with both Petrograd and the Germans.[27]

The Executive Commission of the Emigré Committee in Zurich strongly criticized Lenin's trip. In a meeting on April 11 and 12, a plenary session of the committee approved the Executive Commission's work and labelled Lenin's group "an insignificant part of the emigrés." At the same time, the group also criticized the decision of the defensists to act by themselves.[28]

The defensists organized a committee in Bern, headed by M. Idashkin and Anton Savin. Something of a plebiscite among the Russian socialist emigration ensued as the Zurich and Bern groups competed in soliciting applications for return from the emigrés. According to the last published figures, 226 emigrés sent their applications for return to Russia to the Bern defensist group, while 692 sent theirs to Zurich.[29]

In the middle of April, the emigrés finally became convinced that there was no hope of winning Petrograd's agreement to their return. On April 16, news came of a "clarification," on the part of the Russian Ministry of Foreign Affairs, of the problem of political amnesty and of the return of political emigrés. All former regulations on the issuance of passports and visas were now nullified; missions had orders to grant visas to all emigrés wanting to return. For the emigrés in Switzerland, the regulation had no significance, as French authorities refused admission into France even to Russians with valid passports unless they could prove their

A. Charasch, "Lenins Abreise von Zürich," *Neue Zürcher Zeitung,* Apr. 13, 19, 1921.

27. See the historiographical discussions in Hahlweg, *Lenins Rückkehr.* The protocol of the emigré investigation in IISH.

28. *Biulleten' ispol. kom.,* Apr. 15, 1917.

29. *Ibid.,* May 30, 1917.

loyalty to the Entente cause. The Russian mission in Bern also announced that because of an "interruption of communications between England and Norway at the present time," the passage to Russia was closed.

On April 20, Miliukov publicly admitted that the Allied Powers had a control list which included the names of "those emigrés whose return to Russia is considered undesirable by one of the belligerent powers or by all allied governments together." On April 22, the Emigré Committee finally received a statement directly from Miliukov, saying that he considered "the passage of emigrés through Germany in exchange for civil German internees to be impossible." The committee, noting the arrest in England of Trotsky, Zurabov, and Chudnovsky, denounced Miliukov's statement as "direct treason toward the political emigration."[30]

On April 16, the committee had formally delegated Robert Grimm to travel to Petrograd to present its demands directly to Kerensky. Two days earlier Grimm, supported by Hoffmann, had inquired of Romberg about the possibilities of travelling through Germany. As his purpose he offered the two ideas of facilitating the return of emigrés to Russia and of sounding out the views of the Russian government toward peace, "if possible, giving us his impressions through the Swiss legation in Moscow." Romberg recommended approval of the request: "He can do no damage on the military side, and he may be decidedly useful politically." The German government first approved the request and then attempted to withdraw its approval—in Berlin's eyes, Grimm was probably more dangerous than Lenin—but Romberg had already notified Grimm that permission had been granted.[31]

The emigrés apparently knew nothing of Grimm's diplomatic mission. On April 20, a gathering of Mensheviks in Bern insisted that Grimm should deal only with the Petrograd Soviet and that his specific purpose should be only to win permission for Zimmerwald emigrés to pass through Germany.[32] Grimm left Bern that same day, having been promised that a Russian visa awaited him in Stockholm. Upon his arrival in the Swedish capital on the twenty-fourth, he discovered that the Russian government had not yet acted. Even the direct intervention of the Petrograd Soviet failed to produce the visa, and Grimm remained in Sweden until he was joined by another group of Russian emigrés.

---

30. *Ibid.,* Apr. 28, 1917.
31. Zeman, *Germany and the Revolution,* pp. 47–49.
32. AAM, T120/4818/L243999; Platten, *Die Reise Lenins,* pp. 44–46.

On April 27, the Menshevik Foreign Secretariat requested permission of Romberg for its five members, "together with their associates," to return to Russia "under the same conditions as Lenin's group." On April 30, Platten visited Romberg and hinted that the Russians might welcome discreet financial support in their efforts to return.[33] The German government granted permission to travel, but it apparently gave no financial assistance for the journey. (The Austrians, however, may have.)

So far as the Emigré Committee was concerned, the Mensheviks' initiative represented the "first party of emigrés" to be sent home. Hans Vogel, of the Swiss Socialist Party, agreed to accompany the new group, and he made the necessary arrangements with Romberg, modelled after Platten's agreement and signed on April 30. On May 11, the Zurich Socialist Party held a formal farewell dinner for the travellers in the Eintracht restaurant. Lang, Greulich, and Platten spoke; on behalf of the Russians, Martynov, Manuilsky, and Balabanova responded with great emotion. On May 12, the group departed Zurich. On May 18, with Grimm in their ranks, they crossed the Swedish-Russian frontier. Among the passengers in this second trainload were Martov, Natanson, Lunacharsky, Balabanova, and Manuilsky.[34]

On May 25, the Emigré Committee announced plans to organize another trainload of emigrés. This group left Zurich on June 20 and arrived in Russia ten days later. According to the records of the Emigré Committee, the train of May 12 had 257 passengers, including 58 Mensheviks, 48 Bundists, 34 Socialist Revolutionaries, 25 anarcho-communists, and 18 Bolsheviks. Twenty-two passengers were "wild," that is, without party affiliation, and 12 were classified as not being emigrés. The second trainload of June 20 had 206 participants, including 29 Mensheviks, 25 Bundists, 27 Socialist Revolutionaries, 26 anarcho-communists, 22 Bolsheviks, 19 "wild," and 39 non-emigrés.[35]

The relations between the remaining emigrés and the Russian mission in Bern progressively deteriorated throughout the summer of 1917. A scandal surrounding Grimm's efforts to act as a channel of communications between the Russian and the German governments led not only to Hoffmann's resignation as Swiss Foreign Minister and Grimm's ex-

33. Zeman, *Germany and the Revolution*, pp. 51–53.
34. *Biulleten' ispolnitel'noi komissii*, May 30, 1917; Ernst Nobs, "Lenin und die Schweizer Sozialdemokraten," *Rote Revue* 33:51–52; *Neue Zürcher Zeitung*, May 12–14, 23, 1917.
35. *Biulleten' ispoln. kom.*, June 30, 1917.

pulsion from Russia, but also to the casting of a new shadow over the emigration.[36] The emigrés themselves expressed concern about revelations in the files of the Foreign Agency of the Okhrana, then being examined by a special committee. The refusal of the Russian mission in Bern to permit the emigrés the use of diplomatic channels to communicate with the investigating committee in Paris contributed to the tensions.

Oddly, although the Okhrana had long since ceased to function, Henry Bint received his last payment, 2,680 francs, on September 7, 1917. This money covered even payments to Bint's agents while they sat out their four-month jail sentences in Switzerland. In the Russian service since 1880, Bint, in the meantime, had offered his services to the committee investigating the Okhrana's work.[37]

With the departure of socialist leaders such as Lenin and Martov, the emigration in Switzerland quickly lost the importance which it had enjoyed since 1914. In Bronski's words, "Switzerland's monopoly in the free expression of revolutionary thoughts was ended by the February revolution in Russia."[38] Even the Zimmerwald movement left the country, as Stockholm quickly replaced Zurich and Bern as the center of communications for international socialism and even of diplomatic and political intrigue.

36. On the Grimm affair, see Platten, *Die Reise Lenins,* pp. 44–55; Fritz Fischer, *Griff nach der Weltmacht* (Düsseldorf, 1964), pp. 504–7; *Zimm. Bew.,* 1:573–644.

37. OAr, VIk, f. 8.

38. M. Bronskii, "Uchastie Lenina v shveitsarskom rabochem dvizhenii," *Proletarskaia revoliutsiia,* 1924, no. 4, p. 39.

Epilogue

Seven months after his departure from Switzerland, Lenin stood at the head of a revolutionary government in Russia. To a degree, his rise to power repeated his remarkable rise to leadership within the Zimmerwald movement. Upon his arrival in Petrograd, he appeared to be an extremist out of touch with Russian conditions. As the spring and summer wore on, the political center of gravity veered to the left; Lenin stood ready. Many of his former opponents in the emigration fell in behind him, and the new government, established in November 1917, included a number of them: Trotsky as Commissar of Foreign Affairs, Lunacharsky as Commissar of Education, Sokolnikov-Briliant as the head of the delegation entering into peace talks with the Germans at Brest-Litovsk. Antonov-Ovseenko, one of the founders of *Golos,* led the Bolshevik attack on the Winter Palace; the Rumanian Rakovsky served first in the Ukraine and subsequently in the Soviet diplomatic service.

When the Communist, or Third, International formally came into existence in 1919, it too drew heavily on the former emigration: Zinoviev, Manuilsky, Dridzo-Lozovsky, Bukharin, and even Balabanova. Łapiński, Bronski, Warski, and Walecki all worked in the Communist Party of Poland. The heritage of the Zimmerwald Left was evident in the work of Platten, Münzenberg, and Radek. (Platten was credited with thwarting an assassination attempt against Lenin in 1918.)

Of all the emigrés, Lenin stood out as the one who most successfully exploited his wartime opportunities in Switzerland. Before 1914 he had had no significant foreign audience; by 1917 he had a band of followers from a number of countries. In March 1917 that following still constituted perhaps only a trend; since the Bureau of the Zimmerwald Left had not met for over a year, one hesitates to speak of a formal organization. Nevertheless, the core of the Third International existed.

On the whole, the months following the March revolution in Russia brought disappointment and frustration to most Russian political emigrés in Switzerland. Whereas their comrades in Siberia had been able to return to European Russia immediately, the emigrés found themselves still isolated. The new government did not want them; Russian foreign policy showed no change. Lenin's uncompromising stand loomed more and more as the major alternative, and many of his erstwhile opponents began to come into his camp.

To be sure, the Bolshevik revolution, too, disappointed some of its supporters. For one, Lenin abandoned the idea of revolutionary war, which he had advocated in his theses of September 1915, and instead advocated preserving the gains of the revolution in Russia by making a separate peace with Imperial Germany. He justified his position by arguing, as he indeed had predicted, that the revolution would not sweep Europe in a single wave. Having won in Russia, the revolution needed yet to develop and ripen in other countries. Even longstanding members of the Bolshevik party complained that this constituted a departure from Lenin's call for the conversion of the imperialist war into a revolutionary war, but the interest of the new Bolshevik government in its own survival prevailed.

Ultimately, many of the emigrés found that the revolution could even turn against them personally. At least ten persons who returned with Lenin through Germany in April 1917 fell to the Stalinist purges of the 1930s. The purges struck such major figures as Bukharin, Radek, Trotsky, and even Platten and Zinoviev.

The mosaic of emigrés in Switzerland during World War I also provided leadership for other new governments in Eastern Europe. Felikss Cielens, head of the Latvian group in Bern, served as Foreign Minister of Latvia; Juozas Puryckis, a priest studying in Fribourg, served as Foreign Minister of Lithuania; Gabriel Narutowicz, a professor at the ETH in Zurich, became Poland's first elected president, only to be assassinated a few days later. Erasmus Piltz, Roman Dmowski, and Jan Kucharzewski all played important political roles in postwar Poland.

At the same time, of course, many emigré leaders could not find a place in the new order. Among them were Martov, Axelrod, and even Alexinsky. In an ironic turnabout, Miliukov became a leader of the postrevolutionary emigration. The men who sought power through cooperating with the Germans also met with disappointment. Kesküla resigned from the German service in 1917 and sought to work with Entente agents; he eventually returned to Switzerland. In 1919 Gabrys denounced the new government of Lithuania as a German puppet, and he spent most of the rest of his life in Switzerland.

For the Swiss, the experiences of the First World War brought a turning point in their policies of granting asylum. In the last year before the war, the attention of the political police had begun to turn toward espionage; during the war, faced by a flood of refugees, the government found it necessary to tighten both the conditions for admitting foreigners and the surveillance of alien residents. *Überfremdung,* the danger of being inundated by foreigners, had been a major issue in prewar Switzerland, but now the problem seemed even more acute.

At the same time, the emigration left another mark in the presence of Russians, for example, on Swiss university faculties—Reichesberg in Bern, Manuel Zaitsev in Zurich, and Jean Hersh in Geneva—or even in the government—Jacques Dicker and Valentin Gitermann.

Relations between the Bolshevik government and the Swiss government reflected no romantic illusions about Lenin's years of asylum, particularly after the assassination of a Soviet diplomat in Lausanne in 1923 at the hands of an anti-Bolshevik Russian emigré. Only toward the end of the 1960s did both sides become rather sentimental. The celebration in 1970 of the hundredth anniversary of Lenin's birth gave rise to a campaign by the Soviet government to persuade various Swiss communities to commemorate, in some fashion, Lenin's sojourns within their boundaries. The enthusiastic response which some of these communities gave would have certainly amazed the Bolshevik leader.

Note on Sources

In view of the transitory and unstable character of emigré life, the materials for studying the emigrés' activities are remarkably plentiful. To a certain degree, this may result from the literary talents and ambitious natures of the emigrés. The activists necessarily left a record of their work. On the other hand, the emigrés' role in wartime politics opened a diplomatic dimension which their life had normally lacked in other periods.

As an introduction to the study of the life of the emigrés, we have several useful and interesting works: Jan Meijer's pioneer study of student life in Zurich in the 1870s, *Knowledge and Revolution: The Russian Colony in Zurich, 1870–1873* (Assen, 1955); E. H. Carr's account of the emigrés' personal problems in his *The Romantic Exiles* (London, 1933); and Joseph Conrad's novel *Under Western Eyes.*

In preparing this study, I have relied mostly on archival materials. Prime among them are the archives of the Russian secret police. The Tsarist government showed its concern for the activities of political emigrés by establishing, in Paris, a branch of the secret police, the so-called Foreign Agency (Zagranichnaia agentura) of the Okhrana. Operating from the basement of the Russian consulate, the agency conducted intelligence work throughout Europe and even in the United States, concentrating on the terrorist elements among the Socialist Revolutionaries. During the First World War, the Okhrana employed five cover agents among the emigrés in Switzerland, and these reported to their supervisor, Captain Boris Vitalevich Likhovskoi. Another agent, Jean Henry Bint, a private detective in Paris, maintained a parallel network of informants among local officials in Switzerland. Like any historical documents, the Okhrana reports contain gross errors as well as valuable information; the user must exercise care. Nevertheless, the archive, held by the Hoover Institution in Stanford, California, is indispensable for serious research on the Russian revolutionary movement before 1917. The best introduction to the archive remains the work of the commission appointed by the Russian Provisional Government in 1917: Valerian Konstantinovich Agafonov, *Zagranichnaia okhranka* (Petrograd, 1918).

The files of the German Auswärtiges Amt have been picked over by historians again and again, and yet there always seem to be new materials to be found. Among the most important publications of German documents from these files are Werner Hahlweg's *Lenins Rückkehr nach Russland 1917*

(Leiden, 1957), André Scherer and Jacques Grunewald, *L'Allemagne et les problèmes de la paix* (Paris, 1962), and Z. A. B. Zeman, *Germany and the Revolution in Russia, 1915–1918* (London, 1958). Fritz Fischer's massive *Griff nach der Weltmacht* (Dusseldorf, 1964) still represents the most comprehensive secondary presentation of the materials, although Fischer's interest in the activities of the Russian emigrés was only incidental to his greater interest in German politics. I have relied mostly on the records of the German mission in Bern. The microfilmed records, however, contain only selections of certain important dossiers; the interested historian must also consult the original documents in Bonn.

The Austrians, too, watched the Russian emigrés with considerable interest, as can be seen in the Haus-, Hof-, und Staatsarchiv in Vienna. The East European Research Institute, Philadelphia, Pennsylvania, holds copies of Austrian diplomatic and police documents pertaining to the Ukraine, and many of these have been reproduced in Theophil Hornykiewicz, ed., *Ereignisse in Ukraine 1914–1922* (Graz and Philadelphia, 1966–68).

The files of the Swiss Fremdenpolizei, contained in the Bundesarchiv, Bern, are remarkably thin. One can read in the Okhrana files, however, the comment that the Swiss apparently found little to complain about in the activities of the emigrés from 1914 to 1917. After the revolution in Russia, the Swiss began to pay considerably more attention to their visitors from the East. On the other hand, there is much to be found in local archives. I found it particularly informative to study the files of the Fremdenpolizei of the canton of Zurich and the archives of the University of Zurich, both held by the Staatsarchiv in Zurich, and also the records of the Zurich city administration, in the Stadtarchiv of Zurich. The protocol books of the Socialist Party of the City of Zurich were also extremely informative.

Other governmental archives were not so useful. I found little for these years in either the United States National Archives or the British Public Records Office. The French worked closely with the Okhrana, and Alexinsky apparently served as an advisor on Russian affairs in Paris.

Turning to archives of individuals and organizations, we find them scattered throughout Europe and the United States. In some cases, seemingly unrelated collections prove to be in fact parts of one original whole. Such is the case, for instance, with the archive of the Liga Schweizerischer Hilfsvereine für politische Gefangene und Verbannte Russlands, held by the International Institute of Social History, Amsterdam, and with the Isaac Biske papers, in the Nicolaevsky collection of the Hoover Institution. The former collection has mostly documents from 1914 and 1915, while the latter has corresponding documents for 1916 and 1917.

The International Institute of Social History has done all interested historians a great service with its publication of documents from the archives of Robert Grimm, Ernst Nobs, Paul Axelrod, and others, in Horst Lademacher, ed., *Die Zimmerwalder Bewegung*, 2 vols. (The Hague, 1967). Since the collection, however, reproduced no documents written in Russian, the specialist must still make his way to Amsterdam to examine the archives for himself.

Another important repository for specialized documents is the Schweizerisches Sozialarchiv in Zurich, which has a small file once belonging to the Eintracht Society, as well as the extensive archive and papers of Fritz Brupbacher.

The archive of G. A. Alexinsky, held by the Russian Archive of Columbia University, provides very useful material for studying the first year of the war, including wartime correspondence with Mussolini, Rubakin, Plekhanov, Stravinsky, Gorky, and Manuilsky. The archive also contains most of Alexinsky's own wartime publications, together with the basic documentation for various of the charges which he levelled against other Russians.

Other useful personal archives which I have consulted include the papers of Alexander Keskula (Yale University), Auguste Forel (Bibliothèque cantonale et universitaire, Lausanne), Robert Herron (Hoover Institution), Louis Lochner (Wisconsin State Historical Society, Madison), Jurgis Šaulys (University of Pennsylvania Library, Philadelphia), and Juozas Gabrys (in the possession of Dr. Albertas Gerutis, Bern, Switzerland). I want to make special mention here of the very large collection of papers of Edmond Privat, in the possession of the Bibliothèque de la ville, La Chaux-de-Fonds, Switzerland.

Among the most useful published collections of documents, besides those already mentioned, were Olga Hess Gankin and H. H. Fisher, *The Bolsheviks and the World War* (Stanford, 1960); Georges Haupt, *Correspondance entre Lenine et Camille Huysmans 1905–1914* (Paris, 1963); Leonhard Haas, *Lenin: Unbekannte Briefe, 1912–1914* (Zurich, 1967); and Jules Humbert Droz, *Der Krieg und die Internationale* (Vienna, 1964).

Any study of this sort has to rely also on the emigrés' own publications. I have examined the following Russian periodicals published in Switzerland and Paris: *Biulleten' ispolnitel'noi komissii* (1917), *Biulleten' izdavaemyi ob"edinennymi gruppami PSR* (1916), *Biulleten' zagranichnogo komiteta Bunda* (1916), *Borotba* (1915–16), *Golos* (1914–15), *Golos zarubezhnogo studenchestva* (1915–16), *Informatsionnyi listok Bunda* (1915–16), *Internatsional i voina* (1915), *Izvestiia ZSOK* (1915–17), *Kommunist* (1915), *Listok organizatsii pomoshchi politicheskim zakliuchennym* (1916), *Mysl'* (1914–15), *Na Chuzhbine* (1916), *Nabat* (1915), *Nachalo* (1916–17), *Nashe Slovo* (1915–16), *Novaia Epokha* (1917), *Prizyv* (1915–17), *Rabochee znamia* (1915–17), *Rossiia i svoboda* (1915), *Sbornik 'Sotsial'demokrata'* (1916), *Sotsial'demokrat* (1914–17), *V plenu* (1917), *Vperëd* (1915–17), and *Zhizn'* (1915).

Index

Alexinsky, G. A. (1879–1965), defensist Social Democrat, 19, 29, 35, 114, 136, 170, 175, 220, 222, 234; defines views, 28, 104–12; and *Vperëd*, 43–44, 105, 107; and Parvus, 66, 106–7, 110–12; and Plekhanov, 107–8, 114

Alliance for the Liberation of the Ukraine, 54–55, 64–65, 105–7, 135

Amfiteatrov, A. A., defensist Socialist Revolutionary, 103, 220

Anarchists, 79–80, 135, 223, 231

Antonov-Ovseenko, V. A. (1884–1938), Social Democrat, 18, 76, 154, 233

Argunov, A. A., Socialist Revolutionary, 37, 108

Armand, Inessa (1875–1920), Bolshevik, 16, 40–41, 124, 156, 158, 161, 162, 166, 207, 213, 214, 228

Armenians, 31

Aronson, Moses, 81

Askenazy, Szyman (1866–1935), Polish historian and politician, 140, 185, 195

August Bloc, 16, 155

Austrian diplomatic mission, Bern, 52, 68, 194, 201

Auswärtiges Amt, 56, 61, 64, 66, 70, 139–40, 179, 180, 183, 188–89, 199, 202, 203, 224

Avksientiev, A. A., defensist Socialist Revolutionary, 103, 108, 109, 114

Axelrod, Ida (d. 1917), defensist Social Democrat, 103, 108

Axelrod, P. B. (1850–1928), Menshevik, 9, 24, 36, 77, 120, 134, 144, 148, 155, 165, 223, 234; opposes Lenin, 27, 44–45, 83, 84, 92–93, 96, 116–19, 162; criticized by Lenin, 35, 43, 153, 158; participates in Zimmerwald conference, 80–82, 92–93, 97, 100, 101; at Kiental conference, 156, 158, 159, 161

Bagocki, Sergiusz (b. 1879), Polish socialist, 50, 223

Bakherakht, V. R. (d. 1916), Russian diplomat, 54, 193

Balabanova, Angelica (1878–1965), socialist, 40, 82, 85, 120, 144, 220, 222, 223, 231; and Lenin, 42, 97, 122, 225, 233; and Grimm, 81, 84; at Zimmerwald, 92, 97, 99, 100; and ISC, 144, 145, 157

Bartuška, Vincas, Lithuanian priest, 182–83

Basel, Russians in, 5

Bassok-Melenevsky, M. (1879–1938), Ukrainian socialist, 55, 64

Baugy sur Clarens, Russians in, 9, 20, 172

Belenky, G. Ia. (1885–1938), Bolshevik, 30

Ber, I. (b. 1866), Menshevik, 130

Bergen, Diego v. (1872–1943), German diplomat, 64, 72

Bern, Poles in, 57, 197

Bern, Russians in, 5, 6, 8, 9–10, 12, 21–22, 27, 38–42, 67, 79, 86, 89, 90, 134, 137–38, 165–66, 222

Bern conference of the RSDLP(B), 1915, 38–40, 124, 137–38

Bern University, 6, 7, 8, 9–10

Berzin, Jan (Winter; 1881–1941), Latvian Social Democrat, 86, 90, 92, 93, 98

Bibikov, M. M., Russian diplomat, 73, 193

Bint, Henry (b. 1852), Okhrana agent, 5, 220–21, 232

243